REFORMS, LABOUR MARKETS, AND SOCIAL SECURITY IN INDIA

RIS

Research and Information System for the
Non-Aligned and Other Developing Countries

The World Bank Instit

REFORMS, LABOUR MARKETS, AND SOCIAL SECURITY IN INDIA

Editors
Ramgopal Agarwala
Nagesh Kumar
Michelle Riboud

OXFORD
UNIVERSITY PRESS

OXFORD
UNIVERSITY PRESS
YMCA Library Building, Jai Singh Road, New Delhi 110001

Oxford University Press is a department of the University of Oxford. It furthers the University's objective of excellence in research, scholarship, and education by publishing worldwide in

Oxford New York

Auckland Bangkok Buenos Aires Cape Town Chennai
Dar es Salaam Delhi Hong Kong Istanbul Karachi Kolkata
Kuala Lumpur Madrid Melbourne Mexico City Mumbai Nairobi
São Paulo Shanghai Taipei Tokyo Toronto

Published in India
By Oxford University Press, New Delhi

First published in India 2004

ISBN 019 566609 7

Typeset in Goudy by Laser Print Craft, Delhi 110 051
Printed at Pauls Press New Delhi 110 020
Published by Manzar Khan, Oxford University Press
YMCA Library Building, Jai Singh Road, New Delhi 110 001

Acknowledgements

This volume is published under the joint auspices of the Research and Information System for the Non-aligned and Other Developing Countries and the World Bank Institute.

The findings, interpretations, and conclusions expressed in this volume are entirely those of the co-editors and contributors and should not be attributed in any manner to the World Bank, to its affiliated organizations, or to members of its Board of Executive Directors or the countries they represent. The World Bank does not guarantee the accuracy of the data included in this publication and accepts no responsibility whatsoever for any consequence of their use. The boundaries, colours, denominations, and other information shown on any map in this volume do not imply on the part of the World Bank Group any judgement on the legal status of any territory or the endorsement or acceptance of such boundaries.

Foreword

Effective and sustainable social security systems have emerged as a major issue of concern all over the world. Developed countries, whether it is the United States, Germany, or Japan, are worried about the fiscal viability of the social security systems they had developed as part of a welfare state approach. The socialist economies in transition, like Russia and China, are struggling to change their 'cradle to grave' social protection system into a modern, market-oriented one, which is regarded as crucial not only for long-term sustainability but also for the reform of their state-owned enterprises. The developing countries at various stages of development, from Brazil to the Philippines, are concerned about both the financing needs of the social security systems they have and about the need for new social safety nets which are essential for restructuring of their economies.

In India, the unorganized sector absorbs nearly 90 per cent of the labour force and for them there is no fiscal system of social security. Traditionally, societal structures—such as the tribe, the village, the locality and, most importantly, the family—rather than the over-arching structure of the state, have supported individuals in need. However, the pressures of modernization have led to a weakening of these social support systems.

It would of course be desirable to provide social protection to the entire work force. However, attempting to extend the formal sector schemes to the informal sector would be too simplistic. This highlights the imperative need to find new alternatives to ensure social security in the informal sector. In the organized sector itself, India is also facing the problem of fiscal viability like many other developed and developing countries.

There is an apprehension that the fast pace of liberalization and globalization would increase social tensions, since the system is not geared to the task of providing social security in an adequate manner. It is accordingly urged that the pace of liberalization and globalization should be in conformity with our ability to put in place a suitable social safety net.

It would appear that the nature and structure of social security systems for developing countries such as India during their period of high growth strategy would have to be significantly different from the systems which prevail in more mature economies. The ultimate objective is to combine competitiveness with caring in a context where the needs of the present are as compelling as providing for the future.

The World Bank has been closely associated with social security reforms in different parts of the world over the past decade. I am happy to see that their expertise has been combined with the expertise available in South Asian countries to produce this book which reflects on social security problems of India, home to one-fifth of the world's labour force.

The book throws light on the role and nature of social security systems for economies at our stage of development and provides useful material for policy-makers in the country. I compliment the RIS, the World Bank Institute, and the contributors to the book for this timely contribution to the ongoing debate on these issues in India today.

K.C. Pant
Deputy Chairman,
Planning Commission, India, and
Chairman, RIS

Preface

The Research and Information System for the Non-aligned and Other Developing Countries (RIS) and the World Bank Institute had organized an international conference in New Delhi on 1–3 November 1999 on Social Security Policy. A number of papers were presented on emerging issues and challenges for the South Asian countries in the area of Social Security Policy especially in the context of reforms and liberalization undertaken by them in recent years. These contributions had been prepared by staff members and consultants of the World Bank, and a number of scholars and experts from the region. Besides a number of practitioners and policy-makers in the region had made their observations at the conference. The interest generated by the conference in India on the issues covered prompted us to consider the publication of the papers presented to carry further the debate initiated at the conference. This volume puts together revised versions of a selection of papers presented at the International Conference on Social Security Policy: Challenges before India and South Asia.

We would like to thank K.C. Pant, Deputy Chairman of the Planning Commission, and Chairman, RIS, for kindly agreeing to inaugurate the conference with his perceptive remarks. We are also grateful to him for his foreword to this volume. We also thank V.R. Panchamukhi, the-then Director-General, RIS, for his support to the conference. Joe Delfico of the World Bank Institute played an important role in coordinating the conference.

We would like to thank the contributors to this volume for providing revised versions in a timely manner. We also benefited from the advice and comments of anonymous reviewers of the Oxford University Press.

Nagesh Kumar
DG, RIS
New Delhi

Contributors

Ramgopal Agarwala: International Development Policy Institute, Washington D.C., and Research and Information System for the Non-aligned and Other Developing Countries, New Delhi.
Nishan De Mel: Trinity College, Oxford University, Oxford.
S. Mahendra Dev: Centre for Economic and Social Studies, Hyderabad.
Nagesh Kumar: Research and Information System for the Non-aligned and Other Developing Countries, New Delhi.
Robert Holzmann: World Bank, Washington, D.C.
Estelle James: World Bank Institute, Washington, D.C.
Steen Jorgensen: World Bank, Washington, D.C.
V.R. Panchamukhi: formerly Research and Information System for the Non-aligned and Other Developing Countries, New Delhi.
Michelle Riboud: World Bank, Washington, D.C.
Alakh N. Sharma: Institute for Human Development, New Delhi.
Rajendra K. Sharma: International Development Policy Institute, Washington, D.C.
Ram Upendra Das: Research and Information System for the Non-aligned and Other Developing Countries, New Delhi.
Wouter van Ginneken: International Labour Organization, Geneva.

Abbreviations

AFP	Latin American Countries Pension funds.
BIFR	Board of Industrial and Financial Reconstruction
BOI	Build, Operate, Transfer
BSE	Bombay Stock Exchange
CDF	Cooperative Development Foundation
CMNMP	Chief Minister's Nutrition Meal Programme
CPFC	Central Provident Fund Commission
CPI	Consumer Price Index
DB	Defined Benefit
DC	Defined Contribution
EAS	Employment Assurance Scheme
EFPS	Employees Family Pension Scheme
EGF	Employment Generation Fund
EPF	Employees Provident Fund
EPFO	Employees' Provident Fund Organization
EPS	Employees Pension Scheme
EPZ	Export Processing Zone
FDI	Foreign Direct Investment
FERA	Foreign Exchange Regulatory Act
FTA	Free Trade Arrangements
GDP	Gross Domestic Product
GIS	Group Insurance Scheme
GNP	Gross National Product
HUDCO	Housing and Urban Development Corporation
ILO	International Labour Organization
IMF	International Monetary Fund
IPA	Indian Pension Authority
IPD	Implicit Pension Debt
IRA	Individual Retirement Accounts

IRDP	Integrated Rural Development Programme
JRY	Jawahar Rozgar Yojana
LIC	Life Insurance Corporation
M&A	Mergers and Acquisitions
MFN	Most Favoured Nation
NABARD	National Bank for Agriculture and Rural Development
NDC	National Defined Contribution
NGO	Non-government Organization
NIP	New Industrial Policy
NREP	National Rural Employment Programme
NRF	National Renewal Fund
NSAP	National Social Assistance Programme
NSDP	Net State Domestic Product
NSE	National Stock Exchange
OASIS	Old Age Social and Income Security
OECD	Organization for Economic Cooperation and Development
PAYG	Pay-as-you-go
PDS	Public Distribution System
PFM	Pension Fund Managers
PMRY	Prime Ministers' Rozgar Yojana
POP	Point of Presence
PPF	Public Provident Fund
PR	Replacement Rate
PSU	Public Sector Undertaking
RCA	Revealed Comparative Advantage
RIS	Research and Information System for the Non-aligned and Other Developing Countries
RIP	Retirement Income Security (Provision)
SAARC	South Asian Association for Regional Cooperation
SAFTA	South Asian Free Trade Area
SAPTA	SAARC Preferential Trade Arrangement
SEBI	Securities and Exchange Board of India
SETUP	Self Employment Programme for Urban Poor
SEWA	Self Employed Women's Association
SGSY	Swarnajayanti Gram Swarozgar Yojana
SP	Social Protection
SRM	Social Risk Management
TRYSEM	Training of Rural Youth for Self-employment

UN	United Nations
UNCTAD	United Nations Council for Trade and Development
UNDP	United Nations Development Programme
VRS	Voluntary Retirement Scheme
WTO	World Trade Organization

Tables, Boxes, and Figures

Tables

Boxes

Figures

Contents

1

Reforms, Labour Markets, and Social Security Policy in India: An Introduction

Ramgopal Agarwala, Nagesh Kumar, and Michelle Riboud

1. Introduction

Social security policy reforms have attracted increasing attention over the past decade in industrialized as well as developing countries alike. In the industrialized countries, these reforms have been mainly discussed against the background of a rapidly ageing population and, hence, the fiscal sustainability of the pension systems mostly based on defined benefit (DB) principle. In the developing countries, such as India too, fiscal sustainability of the formal pension system is likely to become a major issue over the long term. However, in the near term attention on reforms of social security systems has been provoked more by the process of industrial restructuring associated with economic reforms and its impact on labour markets. In particular, the recent trends of corporate restructuring, privatization, closures of sick enterprises have led to displacement of a growing number of workers. These trends have raised the concern about protection of vulnerable sections of population from the adverse effects of reforms. Besides social safety nets for the workers adversely affected, there is need for evolving labour redeployment and employment generation policies to create new jobs and alleviate poverty.

The other prominent concern in the Indian context is the poor coverage of social security programmes. Formal pension schemes cover only about 10 per cent of the workforce. Hence, extending the coverage to the remaining 90 per cent of the workforce that is part of the informal sector is a major challenge for the reform. For a large part of the population, deprivation in the form of inadequate income, ill health, or malnutrition is not a contingency to be guarded against, but a continuing certainty of life. The issue in their case is: what kind of social security system can address deprivation? Should social security be defined largely in terms of contingencies as has been done traditionally by the International Labour Organization (ILO) and other international agencies, or should it include promotional measures for poverty reduction as argued by, for instance, Dreze and Sen (1989) and Guhan (1994)?

In the organized sector, one objective of reforms is to improve the fiscal sustainability of pension schemes over the longer term particularly in the context of the demographic transition that is taking place with rising share of retirees over the coming years. The share of population over 60 is projected to rise from 7.5 per cent in 2000 to 10.3 per cent by 2020. The government employees enjoy a non-contributory, indexed, DB pension, funded entirely by the government. The provident fund system for even non-government employees in the formal sector now has a sizable component of DB. Thus there is an issue of how to make the system affordable. Important byproducts of the pension reforms are to increase the flow of long term institutional savings and boost the healthy development of the financial market (Patel 1997). In particular, as the pension funds are long term funds, the bulk of these could be invested in infrastructure projects.

The contributions in this book debate some of these issues in the context of India on the reforms of social security as a part of the ongoing process of economic reforms. The rest of this chapter provides an overview of the issues raised and addressed in the book. The second section briefly summarizes the labour market trends resulting from the reforms and liberalization in India and their implications for social security and social safety nets. The third section discusses conceptual issues on the reforms of pension systems. The fourth section briefly discusses the global experiences in pension reforms and their relevance for India. The fifth section summarizes the issues concerning the reforms of pension systems in India raised in the contributions in the book and elsewhere. The sixth section deals with old age security in the unorganized sector and the seventh section distills the key message emerging out of the discussion in the book on the future policy agenda. Finally, the last section presents the layout of the volume.

2. Reforms, Growth, and Labour Markets

India embarked on the economic reforms process in the 1990s designed to curtail the role of government in production activity, assigning a more important role to domestic and foreign private sector in economic activity, and intensifying their integration with the world economy. The impact of these reforms on the labour market provides a context for the debate for reform of social security in India. It is now widely accepted that growth of employment in the organized sector has not kept pace with the growth of incomes throughout their development experience. In fact, there is evidence that employment growth rates in India in the post reform period have declined further even as the growth rates of Gross Domestic Product (GDP) have increased to around 6 per cent during the 1990s from 3 to 4 per cent during the 1950–80. The employment growth rate has apparently declined from 2.43 per cent during 1988–94 to 1.60 per cent during 1994–7. During 1997–9 employment growth rate has been marginally negative with employment falling from 394 million to 393 million. The growth rates of organized sector employment have been even more marginal at 1.05 per cent during the period from 1988 to 1997 and negligible at 0.24 per cent during 1997–9 (Panchamukhi et al. this volume). Given the negligible growth of jobs, new entrants to the workforce had to find work opportunities in the informal sector.

Reforms and growing competition have also pushed the enterprises to restructure themselves. Corporate restructuring has been associated with increasing outsourcing of certain types of work, contractualization and casualization of the jobs as a way of bringing greater flexibility by enterprises (Panchamukhi et al. this volume). Therefore, an increasing proportion of new entrants to the workforce is either casual or an contractual or become self-employed in the informal sector. Neither of these categories of workers is covered by social security.

An important aspect of economic reforms has covered the restructuring and privatization of public sector enterprises that have a sizeable proportion of the production space in India. The privatization programmes have had significant social effects manifested in the form of worker redundancy, retrenchment, and casualization of workers. An ILO study finds that 23 per cent of the 9.8 million strong employment in Indian public sector enterprises were facing redundancy (Joshi 2000). On the one hand a large number of employees are joining the ranks of the unemployed with retrenchment; while on the other, there is a growing scarcity of trained manpower of certain types, for instance, IT (Information Technology) trained manpower. Very little effort has been made in the area of reskilling and redeployment of the workers that are retrenched. India has established a National Renewal Fund for the retraining of the redundant workers. However, it has been largely used for compensating the retrenched workers under the Voluntary Retirement Scheme (VRS) rather than retraining. Of the 129,000 public sector retrenched, 36,889 were retrained and only 11,623 were redeployed (Sharma, this volume). There are experiences from other parts of the world that suggest that labour can be retrained and redeployed (for example, redeployment of former mining workers in skill-intensive manufacturing activities such as auto and chemicals in the Limburg region of the Netherlands). However, adequate preparation is needed for such schemes.

From the discussion so far it would appear that adoption of economic reforms have accentuated the trend of declining importance of the organized sector as a source of jobs in India. The issues that arise in the light of these trends with respect to the social security policy, besides reform of the existing pension schemes for the organized sector workers, are as follows:

• Employment Generation /Social Safety Nets Policy to be an important aspect of social security policy: employment assurance is important for protecting the vulnerable and underprivileged people against deprivation and falling into the poverty trap. Therefore, employment generation policies are included in the wider concept of social security covering promotional and protective aspects, as defined by Dreze and Sen (1989) and discussed later by Guhan (1994). Given the inability of the organized sector to create jobs for the new entrants to the workforce, policies for creating new jobs have to be established.

In this respect, some initiatives have been taken by the government in India. For instance, the government has launched, among others, the Swarnajayanti Gram Swarojgar Yojana (SGSY)—rural self-employment generation scheme, incorporating the Integrated Rural Development Programme (IRDP), the Jawahar Rozgar Yojana (JRY), and the Employment Assurance Scheme (EAS), Employment Guarantee Scheme (Maharashtra State), the Nehru Rozgar Yojana, the Prime Minister's Rozgar Yojana, the Swarna Jayanti Shahri Rozgar Yojana (Sharma, this volume). However, the effectiveness and focus of these programmes could be substantially improved. Poor coordination among the several programmes having overlapping objectives has been identified as a reason for poor effectiveness (Sharma, this volume).

- Reskilling, rehabilitation, and redeployment of adversely affected workers: it is clear that a considerable proportion of workers are going to be affected adversely in the process of corporate restructuring and privatization. An institutional procedure is needed for reskilling and redeployment of the retrenched workers that could provide counselling on the emerging opportunities for self-employment and alternative jobs, on the respective training and skill requirements and facilitate this process. Even though the National Renewal Fund in India was designed to provide assistance specifically for these tasks besides the payment of compensation, the experience so far has not been encouraging in respect of retraining and redeployment, etc. as observed earlier. There is an obvious need of reform here.
- Extending the protective social security coverage to contract and casual workers besides other workers in the informal sector: with the trend of casualization and contractualization in the organized sector in the post-reforms era, a growing proportion of the organized sector workforce is now outside the social security coverage. These workers are more vulnerable to threat of job losses than the regular employees. There is need to evolve schemes to extend some social security cover to these workers. Besides this, the bulk of the workforce is absorbed in the informal sector and its proportion is actually increasing rather than decreasing. Some social security coverage for the informal sector workers is necessary for preventing deprivation. A number of initiatives have been taken in this direction in India, as observed later (Dev, this volume). The scope of these initiatives needs to be extended and their effectiveness needs to be improved if they are to make a difference.

These issues suggest that a broader definition of social security covering promotional as well as protective aspects as argued by Dreze and Sen (1989) and Guhan (1994) are more appropriate in the Indian context.

The need for creating jobs has attracted attention of the policy-makers in the context of sustainability of the reforms process. The Planning Commission had appointed a Task Force on Employment Opportunities headed by Montek S. Ahluwalia to suggest strategies for generation of 100 million jobs over the next 10 years. The task force in its report submitted in July 2001 placed emphasis on accelerating the growth rate of GDP, on pursuing policies for promoting growth of employment intensive sectors, on improving the quality of the labour force with suitable policies for education and skill development, and on reforms of labour laws. The task force was not convinced of the role of special programmes for creating additional employment, and hence recommended their evaluation before more resources could be devoted to them. The task force report was found to be lacking in certain respects and had apparently not paid adequate attention to the issue of the large backlog of underemployment. Therefore, the Planning Commission appointed a Steering Committee on Labour and Employment for the 10th Five Year Plan (2002–7) and the Special Group on Targeting Ten Million Employment Opportunities per Year Over the 10th Plan Period, both headed by S.P. Gupta, member, Planning Commission. Unlike the task force, the special group argues that there is a specific role for special employment programmes, notwithstanding the complaints of leakage in efficiency.

3. Some Conceptual Issues on Reforms of Pension Systems

The World Bank (1994) argued that the objective of social security programmes should be to

- Facilitate people's efforts to shift some of their income from their active working years to old age, by saving;
- Redistribute additional income to the old who are lifetime poor; and
- Provide insurance against many risks to which the old are especially vulnerable.

Most countries combine all the three functions in a dominant public pillar, a publicly managed scheme that pays an earnings-related DB and is financed out of payroll taxes on a pay-as-you-go (PAYG) basis. The experience, however, suggests that combining all the functions under one public scheme suffers from problems on both efficiency as well as distributional grounds (World Bank 1994; James, this volume). Therefore, the Bank has been favouring a multi-pillar approach. The first mandatory pillar is the redistributive social safety net pillar, providing means tested, minimum pension guarantee, which is publicly managed. The second pillar is a mandatory defined contribution (DC) funded plan, and is privately managed. The third pillar consists of fully funded voluntary savings or occupational plan. All of these pillars can be thought of as really part of one package of a very diversified risk protection. The first pillar basically keeps people out of poverty. The second pillar links the benefits very closely to the contributions and thereby reduces labour market distortions. It can also have beneficial effects on workers' willingness to continue working rather than retire early. But it is very important that these funds should be competitively managed in a diversified portfolio because this is the way one gets the best allocation of capital that will maximize the returns to the fund and also returns to the economy as a whole. The third pillar provides additional protection for people who want more income and insurance in their old age (James, this volume).

In recent times, there has been a lot of discussion on the transition of pension schemes from PAYG to funded schemes and from central public management to private management of these schemes, even in India (for example, the debate following the submission of OASIS (Old Age Social and Income Security) report, as seen later). De Mel (this volume) shows, however, that these transitions are not free from problems and do imply costs. Therefore, De Mel feels that adoption of any particular form of retirement income package may not constitute appropriate reform for a country. Therefore, the pension reform for a country has to be designed keeping in mind the peculiarities of the country such as existing mechanisms and schemes, structure of labour and financial institutions, capacity for professional fiscal management, and the socio-political priorities.

Rethinking on the social security reforms has been going on. Holzmann and Jorgensen (this volume) define social protection as human capital oriented intervention with two main objectives to assist individuals, households, and communities: first, to better manage risks and second, to provide support for the critical poor. This concept provides for a safety net but it does not want to let people sit idle. It aims at getting people back into gainful work and out of poverty. Second, this new concept of social protection is viewed as one type of investment, helping the poor to avoid irreversible negative effects on their human capital during adverse shocks. The third point is that the new concept focuses less on the symptoms but more on the causes of poverty and last, but not least, it takes into account the reality of the countries trying to reform their social protection system.

Holzmann and Jorgensen's (this volume) conceptual framework has its foundations in risk management. But as mentioned earlier, in India, the problems of old age, out of season unemployment, and chronic poverty are a certainty as is the specially disadvantaged position of women in old age. Nearly 90 per cent of the workforce is in the informal sector and the standard forms of social security system do not reach them. Dev (this volume) argues that the links between social security provision, human development, and economic growth may have to be first worked out in greater detail before we enter into these components of risk management.

Following the conceptual framework developed in India by Guhan (1994), it is argued that social security programmes in South Asia should comprise three levels. The first level covers primary education, primary health, and nutrition, the second level concerns provision of assets and employment to the poor, and the third level covers social assistance schemes. The first two levels could be called promotional measures; the third could be called protective. The three levels could also be defined in terms of time span for effectiveness. The first measure takes a long time to make an impact on economic growth. The second takes about five to ten years, and the third is immediate in its impact on livelihood but its impact on growth is not very well known. Also important is that they affect three different age groups: the first one basically affects children: the second affects adults in the working age group; and the third influences the old and the destitute. These are not mutually exclusive programmes although they do address different categories and, therefore, they may need to be undertaken in a complementary manner. In Indian conditions the importance of a broader approach to social security cannot be over emphasized.

4. Global Experiences of Pension System Reforms

Reform of pension systems in Chile is highlighted for its success in contributing to economic growth through development of capital markets (James, this volume) and it has been followed by a number of other Latin American countries also (UNRISD, 2000: 37). However, there have been criticisms of the Chilean approach. Perhaps a more relevant case for India is the example of Malaysia which began with a PF system similar to what most South Asian countries have and gradually broadened its coverage for social protection and modified its investment rules with growing maturity of financial system. The Malaysian system achieved reasonable protection for the elderly and contributed to the funding of infrastructure investment in the country. By avoiding the temptations of moving toward a DB system (as India did in 1995) its PF system did not impose any burden on the budget.

The Malaysian Employee Provident Fund (EPF) was established in 1951 and is now the largest financial institution in Malaysia (Ghaffar 1999). Over time, coverage has been widened to include every non-pensionable wage. The contribution has changed over the years: in 1952 it was 5 per cent on both sides—the employee and the employer—and it moved up gradually until in 1996 it was 11 per cent from the employee and 12 per cent from the employer. An individual has three accounts where 60 percent of a member's savings go into Account One that may only be withdrawn upon retirement at the age of 55. Account Two consists of 30 per cent of total savings and can be withdrawn for housing or when the member is 50. The remaining 10 per cent is kept in Account Three for medical coverage. Given the shortcomings of the lump sum withdrawal at age 55, members are also given the option to withdraw their savings through the annual dividend withdrawal scheme as well as the periodic payment scheme (Ghaffar 1999).

To improve the outreach to members, the Malaysian EPF has decentralized most of its operational functions to the State levels. The default rate has been reduced from about 27 per cent in 1989 to 4.6 per cent in 1998. The management expenses of the fund have been kept below 3 per cent of its income. In terms of assets allocation, the original Act provided that not less than 70 per cent must be in government securities. In the past, Malaysian EPF has been able to play the traditional role of a non-inflationary financier of the government's development But this has changed over the years and in 1998, only 31 per cent of the investment was in government securities. The rest are made of private sector bonds and loans as well as equity. The contributors are also allowed to withdraw the money to invest in any Unit Trust of their own. The Act has been continuously amended over time to enable greater flexibilities in the fund's investment approach. The annual real rates of return on EPF funds have been over 4 per cent over the last 15 years.

5. Reforms of Pension Systems in India

India has a highly dualistic structure of pension system in which a small privileged minority is given generous pension benefits with considerable risk to the fiscal health of the country, while the vast majority has very little social protection. (Agarwala and Sharma, this volume). For government workers it allows, through a system of provident funds, non-contributory pensions and gratuities, for a generous replacement rates of 95 per cent or above.[1] Pensions are adjusted not only for price increases but also salary increases for current employees. The provident fund systems for non-government employees in the organized sector also have a sizeable component of DB. The pension system in the formal sector may thus be a potential fiscal time bomb. In order to defuse this, it would be necessary, among other things to: (a) re-examine the concept of age of retirement, (b) improve the rates of return on provident funds (c) introduce a contributory part in the pension schemes for civil servants and gradually move toward a DB system; and (d) revisit the Employees Pension Scheme (EPS) of 1995 (Agarwala and Sharma, this volume).

An alternative view is that the main problem in India's pension system is the low rate of return on investments, which is due to

[1]In the Union Budget 2003–4, the finance minister announced a restructured pension scheme which '...will apply only to new entrants to government service, except to the armed forces, and upon finalisation, offer a basket of pension choices. It will also be available on a voluntary basis to all employers for their employees, as well as to the self-employed'.

'This new pension scheme, when introduced, will be based on defined contribution, shared equally in the case of government employees between the government and the employees. There will be course be no contribution from the government in respect of individuals who are not government employees. The new pension scheme will be portable, allowing transfer of the benefits in case of change of employment, and the individual pension accounts with pension funds. The ministry of finance will oversee and supervise the pension funds through a new and independent PensionFund Regulatory and Development Authority.' (Government of India, 2003) investment guidelines set by the government, whereby up to 90 per cent of funds are preempted by government. By improving the rates of return on provident funds and reducing early withdrawals from them provident funds, reasonable provision for old age income security can be made without any serious fiscal risk to the government (Dave 1999; Project OASIS 2000).

Improving the rate of return on pension and provident funds consistent with acceptable risks to the beneficiaries is a key objective for pension system reforms in India. There is a lively debate in the country on the issue of the guaranteed rate of return on provident funds. Some argue that it penalizes the pensioners because the funds can earn a higher rate of return elsewhere. Some, while accepting the point that the government is getting the captive funds at below market rates, argue that it is a legitimate taxation role of the government. Still others argue that the government is not earning enough on these funds to justify the assured fixed return and it is assuming an unnecessary risk and easy availability of these funds creates temptations for lax fiscal management.

In this context the recommendations of the Project OASIS are worth noting. The Project OASIS was the result of the formation of an eight-member expert committee by the Ministry of Social Justice and Empowerment in 1998 to look into the issue of social security reforms. The report makes several recommendations that include augmentation of existing schemes by a system of Individual Retirement Accounts (IRAs) directly linked to workers with a unique account number and tax exempt contributions between Rs 500 to Rs 60,000 per year, establishment of a system of points of presence comprising post offices and banks to collect contributions and distribute benefits, and creation of a depository to pool these contributions and pass them on to fund managers (Project OASIS 2000). It proposes to give to the contributors a choice regarding the investment of their funds. A system of six competing private pension fund managers is proposed and each fund manager would offer three investment portfolios, distinguished by level of risk and return depending upon the proportion of funds invested in fixed income securities and stock markets from which workers could freely choose. The committee recommended the restructuring of the EPF on the lines of IRAs with workers given the option of switching over to IRA plan and opt for the investment strategy used for IRAs.[2]

[2]The DC scheme applicable to all employees in industrial establishments with more than 20 workers are required to contribute under the EPF Act 1952.

The government contributions to the EPS should be discontinued and EPS should implement a uniform 10 per cent employer contribution, adopt IRA investment guidelines, perform an annual acturial review, and adjust parameters to assure the system of self-financing.[3]

The OASIS recommendations, however, have provoked a lot of debate especially on the relevance of increasing the share of equities (domestic and foreign) in the investment portfolio of provident and pension funds and involvement of private fund managers to manage these schemes for increasing the return.[4] On the issue of switch from fixed income securities to equities in provident fund portfolio, it can be argued that if we accept the hypothesis of efficient allocation by market, the observed differences in rates of return in securities and equities reflect the investor's trade-off between rates of returns and risks and the case for investment in equities cannot be made solely on the basis of observed higher rates of return on equities. The experience of pension reforms in Chile shows that many expectations of efficiency, higher yield, increased competition, coverage, and growth of capital markets from privately managed pension schemes investing in equity markets have not come true (UNRISD 2000: 37). To some extent the real rate of growth of the country was responsible for higher return and not necessarily the fund managers. In India, the investors seem to have concerns about the volatility of share markets and scams and their potential to erode their savings. Investment in equity indices could be a way of diversifying investment portfolio in favour of equities. Only a minority of active managers has been found to outperform indices in developed countries (Shah and Fernandes 1999).

The case for the diversification of the investment portfolio to cover international markets requires further study. India is trying to attract private investment into infrastructure and these investments come at relatively high rates of interest. It is not clear why provident funds that will enable large infrastructure investments for the country should be invested abroad at rates of return which are likely to be lower than demanded by foreign investors in view of their perceived risks. Second, pensioners who put their money abroad will be taking exchange risks in

[3]The DB currently funded by employer and government contributions is respectively 8.33 per cent and 1.16 per cent.

[4]See Gilingham and Kanda (2001) for other problems with OASIS recommendations.

addition to the risks on rates of return. Moreover, with the increasing globalization of securities markets, the international markets seem to be moving in parallel and the presumed advantages of diversification are not as great as assumed. In any case such diversifications are not possible without capital market liberalization and particularly after the experience of financial instability in East Asian countries in the wake of their capital account liberalization, capital account convertibility may not happen in the near future. Others argued that even if it was not necessary or feasible to make large investments abroad, it was useful to get the taste of the system and allow a limited degree of international investments just as India has allowed foreign portfolio investments through foreign institutional investors.

6. Old Age Security in the Unorganized Sector

With over 90 per cent of the workforce in the unorganized sector, a crucial challenge for India is how to design a system, which can provide income security to the elderly during old age. The problem is particularly serious for women who have longer life expectancy than men and often do not have any independent source of income. The social taboos towards widowhood in India make their situation particularly difficult.

There is one line of argument (James 1999) that in conditions of South Asian countries, it may be neither feasible nor desirable to extend the coverage of the formal pension system. In these cases, there are many small employers and self-employed people and it is difficult to collect a pay roll tax from them. And it may not be desirable because it may be more important for the poor families to use the money today than to put it aside for tomorrow. There is no argument against increasing coverage on a voluntary basis. But that is workable only if safe financial instruments can be made available in villages and a legal framework can be set up that enables employers to establish pension programmes on a voluntary basis.

An alternative is some kind of means-tested social assistance that will help out the neediest of the 90 per cent. The means-testing programmes can be made cost effective through self-selection mechanisms which provide, for example, soup kitchens, dormitories, and other in-kind benefits where the quality of services that is offered will be low enough so that only the neediest of the needy will seek to use those services.

Among the various social assistance programmes initiated by the government is the National Old Age Pension Scheme that provides a benefit of Rs 75 per month to the poorest elderly over 65. However, relatively few elderly have applied for this benefit (Gillingham and Kanda 2001). A number of state governments in India have also taken initiatives to provide various protective social security measures for the unorganized sector (Dev, this volume). The important ones among these are programmes in Kerala, Tamil Nadu, Maharasthra, and Andhra Pradesh. The social security programme is most advanced in Kerala. In 1992–3, the state spent about Rs 80 crore on these schemes which is about 2.8 per cent of the revenue budget. The most important schemes in terms of coverage are: old age pensions and programmes for destitute and agricultural labourers. Social security programmes were introduced in Tamil Nadu in 1989–90 of which the main initiative was a liberalized pension programme. The employment guarantee scheme of Maharashtra is one of the biggest social security programmes for the unskilled workers in India. In Andhra Pradesh, innovative approaches have been adopted that integrate traditional and modern institutions and their integration of self-help groups with the state has led to near universal coverage and has reduced the transaction cost.

The main problem is inefficient utilization of resources in these programmes. Kerala is a relatively successful case; but that is due to several special factors such as greater expenditure in social sectors, greater vigilance of political parties and their unions, the history of left movement, the historical legacies of policies of princely states, and social movements including the contribution of Christian missionaries. These features are not easily replicable elsewhere; and there is an issue as to how long Kerala itself can sustain expenditures on these programmes without economic growth.

While being aware of the difficulties of devising an effective system of old age security for the unorganized sector, it is important to emphasize that old age income and consumption is needed for the poor as well as for the rich, for the unorganized as well as the organized sector. And in their own ways, the elderly in the unorganized sector have been by and large finding that support. The old system of family-based old age security can be regarded as an informal PAYG system. Under this system each generation is implicitly paying the taxes to provide income support to the elderly in the informal sector. However, the system is under stress for the same reasons that the formal PAYG system is under stress. There are fewer and fewer family members to support the elderly and the life expectancy of the elderly is increasing along with costs of maintenance, particularly medical expenses. As in the formal system, many people approaching old age are trying to set up their own funds so that they can draw upon their own resources rather than depend on their children. This is particularly true for the informal sector group which is above the poverty line and may constitute as much as 60 per cent of the workforce in India. The task of public policy is to see if the old age security needs of this group can be met through some flexible pension plans which can inspire the trust of this group and has low transaction costs.

There are some localized successful experiences in India which need to be studied and could be extended to other parts of the subcontinent. One example is the pension scheme by the Cooperative Development Foundation (CDF), an institute which aims at strengthening cooperatives and is mainly working with thrift and credit groups in Andhra Pradesh, as well as in Tamil Nadu, Karnataka, and Kerala. This scheme provides a form of life insurance, that is, a payment on the death of a member. On reaching the age of 60 years or on withdrawing from the scheme, the deposit amount is returned with a 2 per cent bonus (van Ginneken, this volume). In India the benefits of social insurance have also been available to different categories of vulnerable groups under the various Group Insurance Schemes (GIS) subsidized with the social security fund under the Life Insurance Corporation (LIC). The most prominent example is the Rural Group Life Insurance Scheme introduced on 15 August 1995 in which insurance is available between ages 20 and 60 years for an assured amount of Rs 5000, the premium being around Rs 60 per annum. The other interesting case is of SEWA (Self Employed Women's Association) Bank's insurance schemes that provide coverage for life insurance, widowhood, maternity, sickness, and calamity to members of SEWA, a trade union comprising 2,20,000 poor, self-employed women workers paying a subscription. The SEWA example shows that the poor can manage their own social security systems in a viable way and, hence, there is need for rethinking on indigenous new forms of participatory and decentralized organizational structures (Bhatt 2000).

The Public Provident Fund (PPF) Scheme in India is ideally suited to meeting the needs of the middle group which constitutes about 60 per cent of the workforce. This scheme offers highly attractive tax facilities; contributions are tax exempt up to Rs 60,000 per year, income on these funds are tax free, and there is no tax when they are withdrawn. These funds can be bought with cash (which makes it easier for the lower income groups who may not have bank accounts) through banks or post offices. Withdrawal rules are liberal. Loans can be taken after three years and withdrawals up to half the balance can be taken after six years. The account can be closed after 15 years. At present, however, this scheme is not highly publicized. It is confined mainly to the urban middle class and has become an instrument of tax avoidance. This scheme can be modified (with stricter rules on withdrawals and better investments of funds) to be a vehicle for income security for the informal sector. In view of the externalities of providing for the old age for the informal sector and the potential of the scheme to generate long term savings, this scheme should be publicized along the line of family planning. The social marketing campaign can be combined with incentives in the form of tax benefits, and by allowing account holders to use part of their balances as collateral for credits from the formal sector.

7. The Way Forward

In the foregoing sections we have summarized and overviewed some of the issues that the contributors to this book have raised and addressed. The issues that emerge from the debates raised in the volume are the following:

- First, it is clear that there is a need for more serious efforts to synchronize the programmes of liberalization and corporate restructuring and reform of social insurance systems in the country including retraining and redeployment programmes. In fact, social security system reforms, which are called second generation reforms, could be the first generation reforms.
- Second, the informal sector which includes contractual and casual labour is emerging as the most dynamic part of the labour market. There is need for modernizing this sector, with better provisions for training and social protection of workers but at the same time care has to be taken to avoid the pitfalls of introducing labour laws unsuitable for the conditions in India and which have contributed to the disappointing performance of the formal sector over the last 50 years.
- Third, the pension system for the government employees imposes

a heavy and growing burden on the fiscal system in the country. Urgent explorations should be made to see how to defuse this fiscal time bomb.

- Fourth, improving rates of return on pension funds is a priority and a greater share of investment portfolio of pension and provident funds should be allocated to equities. At the current stage of development in India, such investment could be largely in the form of investment in share market indices. But, as in other countries, portfolio options and limits could be modified over time.
- Fifth, for the informal sector, mandatory systems of pensions or provident funds do not appear realistic. For the 30 per cent people below poverty line, safety net schemes are the only realistic options but these schemes should be integrated with poverty reduction programmes. There is also need for rethinking on indigenous new forms of participatory and decentralized organizational structures, that could handle the social security for participants, as the SEWA example shows. For the middle 60 per cent of the workforce, which is in the informal sector but has saving capacity, voluntary schemes should be developed to enable them to make savings for the old age. These savings could be a big source of funding the much needed infrastructure development in the country.
- Finally, there is an urgent need for better collection of data on various aspects of social security in India. Despite a formidable statistical system, there is a lack of good information on employment and other vital data on labour markets in India. When it comes to the informal sector, there is very little information about even the basic numbers, about the size of the sector, and its mode of functioning. There has been very little analysis of how serious the implicit debt burden is due to the pension obligations. Even for the government sector, there is no readily available information about the size, age composition, and mortality tables of the workers covered by the pension system. Similarly, for the non-government employees' provident funds, there is very little known about the rate of compliance in collection of contributions, etc. essential for estimating the pension burden that the fiscal system will have to face in the future. There are several experiments in social security measures initiated by the various states in India but very little has been done to evaluate them and draw lessons for the future shape of social security systems. In general, there is very little high quality research work done on reforms of pension systems in India. Now that the importance of

the issue has been fully registered, one hopes that there would be greater efforts for in-depth research in these areas. This is clearly one area where knowledge can help improve public policy and public welfare.

8. Plan of the Book

The contributions in this volume have been grouped in two parts. Part I combines three contributions raising conceptual issues by Holzman and Jorgensen, Estelle James, and Nishan De Mel. Part II comprises five contributions covering the reforms, labour markets, and social security issues in India. Panchamukhi et al. discuss the nature of reforms and their implications for labour markets. Agarwala and Sharma deal with reforms of pension systems. Van Ginneken and Mahendra Dev in their papers deal with social security issues in the informal sector. Finally, Sharma discusses the employment generation policy and social safety nets in India.

References

Asher, Mukul G. (2000) 'Recent International Experience and Pension Reform: Implications for India', paper presented at the seminar on *Social Security for the Elderly*, organized by the Social Security Association in New Delhi, India, August 2000.

Bhatt, Ela (2000) Foreword to Renana Jhabvala and R.K.A. Subramanya (eds) *The Unorganized Sector: Work Security and Social Protection*, New Delhi, Sage.

Dave, Surendra (1999) 'Restructuring Pensions for the Twenty-first Century', in James Hanson and Sanjay Kathuria (eds) *India: A Financial Sector for the Twenty-First Century*, New Delhi, Oxford University Press, pp. 305–35.

——— (2000) 'Economic Liberalization and Employment in South Asia', *Economic and Political Weekly*, 8 and 15 January 2000.

Dev, S. Mahendra (1999) 'An Overview of Social Security in India', *The Indian Journal of Labour Economics*, 42 (3) July–September 1999.

Dreze, J. and A. Sen (1989) *Hunger and Public Action*, Oxford, Clarendon Press.

Ghaffar, Roslan A. (1999) 'Managing the Malaysian Employees Provident Fund', paper presented at the International Conference on Social Security Policy: Challenges before India and South Asia, New Delhi, 1–3 November 1999, RIS and the World Bank Institute.

Gillingham, Robert and Daniel Kanda (2001) Pension Reform in India, IMF Working Paper WP/01/125, Washington, D.C..

——— (1994) 'Social Security Options for Developing Countries', *International Labour Review*, 133(1) pp. 35–53.

Government of India (2003) Union Budget (2003–2004), speech by minister for finance, http://indiabudget.ric.in/ub2003–04/bs/speecha.htm.

Guhan, S. (1993) 'Social Security for the Poor in the Unorganized Sector: A Feasible Blueprint for India', in K.S. Parikh and R. Sudarshan (eds) *Human Development and Structural Adjustment*, Madras Macmillan, pp. 203–37.

James, Estelle (1999) 'Coverage under Old Age Security Programmes and Protection for the Uninsured', paper presented at the International Conference on Social Security Policy: Challenges before India and South Asia, New Delhi, 1–3 November 1999, RIS and the World Bank Institute.

Jhabvala, Renana and R.K.A. Subrahmanya (eds) (2000) *The Unorganised Sector: Work Security and Social Protection*, New Delhi, Sage.

Joshi, Gopal (2000) (ed.) in 'Overview of Privatization in South Asia', *Privatization in South Asia*, New Delhi: ILO–SAAT.

Jutting, Johannes (1999) 'Social Security Systems in Low Income Countries: An Overview from an Institutional Perspective', *The Indian Journal of Labour Economics*, 42 (3) July–September 1999.

Patel, Urjit R. (1997) 'Aspects of Pension Fund Reform: Lessons for India', *Economic and Political Weekly*, 20 September 1997.

Planning Commission (2002) *Report of the Special Group on Targeting Ten Million Employment Opportunities per year over the Tenth Plan Period*, Government of India, May.

—— (2001) *Report of the Steering Committee on Labour and Employment for the Tenth Five-Year Plan*, Government of India, December.

—— (2001) *Report of the Task Force on Employment Opportunities*, Government of India, July.

Prabhu, K. Seeta and Sandhya V. Iyer (2001) 'Public Provision of Social Security: The Challenge in South Asia', *South Asia Economic Journal*, 2(1), pp. 31–66.

Project OASIS (2000) *Project OASIS Committee Report*, Ministry of Social Justice and Empowerment, New Delhi, Government of India

Shah, Ajay and Kshama Fernandes (1999) 'The Relevance of Index Funds for Pension Investment in Equities', paper presented at the International Conference on Social Security Policy: Challenges before India and South Asia, New Delhi, 1–3 November 1999, RIS and the World Bank Institute.

UNRISD (2000) *Visible Hands*, Geneva: United Nations Research Institute for Social Develoment.

World Bank (1994) *Averting the Old Age Crisis: Policies to Protect the Old and Promote Growth*, World Bank, New York, Oxford University Press.

Gu[illegible] (2005) [illegible] A Flexible Blueprint for India [illegible] Development [illegible] pp. [illegible]

Jo[illegible] (19[illegible]) [illegible] Protection [illegible] Social [illegible] Delhi [illegible] Institute.

Ib[illegible] Security [illegible]

Ko[illegible] (2003) [illegible] Education [illegible]

[illegible] Countries: An Overview [illegible] Labour [illegible]

In[illegible] Rural [illegible] for India [illegible] 1996.

[illegible] Commission [illegible] Million [illegible] of [illegible]

[illegible] for the [illegible]

[illegible] Report [illegible] Government [illegible]

[illegible] Social Security: The Challenge [illegible] pp. 11–65.

[illegible] Social Justice and [illegible]

Shah [illegible] for Pension [illegible] New Delhi.

[illegible] Institute for [illegible]

World Bank [illegible] the Old and [illegible] Oxford University Press.

PART I

Conceptual Issues to Social Security Reforms

2

Social Risk Management
A new conceptual framework for social protection, and beyond

Robert Holzmann and Steen Jorgensen[*]

The revolutionary idea that defines the boundary between modern times and the past is the mastery of risk: the notion that the future is more than a whim of gods and that men and women are not passive before nature.

Peter L. Bernstein (*Against the Gods — The Remarkable Story of Risk,* 1996)

1. Introduction and Overview

Social protection (SP), generally defined as public measures to provide income security for individuals, is back on the international agenda.

*This paper is a complete revised version of Holzmann and Jorgensen (1999). This served as a conceptual background paper to the development of the Social Protection Sector Strategy of the World Bank that was published in early 2001 (World Bank 2001). It reflects the many constructive critiques, comments and suggestions received during presentations at conferences, consultations with internal and external partners during the preparation of the paper. Special thanks for encouragement in the pursuit of the social risk management framework go to Ashraf Ghani, Margaret Grosh, Michael Lipton, Paul Siegel, Michael Walton, and Tara

The experience of East Asia has demonstrated that high economic growth rates over many decades can impressively reduce poverty. The recent financial crisis, however, also showed that if appropriate income protection measures and safety net programmes are not in place, when GDP falls dramatically, wages decrease and/or unemployment rises individuals become very vulnerable. In OECD (Organization for Economic Cooperation and Development)-type economies, where SP programmes such as active labour market policy, social insurance, and social assistance do exist, the high and often rising public expenditure levels generate concern, particularly in view of an aging population and rising international competition. On the other hand, developing economies have few public resources and can spend little for the income security of their populations despite the high levels of poverty and income insecurity of individuals.

This tension between the need for income security and the apparent non-affordability of providing it, while relevant, provides little comfort for the more than 1 billion individuals in the world living on less than a dollar a day, the unemployed as a result of structural adjustment or globalization, and the rising number of disadvantaged elderly. The traditional definition of SP, labour market interventions, social insurance, and social safety nets, may be partly responsible for the tension. First, the traditional definition overemphasizes the role of the public sector. Second, the common conceptualization of SP tends to emphasize net costs and expenditures while overlooking potential positive effects on sustainable economic development. Third, categorizing SP interventions into sectoral programmes obscures what they have in common and how they can support each other. Fourth, and most importantly, the traditional thinking provides limited guidance for a strategic outlook on effective poverty reduction beyond the general exultations not to forget the poor who cannot participate in a labour intensive growth process.

This chapter develops a new definition and conceptual framework named 'Social Risk Management' (SRM) which should allow for better design of SP programmes as one component of a revised poverty reduction strategy. While the focus of the chapter is on developing

Vishwanath. The paper profited also from comments and suggestions during the conference in New Delhi and a session at the Seville conference of IIPF in August 2000. However, all errors are our own.

countries and poverty reduction, it is our view that the proposed framework can be productively applied also in developed economies to guide a needed restructuring of their SP programmes.

The proposed definition sees 'SP as public interventions to (i) assist individuals, households, and communities better manage risk, and (ii) provide support to the critically poor.' This definition and the underlying framework of SRM:

- Present SP as a safety net as well as a springboard for the poor. While a safety net for all should exist, the programmes should also provide the poor with the capacity to come out of poverty or at least resume gainful work.
- View SP not as a cost, but rather, as one type of investment. A key element of this concept involves helping the poor keep access to basic social services, avoid social exclusion, and resist coping strategies with irreversible negative effects during adverse shocks.
- Focus less on the symptoms and more on the causes of poverty by providing the poor with the opportunity to adopt higher risk–return activities and avoid inefficient and inequitable informal risk sharing mechanisms.
- Take account of reality. Less than a quarter among the world population of 6 billion have access to formal SP programmes, and less than 5 per cent can rely on their own assets to successfully manage risk. Meanwhile, eliminating the poverty gap through public transfers is beyond the fiscal capacity of most developing countries.

The basic thrust of the SRM framework is supported by two established facts: (i) the poor are typically most exposed to diverse risks, whether they are natural (such as earthquakes, flooding, or illness) or man-made (such as unemployment, environmental degradation or war), and (ii) the poor have the fewest instruments to deal with these risks (such as access to government provided income support and market-based instruments like insurance). These facts have important consequences, most importantly: (i) the poor are the most vulnerable in society as shocks are likely to have the strongest welfare consequences for them. For welfare reasons, therefore, they should have increased access to SRM instruments; and (ii) the high vulnerability makes them risk averse and thus unable or unwilling to engage in higher risk–return activities. Hence, access to SRM instruments would tend to make the poor more risk-taking and thus provide the opportunity to gradually move out of poverty.[1]

The main elements of the new framework are derived from introducing the notion of asymmetric information in a world of diverse risks in a more explicit way than has been done generally. Compared to an Arrow–Debreu world, this has several consequences for managing risks, most importantly: (i) the sources and the forms of risk matter, for example, whether a particular risk is idiosyncratic or covariant. For the former, more reliance can be given to informal or market-based risk management instruments; for the latter, more government involvement tends to be required; (ii) since risk is not necessarily exogenous, there are many more strategies to deal with risks than simple insurance, including risk reduction, risk mitigation, and risk coping strategies; (iii) as private insurance markets tend not to emerge or break down in view of asymmetric information, there are three main institutional arrangements for dealing with risk: informal, market-based and publicly-provided mechanisms; and (iv) there are multiple suppliers of Risk Management (RM) instruments (including individuals, households, communities, non-government organizations (NGOs), market institutions, government, international organizations and the world community at large) and distinct demanders (such as the formal urban, the informal urban, the formal rural, and the informal rural worker).

The application of the risk management framework goes well beyond SP since many public interventions such as sound macroeconomic policy, good governance, and access to basic education and health care all help to reduce or mitigate risk, and hence, vulnerability. It also extends SP as traditionally defined since it goes beyond public provision of RM instruments and draws attention to informal and market-based arrangements, and their effectiveness and impact on development and growth.

This chapter serves to highlight the rationale, main ideas, and open questions of the new framework with a view to stimulate further discussions. The second section presents the background and motivation for the conceptual framework, which is grounded in the

[1]The recognition of the importance of risk management for the poor, together with the need for the creation capacities and opportunities, and for voice and empowerment, also form the centrepiece of the World Development Report, 2000–1 (World Bank, 2000a).

needs, challenges, and opportunities of RM. The third section outlines the principal dimensions of the conceptual framework, including sources and forms of risks, three strategies of dealing with risk, three main levels of formality of RM, and the many relevant actors. The fourth section identifies the implications of the framework and unresolved questions, including boundaries and overlaps among RM approaches, SP beyond public provision, and new guiding principles. Finally, the conclusion is presented in the fifth section.

2. Purpose, Challenges, and Opportunities

Dealing with risk, and income risk in particular, is not a new challenge for mankind.[2] But new challenges are emerging, for instance, from globalization, which raises the need for managing risk in a proactive manner to be able to grasp opportunities for economic development and poverty reduction. This section provides the background and rationale for the new conceptual framework.

2.1. Risk Management: Old and New Issues

Natural disasters (for example, earthquakes and volcanic eruptions), bad weather (for example, floods and droughts), and health-related problems (for example, individual or epidemic illness, disability, old age, and death) have always been a concern to individuals and society. Risks associated with these sources gave rise to individual precautionary strategies (for example, crop diversification and building-up of stocks) and, perhaps more importantly, the creation of informal exchange-based risk sharing mechanisms through extended families, mutual gift giving, egalitarian tribal systems, crop-sharing arrangements with landlords, etc.. Much of the population in developing countries still relies largely or exclusively on these informal arrangements to deal with risk.

Industrialization and urbanization brought two important changes: a break-down of traditional and informal risk-sharing mechanisms and

[2]The notion of risk typically refers to uncertainty or unpredictability that result in welfare losses. For convenience we use the word 'risk' in its broadest sense to include both predictable and unpredictable elements. For individuals lacking RM tools, predictable events (such as seasonal drought) will also have negative welfare effects, thereby creating welfare risks. Yet a more precise notion such as 'undesirable fluctuations' (Sinha and Lipton 1999) is somewhat cumbersome.

the introduction of new risks, most importantly work related accidents and unemployment. The resulting 'social question' haunted governments and society in the newly industrialized nations in the second half of the 19th century and gave rise to the introduction of 'social insurance' programmes around the notion of social risks (Hesse 1997). Starting with mandated work-injury, health and old-age social insurance in some developed countries at the end of the 19th century, some 100 years later, most industrialized countries have public provisions to deal with the 'social risks' (such as work injury, sickness, disability, death, and unemployment) for a major share of their populations.

The evolution of the modern state in the north and emergence of new states in the decolonialized south brought to the forefront other types of risk arising from economic policy and the developmental process such as economic policy-induced inflation and devaluation, technology- or trade-induced changes in relative prices, default on social programmes, and changes in taxation. They all have an important bearing on the welfare position of individuals, households, and communities. Also, the development process itself, which can include resettlement and environmental degradation, can and does increase risks, as witnessed by the rising number of natural catastrophes leading to more severe consequences for the population, which is often poor (IFRC & RCS 1999).

Recent trends in the evolution of trade, technology, and political systems have generated great potential for improvements in welfare around the world. Globalization of trade in goods, services, and factors of production has the world community poised to reap the fruits of global comparative advantages. Technology is helping to speed innovation and holds the potential to remove the major constraints to development for many people. Political systems are increasingly open, setting the stage for improved governance by holding those in power accountable to larger segments of the population. Combined, these trends create a unique opportunity for unprecedented social and economic development, poverty reduction, and growth.

On the other hand, the same processes that allow for welfare improvements also heighten the variability of the outcome for society as a whole and even more so for specific groups. The global financial crisis in 1998 demonstrated this on a worldwide scale. There is no certainty that improvements will be widely shared among individuals, households, ethnic groups, communities, and countries. Expanded trade or better technology can sharpen the differences between the haves and have-nots just as it can increase the opportunity for all, depending on the prevailing social context and policy measures. Globalization-induced income variability combined with marginalization and social exclusion can, in fact, increase the vulnerability of major groups in the population. In other words, the risks are as large as the potential rewards. To further complicate matters, the trend towards globalization and the higher mobility of production factors reduces the ability of governments to raise revenues and pursue independent economic policies and, thus, to have national policies to help the poor when they are needed most (Tanzi 2000).

2.2. Importance of Good Social Risk Management

The existence and use of appropriate SRM instruments to effectively and efficiently handle risk in its various forms[3] is important because they (i) enhance individual and social welfare in a static setting; (ii) contribute to economic development and growth from a dynamic perspective; and (iii) serve as crucial ingredients for effective and lasting poverty reduction. All three dimensions are interrelated but will be discussed separately and briefly in turn.

(i) Static welfare-enhancing aspects

There are three main welfare-enhancing results of good SRM even in a static setting: reduced vulnerability, enhanced consumption smoothing, and improved equity.[4]

[3]The SRM framework can be best understood in the form of income risk, encompassing market income, imputed income, income in-kind, etc.. This broad definition of income also takes care of concerns about social services that cannot be readily bought in the market. Hence, SRM is not restricted to the monetary aspect of income/consumption of individuals or households, but merely emphasizes the income equivalent for analytical reasons. The notion 'social' refers to the form of risk management which is largely based on interpersonal exchanges and not to the form of risk.

[4]The term equity can be given many interpretations. In its most prominent use, it is linked with equality of outcomes (such as income, consumption, or wealth) and a sense of fairness. Yet there are diverse variables that enter into an assessment of equity, and the lack of adequate valuation functions over all variables means they cannot be aggregated into a single scalar measure. This has led Sen to argue for some

Reduced vulnerability. Vulnerability can be defined as the likelihood of being harmed by unforeseen events or as susceptibility to exogenous shocks and it extends the traditional view on poverty (Lipton and Ravallion 1995). The likelihood of being harmed by a shock depends on (i) a person's resilience to a given shock—the higher the resilience, that is, the capacity to deal with a shock, the lower the vulnerability and (ii) the severity of the impact — the more severe the impact, if risks cannot be reduced, the higher the vulnerability. The susceptibility to a shock depends on the capacity of avoidance, another aspect of risk management. The poor and the very poor, in particular, are especially vulnerable since they are typically more exposed to shocks and have less instruments to manage risk, and even a small drop in welfare can be disastrous. Enhancing the RM capacities of the poor and the non-poor reduces their vulnerability and increases their welfare and should thereby contribute to a decline in transitory poverty as well as provide a way out of chronic poverty (Morduch 1994).

Enhanced consumption smoothing. Economic considerations and empirical evidence suggest that economic units have a preference for smooth consumption, spreading the consumptive use of expected income over a long period, even a lifetime (Alderman and Paxson 1992; Besley 1995; Deaton 1997; and Gerowitz 1988). Income realization is mostly stochastic and during periods of negative shocks can be very low or even negative but appropriate instruments do not exist to store and transfer income to the future. The access to RM instruments, such as saving and dis-saving possibilities is crucial in order to achieve a welfare-enhancing smooth consumption path.

Improved equity. It is also a result of good SRM. If society values a more equal welfare distribution across individuals, better RM can enhance the welfare distribution and societal welfare without actually re-distributing income among individuals. Under the likely scenario that the lower income strata are more constrained in their ability to smooth consumption, improved RM arrangements can ease this constraint and thus help improve welfare more for the lower income segments leading to a more equal distribution of individual welfare (Holzmann 1990).

time that one should think of equity in terms of a checklist and use the results for 'the identification of patent injustice' (Sen 1998). Here, the use of equity is more germane to the traditional term 'equality'.

(ii) Dynamic economic development and growth aspects

Deficient or inappropriate SRM instruments will negatively impact economic development and growth and can perpetuate or even deepen poverty. This is illustrated in the examples that follow.

Income and consumption smoothing. Household welfare smoothing can take two forms: (i) households can smooth income by making conservative production and employment choices and diversifying economic activities, or (ii) households can smooth consumption by borrowing and saving, accumulating and depleting assets, adjusting labour supply (including that of their children), and employing formal and informal risk-sharing arrangements (Morduch 1995). The absence of efficient market-based or consumption-smoothing instruments provided by the government often results in the use of costly informal coping mechanisms once the adverse income shock hits, such as pulling children out of school, reducing nutritional intake, selling productive assets, or neglecting human capital accumulation. Very poor people are so close to a 'survival line' that they become extremely risk adverse, and may exhibit non-linearities in behaviour and outcome (Ravallion 1997). An awareness of insufficient consumption-smoothing instruments and risk aversion will lead households to engage in low-risk and low-yield activities. Estimates for the agricultural sector in India indicate that income smoothing can reduce farm profits by 35 per cent for the bottom wealth quartile (Binswanger and Rosenzweig 1993).

The effectiveness and costs of informal provisions. Informal risk-sharing arrangements are often associated with high transaction and hidden opportunity costs. These arrangements are essentially a form of mutual insurance that provides for those in need, are guided by a principle of balanced reciprocity, and are not insurance in the conventional sense.[5] These arrangements are informal because there

[5]Balanced reciprocity means that for any 'gift' there is a strong assumption that at some time in the future there will be a counter gift. In this sense, informal insurance arrangements may be similar to a loan where the repayment loan is state-contingent (Platteau 1996; Ligon et al. 1997). Evidence for the latter is provided by Udry (1990; 1994) for Nigeria. On an average a borrower with good realization repays 20.4 per cent more than he has borrowed while a borrower with bad realization repays 0.6 per cent less than he borrowed. Moreover, repayment is contingent on the lender's realization. A lender with a good realization receives on average 5 per cent less than he lent, but a lender with a bad realization receives 11.8 per cent more than he lent.

are no legal means within traditional agrarian societies to make binding commitments or enforce promises of reciprocity, which bears several implications:

- the very poor are often excluded since no counter-gift can be expected;
- they tend to break down or become ineffective in case of large and covariate shocks;
- strong social pressure is exerted to enforce commitment, and this is often linked with growth-inhibiting social structures (Platteau 1999); and
- a 'commitment technology' of ceremonial and expensive gift exchanges is often used, which can amount to a major share of income (Walker and Ryan 1990).

The costs of public provisions. The provision of public RM instruments such as PAYG pension system, unemployment insurance, or social assistance can enhance the welfare of individuals and the development path of countries. However, poorly designed and/or implemented systems, governance problems, or exaggerated generosity and the budgetary costs this entails, are likely to lead to significant welfare costs for the individual and the society at large. Examples include the functioning of the labour market in OECD countries (OECD 1994 and 1999), the impact of an overly generous pension system on public finance and macroeconomic stability in Brazil, and the potential implication of high social expenditure for competitiveness and economic growth while significant pockets of poverty continue to exist. These examples indicate that industrialized countries also need to review their current SRM instruments for the benefit of the population at large and more especially for the poor.

(iii) Poverty reduction aspects

It should have become clear by now as to why SRM is of particular importance for reduction of poverty. The main elements are threefold: it reduces transitory poverty, it prevents the poor from falling deeper into poverty, and it provides an avenue out of poverty.

Most panel data, including Table 2.1, suggest that between one-fifth and three-fifth of the people below the 'poverty line' at the time of a survey are not permanently poor but have been pushed into consumption poverty by life-cycle events (such as family formation) or more often by income losses (such as unemployment and sickness), special needs (such as medical treatment) or the lack of income transfer over time (Sinha and Lipton 1999). Access to appropriate SRM instruments could importantly reduce transitory poverty as fewer individuals with a lifetime income above the poverty line would become consumption poor at a moment in time.

Table 2.1
Mobility Into and Out of Poverty for Selected Countries

		Percentage of Households who are:		
		Always poor	Sometimes poor	Never poor
China	1985–1990	6.2	47.8	46.0
Côte d'Ivoire	1987–8	25.0	22.0	53.0
Ethiopia	1994–7	24.8	30.1	45.1
India	1976/76–83/84	21.9	65.9	12.4
Indonesia	1997–8	8.6	19.8	71.6
Pakistan	1986–1991	3.0	55.3	41.7
Russia	1992–3	12.6	30.2	57.2
South Africa	1993–8	22.7	31.5	45.8
Vietnam	1992/93–97/98	28.7	32.1	39.2
Zimbabwe	1992/93–1995/96	10.6	59.6	29.8

Source: Baulch and Hoddinott, 2000 and Vietnam Draft Poverty Report, 1999.

The poor are typically the most vulnerable in a society because often they are the most exposed to a whole range of risks and have the least access to appropriate risk management instruments. Risk reduction through preventive measures is largely impossible because this goes beyond the capacity of a single person, household (in many cases), or community. Personal and informal risk-management instruments are effective only in face of smaller and household-specific risks but tend to break down once a large adverse shock hits the whole community. Then the poor have only recourse to coping mechanism, such as pulling children out of school, distress sale of their assets at very low price, and the reduction of food intake, all of which endanger their future earning capacities leading to even deeper poverty and perhaps destitution.

This threat of destitution and non-survival renders the poor very risk averse and as a result makes them very reluctant to engage in higher risk/higher return activities. As a consequence, the poor are not only incapable of seizing opportunities, which emerge in a globalizing world, but are even more exposed to the increased risks, which the process is likely to entail. Without the opportunity of risk taking and engagement in more profitable production, proverty is likely to be perpetuated for them and their children. Improving the risk management capacities of the poor thus becomes an important policy for 'lasting poverty reduction', not only for dealing with 'transitory poverty' (see World Bank, 2000b, Baulch and Hoddinott, 2000).

3. Main Elements of the New Conceptual Framework

3.1 Definition and Key Concepts

A new broad definition of SP centres on the concept of social RM:

SP consists of public interventions (i) to assist individuals, households, and communities better manage risk, and (ii) to provide support to the critically poor.

This definition combines the traditional SP tools which include labour market interventions, social insurance programmes, and social safety nets, under a unifying theme. It extends beyond the public provision of RM instruments and covers public actions to improve market-based and non-market-based (informal) instruments of risk management. The concept of SRM exceeds the new definition of SP and comprises RM policies such as agricultural projects, which reduce the effects of drought, and economic policy, which in turn reduces macroeconomic shocks. On the other hand, the definition of SP goes beyond SRM and includes measures to support the critically poor.[6]

The main elements of the SRM framework consist of:

- RM strategies (risk reduction, mitigation, and coping);
- RM arrangements by level of formality (informal, market-based, and publicly provided or mandated), and
- Players in RM (from individuals, households, communities, NGOs, market institutions, and government, to international organizations and the world community at large).

These are set against the background of (i) different levels of asymmetric information and (ii) different forms of risk.

The next sub-sections will present each element in turn, starting out with the issue of asymmetric information and main forms of risk since both are fundamental for the other elements of the framework.

[6]The critically poor are those, who could not provide for themselves even if employment opportunities did exist.

3.2 The Importance of (A-)Symmetric Information for RM

Asymmetric information among market partners, individuals, groups, and government has an important bearing on the form and effectiveness of RM instruments and on government's capacity to achieve more equality in income and assets distribution.

The sources and characteristics of risks have no bearing on RM under symmetric information among all economic players and complete markets. Full insurance/state contingent contracts emerge as the best and the only instrument to deal with any kind of risk (Box 2.1). Yet, once this theoretically important but unrealistic counterfactual is abandoned, RM becomes complex. When individuals, households, or communities hold back private information, some risk markets may not emerge, would tend to break down, or function poorly. Insurance becomes the one and only and often not even the best choice to address risks, and for many risks insurance markets do not even exist. Debt and labour contracts emerge as a device to circumvent costly state verifications. Informal risk sharing mechanism substitutes for market-based instruments, in particular at the beginning of economic development since the financial systems are vulnerable to private information. In principle, there is an important role for the government to help establish, regulate, and supervise risk markets and to provide risk instruments where markets are bound to fail. Yet, asymmetric information applies also to the relation between the citizen and the government leading to government failure and political risk. As a result, a variety of RM instruments do exist in reality, provided by a multitude of players of which all hold different advantages which change over time and differ among countries.

3.3 Forms and Measurement of Risk and their Importance for RM

As discussed so far, in a world of asymmetric information the sources of risks and their characteristics have a bearing on the selection of RM instruments and, furthermore, the measurement of risk is not restricted to mere variance/standard deviation.

The capacity of individuals, households, or communities to handle risk and the appropriate RM instrument to be applied depend on the characteristics of risk: their source, correlation, frequency, and intensity. The sources of risk may be natural (for example, floods) or the result of human activity (for example, inflation resulting from

Box 2.1: Implications of (A)Symmetric Information for RM

In an ideal world á la Arrow–Debreu with symmetric information and complete markets which assumes that all decision-makers in an economy can specify, agree, and eventually verify states of the world in which they know each other's preferences and beliefs, all risks can be addressed with market-based solutions, and government may intervene for distributive purposes in a non-distortionary manner:

- Since each risk is fully known, an actuarial fair price can be established, and able-bodied individuals can and will fully insure themselves. Insurance (state contingent claims) under such a setting is the only and best instrument for dealing with all risks (including natural disasters).
- All non-able-bodied individuals would rely on public or private transfers (provided for altruistic or other reasons).
- A more equal distribution of income or assets can be achieved through lump-sum taxes and transfers in a non-distortionary manner but requires an inter-personal redistribution of income or wealth.
- In this framework, where any Pareto-efficient outcome can be described as an equilibrium of perfectly competitive markets, efficiency and equality are separable.

The above world is an important but only theoretically counter-factual, while asymmetric information in the real world, inter alia, gives rise to:

- Moral hazard, adverse selection, and insufficient property rights, which lead to poor functioning or the breakdown of risk markets (and the need for public provisions and regulations);
- Transaction costs and the development of specific institutions, such as debt and labour market contracts to circumvent costly state verification, or informal risk sharing arrangements;
- Non-exogenous risk, which can be controlled or influenced by economic players;
- Situations in which full insurance/state contingent contracts are no longer the first or even second best instrument to manage risk;
- The relevance of the sources and forms of risk to the design and selection of the most appropriate risk management instrument(s);
- Entanglement of efficiency and redistributive considerations — public interventions to increase efficiency now have distributive effects; redistributive actions have efficiency effects; and, as a result, a more equal welfare distribution can be achieved without inter-personal income redistribution;
- Unequal distribution of asymmetric information, in which there are many players with different advantages in risk management, and, as an implication, the emergence of information as a commodity and an instrument of power; and,
- Market and government failures in the provision of risk management instruments, which lead to specific market and political risks that need to be taken into account when designing programmes.

Source: Stiglitz (1975 and 1988); Eichberger and Harper (1997); Kanbur and Lustig (1999).

economic policy); risks can be uncorrelated (idiosyncratic) or correlated among individuals (covariate), over time (repeated) or with other risks (bunched); and they can have low frequency but severe welfare effects (catastrophic) or high frequency but low welfare effects (non-catastrophic). Box 2.2 presents the main sources of risk and the degree of covariance which can range from pure idiosyncratic (micro), to regional covariant (meso), to nation-wide covariant (macro) events. While informal or market-based RM instruments can often handle idiosyncratic risks, they tend to break down when facing highly covariate, macro-type risks.

Box 2.2: Main Sources of Risk

	Micro (idiosyncratic)	Meso	Macro (covariant)
Natural		Rainfall Landslides Volcanic eruption	Earthquakes Floods Drought Strong winds
Health	Illness Injury Disability	Epidemic	
Life-cycle	Birth Old age Death		
Social	Crime Domestic violence	Terrorism Gangs	Civil strife War Social upheaval
Economic		Unemployment Resettlement	Output collapse Balance of payments, Financial or currency crisis
	Business failure	Harvest failure	Technology- or trade-induced terms of trade shocks
Political	Ethnic discrimination	Riots	Political default on social programmes Coup d'état
Environmental		Pollution Deforestation Nuclear disaster	

Source: Adapted from Holzmann and Jorgensen (1999); Sinha and Lipton (1999); World Bank (2000b).

Risk and its measurement is traditionally related to variability of income or consumption, typically measured by its variance or standard deviation. Yet, if one wants to measure the welfare implication of risk, in particular for the poor, such a measure may prove inappropriate in many circumstances. Three measures of risk can be derived from three broad classes of household RM objectives that have different information requirements and implications for household and social RM strategies (Box 2.3). Since for the very poor the relevant risk measure is the maximum possible welfare loss, the most appropriate RM instruments are those which minimize that loss, for example, through the provision of basic health care or emergency food. Since for

Box 2.3: RM Objectives and Risk Measurement

RM Objective I: Minimize the size of the maximum possible welfare loss. Such an objective function is particularly relevant for the very poor and vulnerable since their maximum loss is likely to be destitution or death. The decision rule is the 'min-max principle' which is to avoid actions with a maximum possible loss of welfare. This decision rule does not require information on probabilities, just on the universe of loss functions, and the measured risk is a quantity — the loss.

[min max (loss)]: *quantity*

RM Objective II: Minimize the probability of a loss in consumption below a given threshold. Such an objective function is particularly relevant for individuals around the poverty line. The decision rule is 'safety-first', which means avoiding actions that generate an expected consumption level below a predetermined threshold. The decision-maker needs information on expected income from alternative activities and threshold consumption, and the measured risk is a probability.

[min $Pr\{c_t \leq c_{min}\}$]: probability

RM Objective III: Maximize the expected rate of return given a level of variability of returns. Such an objective function is particularly relevant for individuals with higher income levels for which the downside risk is not related to poverty or destitution. The decision rule is to maximize the expected utility function, constrained by levels of income variability associated with the activities of the decisions. The decision-maker needs information on risk preferences, expected returns generated by the asset portfolio and the distribution of returns from different asset allocations. In the special case of a utility function $V(\mu, \sigma)$ which depends only on the first two moments of a probability distribution of an asset allocation, the objective function can be easily written and the standard deviation σ becomes an easy measure for risk.

[max $V(\mu, \sigma)$]: *standard deviation* (σ)

Source: Authors, based on Siegel and Alwang (1999).

individuals around the poverty line the relevant risk measure is to minimize the probability to fall below a set consumption level, the most appropriate RM instruments are likely to be those which allow consumption smoothing through saving- or dis-saving instruments. Since for the higher income groups the relevant risk measure is the standard deviation of income, the most appropriate RM instruments are likely to be portfolio diversification and insurance.

3.4 Main Categories of RM Strategies and Levels of Formality

Given the existence of asymmetric information in the real world and the importance of the form of risks for the selection of RM instruments, there are different risk strategies and levels of formality among which one can usefully differentiate. The proposed differentiation has already been extended to fit regional (for Africa, see World Bank 2000b) and analytical purposes (Siegel and Alwang 1999).

(i) RM strategies fall in three broad categories:

a. *Prevention strategies—to reduce the probability of a down-side risk.* These are introduced before a risk occurs. Reducing the probability of an adverse risk increases people's expected income and reduces income variance (both increase welfare). Strategies to prevent or reduce the occurrence of income risks have a very broad range that surpasses the traditional scope of SP. These include policies regarding sound macroeconomics, public health, the environment, and education and training. Preventive SP interventions are typically linked to measures to reduce the risks in the labour market, notably the risk of unemployment or underemployment or low wages due to inappropriate skills or poorly functioning labour markets. They are concerned with labour standards and the (mal) functioning of the labour market resulting from skill-mismatch, bad labour market regulations, or other distortions.

b. *Mitigation strategies—to decrease the potential impact of a future down-side risk.* As with reduction strategies, mitigation strategies are also employed before the risk occurs. Whereas preventive strategies reduce the probability of the risk occurring, mitigation strategies reduce the potential impact if the risk were to occur. Risk mitigation can take several forms:

- Portfolio diversification: It reduces the variability of income by relying on a variety of assets from which returns are not perfectly correlated. This requires the acquisition and management of different assets such as physical, financial, human, and social capital in their different forms. For example, even if individuals can invest only in human capital, they can still diversify in different occupations but perhaps to the detriment of the return. If women cannot own or inherit land and have no access to safe financial instruments, they may acquire gold and jewellery. Since these assets often generate a low rate of return and insufficient risk protection, access to a broad range of assets is vital for RM, especially for the poor.

- Informal and formal insurance mechanisms: These are characterized by risk sharing (that is, risk pooling) through a number of participants whose risks are not (very) correlated. While formal insurance benefits from a large pool of participants, which results in less correlated risks, informal insurance has the advantage of low information asymmetry. The characteristics of formal or market-based insurance—the payment of a risk-based insurance premium gives rise to future state-contingent payments—are straightforward. Informal insurance arrangements are more difficult to describe as they come in different and often disguised forms because the same 'institution' serves insurance as well as non-insurance type functions (such as the family and the community).
- Hedging: It has an increased importance for financial markets (for example, forward exchange rate contracts) and is based on risk exchange or payment of a risk price to somebody for assuming that risk. Yet these arrangements do not appear to work in a labour–income related and formal provision environment, the effects of asymmetric information are too strong. However, elements can be found in informal arrangements also. For example, various family arrangements (marriage) and some labour contracts are more akin to hedging than insurance.

c. *Coping strategies—to relieve the impact of the risk once it has occurred.* The main forms of coping consist of individual/households dis-saving/borrowing, migration, enhancing labour supply (including that of children), reduction of food intake, or the reliance on public or private transfers. The government has an important role in assisting people in coping, for example, in the case where individual households have not saved enough to handle repeated or catastrophic risks. Individuals may have been poor for their entire lifetime with little or no possibility to accumulate assets, being rendered destitute by the smallest income loss and running the risk of being faced with irreversible damages.

(ii) The level of formality can distinguish the arrangements used under each of these three RM strategies. Three distinctions are proposed:

a. *Informal arrangements* (such as marriage, mutual community support, and savings in real assets such as cattle, real estate, and gold). With the lack of market institutions and public provisions, the response by individual households is self-protection through informal or personal arrangements (Alderman and Paxson 1994; Besley 1995; Ellis 1998). These arrangements sidestep most information and coordination problems that cause market failure but may be limited in their effectiveness and be expensive in terms of direct and opportunity costs (Coate and Ravallion 1993; Morduch 1999a). Examples include the buying and selling of real assets, informal borrowing and lending, crop and field diversification, the use of safer production technologies (such as growing less risky crops), and the storing of goods for future consumption.

b. *Market-based arrangements* such as financial assets—cash, bank deposits, bonds and shares—and insurance contracts. The supply of money in a low-inflation environment, financial assets with market-determined and positive rates of return, and actuarially fair insurance contracts dramatically increases the capacity of households (including the poor) to manage risk. Their supply, however, requires diverse, well-functioning financial market institutions such as a central bank, banking system, securities markets and insurance companies. Experience, however, indicates that their development takes time and involves overcoming many obstacles. Also, some degree of financial literacy is necessary for individuals to use these instruments in a welfare-enhancing manner. Since the development of good financial market institutions is time consuming and even good banks have little inclination to lend money to individuals without collateral, well-functioning microfinance institutions in various forms have an important role in the development process.

c. *Publicly mandated or provided arrangements* (such as social insurance, transfers, subsidies, and public works). When informal or market-based RM arrangements do not exist, break down, or are dysfunctional, the government can provide or mandate (social) insurance programmes (such as for unemployment, old age, work injury, disability, survivorship and sickness). The mandatory participation in a risk pool can circumvent issues of adverse selection and create beneficial welfare effects. Since these programmes are typically linked to formal employment, the coverage in developing countries is generally low. On the other hand, governments have an array of instruments to cope with the consumption effect of lost income after a shock hits, such as social assistance (that is, providing means-tested transfers in cash and in kind), subvention of basic goods and services, and public works programmes. It can also provide basic income in a universal manner to the total population or a sub-group (such as the elderly). The choice will depend on distributive concerns, available fiscal resources, administrative capacities, and the type of risk.

(iii) Examples of social RM, broken down according to type of strategy and level of formality are shown in Table 2.2.

3.5 Main Actors and Their Role in SRM

As the issue of SRM emerges as a result of private (asymmetric) information, the role of the actors/institutions need to be considered in their capacity to best deal with this situation. As information asymmetry also gives rise to imperfect market institutions (market failure) as well as non-benevolent government behaviour (policy failures), the relative roles have to be viewed in perspective.

As individuals/households hold essentially all private information, much of the risk management can take place at this level. Risk-mitigation (through the acquisition of different assets and insurance contracts) and risk-coping (through dis-saving/borrowing decisions) optimize the consumption path for a large range of risks. The better the market-based instruments, the more RM can take at this level (Hoogeveen 2000). Correspondingly, the absence of appropriate market instruments leads to a strengthening of informal RM arrangements at the household level, which are often less effective and dynamically inefficient and can have undesirable social consequences, such as child labour.

Next to households, communities have a large stock of private information. Hence, lacking the appropriate market institutions, communities have developed various informal mechanisms of risk sharing in developing countries. These mechanisms provide diverse instruments for risk mitigation and coping, deliver protection and

Table 2.2
Strategies and Arrangements of Social Risk Management—Examples

Arrangement Strategies	Informal	Market-based	Public
Risk Reduction	• Less risky production • Migration • Proper feeding and weaning practices • Engaging in hygiene and other disease preventing activities	• In-service training • Financial market literacy • Company-based and market-driven labour standards	• Good macro-economic policies • Pre-service training • Labour market policies • Labour standards • Child labour reduction interventions • Disability policies • AIDS and other disease prevention
Risk Mitigation			
Portfolio	• Multiple jobs • Investment in human, physical, and real assets • Investment in social capital (rituals, reciprocal gift-giving)	• Investment in multiple financial assets • Microfinance	• Pension systems • Asset transfers • Protection of property rights (especially for women) • Support for extending financial markets to the poor
Insurance	• Marriage/family • Community arrangements • Share tenancy • Tied Labour	• Old-age annuities • Disability, accident and other insurance (for example, crop insurance)	• Mandated/provided insurance for unemployment, old age, disability, survivorship, sickness, etc.
Hedging	• Extended family • Labour contracts		
Risk Coping	• Selling of real assets • Borrowing from neighbours • Intra-community transfers/charity • Sending children to work • Dis-saving of human capital • Seasonal/temporary migration	• Selling of financial assets • Borrowing from banks	• Disaster relief • Transfers/Social assistance • Subsidies • Public works

Source: Authors, based on Holzmann and Jorgensen (1999)

services that market-based instruments cannot provide, and are part of 'social capital.' Examples include 'susu' schemes in West Africa, mutual support arrangements reinforced through celebration and rituals in South Asian countries, and burial societies in Andean countries. Despite their risk-sharing functions, some of them may be socially undesirable because they perpetuate dependency structures or impede on economic development (Platteau 1999).

NGOs may or may not have as much private information as tightly-knit communities, but their local and informal character allows them to monitor individual behaviour better than formal market institutions. This explains the existence and importance of NGO-sponsored savings and microcredit schemes in many developing countries around the world.

Market institutions such as banks and insurance companies have to rely on public information and, as a result, are confronted by issues of moral hazard and adverse selection. On the other hand, if they are well-regulated and supervized, the shareholder value concept leads them to transparency and high efficiency, providing individuals nationwide with a broad variety of RM instruments. Market institutions in a competitive environment can also be efficient instruments to deliver services financed by the public sector (such as job placement, social assistance payments, etc.). The main challenge in coping with the new principal-agent problem in this context is to draft contracts that circumvent the private information problem as much as possible.

The government has many important roles in the area of SRM. The most important of these are: (i) to implement policy actions for risk prevention; (ii) to facilitate the establishment of market-based financial institutions, provide the enabling legal environment, ensure their regulation and supervision, and help facilitate the flow of information; (iii) to provide RM instruments where the private sector fails (for example, unemployment insurance) or where individuals lack the information for self-provisions (myopia); (iv) to provide social safety nets for risk coping; and (v) to enact income redistribution if market outcomes are considered unacceptable from a societal welfare point of view.

International institutions such as the International Monetary Fund (IMF), World Bank, ILO, and UN (United Nations) organizations, bilateral donors, and the world community at large are pivotal actors in SRM although their roles are sometimes controversial (Deacon et al.

1997). The Bretton Woods institutions are important in the provision of adjustment and emergency funds during economic and financial crises, while UN organizations and bilateral donors engage in relief efforts after natural catastrophes. Beside this support for coping with adverse risks, international institutions and many international NGOs are also involved in areas of risk reduction (for example, environment and labour standards) and risk mitigation (for example, improvement in the functioning of financial markets).

All these actors not only offer RM arrangements but can also be important generators of risk themselves, for example, through the support of development programmes that increase some risks for some people, the impact of aid in kind at domestic producers' risk, or by the fact that some of the service providers are in a monopolistic situation and extract rent, thereby increasing risk. This requires one to place SRM in a political context and ask under what types of conditions the actors are more or less likely to generate risk or offer good RM arrangements. The answer to these questions will depend crucially on the power relationships and the degree of asymmetry of information.

4. Main Implications of the New Conceptual Framework and Some Questions

The SRM framework holds many implications for areas ranging from the conceptualization of SP to programme design and implementation. This section reviews three main areas of interest: extending the traditional boundaries of SP, SP beyond public provision, and new guiding principles for SP.

4.1 Extending the Boundaries of SP

A first question relates to the overlap between SRM and a traditional view of SP. This has three main dimensions:

- Many areas of risk prevention and mitigation, such as economic and other governmental policy reduce vulnerability and income variability and thereby support SP objectives, but they are well outside SP. What is the appropriate delineation among these activities and what is the role of SP?
- Public income redistribution goes well beyond transfers to the critically poor. Where are the boundaries with SP?
- An extensive version of SP stresses problems associated with

exclusion and the need for inclusive public policies. Do they fall within the limits of SRM? Figure 2.1 presents the set of the three policy areas and their overlaps and likely boundaries.

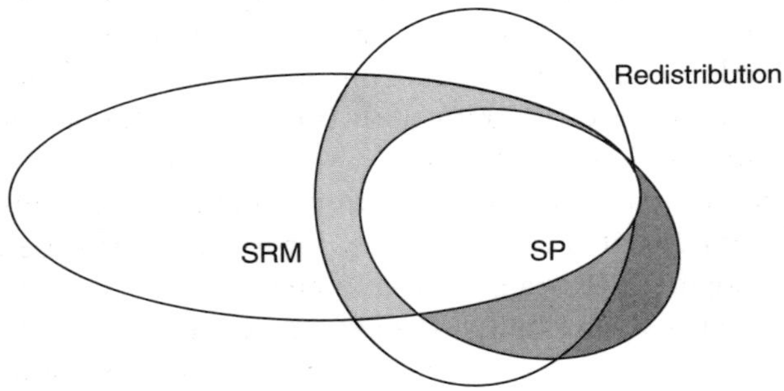

Fig. 2.1: Overlaps and Boundaries of SRM, SP, and Redistribution

In Figure 2.1, the dark shaded area of the SP set constitutes issues beyond redistribution and SRM such as social exclusion, the grey-shaded area the intersection of redistribution outside SRM such as income support for the critically poor, and the unshaded area SP as part of SRM, as discussed earlier. The light-grey-shaded area represents issues of income redistribution as part of SRM but outside SP, such as infrastructure investments in poor areas to prevent or mitigate risk especially for poorer people. The unshaded areas of the redistribution set represents public measures to achieve a more equal income distribution outside RM considerations, such as progressive income taxation. Finally, the unshaded area of the SRM set presents risk management outside SP.

(i) Risk management outside SP, and the role of SP

There are many areas of public policy that impact vulnerability and income variability that are clearly outside SP, such as macroeconomic stability, preventive measures against natural catastrophes, and infrastructure investment (for example, roads and water supply). Against the background of the SRM objectives, this suggests an advocacy and analytical role for SP, a role that assesses the risk reducing/mitigating as well as coping–avoiding effects of these policies.

Advocating and building greater awareness about the importance of broad policies to create a less risky environment for households and communities is important. There is still an insufficient understanding among some academics in the developed world and policy-makers in developing countries that sound macroeconomic policy, sound financial markets, enforcement of property rights, respect of basic labour rights, and growth-oriented policies are the best ingredients for dealing with risk and enhancing welfare.[7] If these policies are in place, households are less susceptible to risk and thereby less vulnerable and should be able to achieve most of their consumption smoothing with informal and market-based instruments. This calls for measures to build greater awareness within developing countries and among donors.

There may be a specific role for SP practices in alerting others to the fact that preventive measures are required and are cost efficient in present value calculation. Recent examples are the effects of 'El Niño' and the welfare implications of this catastrophic shock for the worldwide population. Ex-post measures of governments' ability to cope with the negative income effects may prove to be more expensive in present value terms than ex-ante measures such as investments in public infrastructure (Vos and de Labadista 1998).

The concept of SRM can be a powerful analytic instrument to assess many policy or project measures (such as road construction or irrigation schemes) on one aspect of their potential poverty reduction impact, namely their RM effects. The construction of a road between an isolated village and a market town reduces the vulnerability of the community as it enhances the use of trade for risk sharing purposes (Collier and Gunning 1999). Similarly, irrigation projects are a central instrument to reduce the risk in agriculture when rainfall is unpredictable.[8]

(ii) Income redistribution inside and outside SP

Income redistribution features importantly in SRM and SP activities, but compared to a more traditional view for SP or the welfare state

[7]More recently, the ILO, international trade union organizations (such as ICFTU), and international NGOs have become aware of and more vocal about the positive welfare consequences of macroeconomic stability and have enhanced their interaction with the Bretton Woods Institutions in this regard.

[8]In the past these investments have largely been evaluated by their estimated rate of return. In the future, a further estimate may be added: how the investment affects vulnerability. This will require new data and analytical techniques.

(Barr 1998), it is not necessarily the primary or only goal. For some academics and politicians, the main objective of SP is income redistribution, and the correction of the primary and market-determined income distribution toward a more egalitarian final and government-corrected income distribution. In the SRM framework income redistribution enters as an equality objective linked with negative shocks and emerges as an important outcome of good SP programmes at different levels:

- The support of the critically poor is the main objective of SP. Since the financing of the needed transfers in cash or in kind requires taxes on workers or non-working wealthy, it leads to an income redistribution as a result, but not as a primary objective.
- The objective of SP to enhance equity offers a second chance for redistributive actions. At a minimum, it enters at the level of equality of opportunity, and at the maximum it corrects the outcome as a result of negative shocks.
- Enhancing risk management capacity has high redistributive effects for individual welfare positions, yet it does not require direct interpersonal income redistribution to achieve a more equal welfare distribution (Holzmann 1990).
- However, many redistributive efforts by the government that emerge through a tax-transfer mechanism with a clear income redistributive objective or through the distributive effects of public goods provision are largely outside SRM and SP.

(iii) Social Protection and Social Inclusion

Advocates of policies to combat social exclusion argue that modern social protection should not be limited to traditional forms of income support but should include measures to promote social cohesion, solidarity, and inclusion (Silver 1995). This raises the question of whether social inclusion is legitimately part of the remit of social protection.

At one end, social inclusion, cohesion, solidarity, and stability are the desired outcomes of SRM, which is merely directed toward income aspects of risk, however widely defined. All these social policy objectives can be defined as positive externalities resulting from well-designed and implemented SRM. For example, a well-designed income support system for the unemployed will not only enhance individual welfare through lower vulnerability and better consumption smoothing but will also help achieve qualitative objectives such as social stability. Providing income support for the elderly not only enhances their consumption possibilities but also allows them to better participate in social life. On the other end, social protection measures would go well beyond mere financial and income-oriented considerations to include a more holistic, proactive policy to influence the social structure of an economy. This approach would include investments in the socio-cultural infrastructure by supporting informal arrangements and upgrading the non-profit sector. It would quite likely include a strengthening of the 'social rights approach' of social policy. Finally, it would include an extended view of instruments and institutions to be used under social protection, including the concept of 'social capital' (Badelt 1999).

4.2 SP beyond Public Provision

One main implication of the framework is that social protection is often or predominantly provided outside the public sector through the informal and private sector, and involves many actors, ranging from individuals, communities, and NGOs to governments, and international institutions. This raises three important questions: What are the possibilities of the public interventions to facilitate RM in the other sectors? What is the trade-off in developmental terms to support or restrict SRM in different sectors? And since all of the actors operate in their own interest and under asymmetric information constraints, what are the implications for design and sustainability?

(i) Public intervention and SRM in the non-government sector

The core institution for managing idiosyncratic risks was, and quite likely still is, the family. While the break-down of the extended family in some parts of the world has required the introduction of alternative measures, such as public or privately provided pensions, even the core family or single parent family of today's industrialized countries employs many of the RM strategies. But the power within families is not equally distributed, the effectiveness and the efficiency of SRM may not be gender neutral, and the legal or informal position of women and children may not be secured. This raises the issue of the possibility of government to positively influence informal SRM through legislation, monetary and non-monetary incentives, and the provision of information, etc..

Similar uncertainties exist with regard to communities and NGOs too. Both are important actors in the provision of RM instruments, and many have developed independent of government intervention. Informal risk sharing mechanisms at the community level are a result of repeated interactions and a commitment technology developed over time. In these areas of informal SRM, we know more about what governments have done to crowd out desirable RM activities, something on what governments can do to crowd out undesirable coping mechanisms (for example, child labour), and little about what governments can do to 'crowd in' desirable RM interventions.

In contrast to informal provisions, the potential of government in helping to establish and influence market-based RM instruments seems to be better understood. There is a growing knowledge of the role of government in sound regulation and supervision of financial market institutions, ironically helped by recent worldwide financial crises. But regarding the most vulnerable and marginalized, formal sector institutions serve them little or not at all. Here, a lot of hope has been placed on the development of microfinance institutions, but as some authors suggest, the promise of microfinance may have pushed far ahead of the evidence (Morduch 1999b). What developing as well as developed economies have in common is the need for 'financial market literacy', that is, an understanding of the role and functioning of financial institutions and the instruments provided.

(ii) SRM and economic development

SRM is not neutral to economic development (Ahmad, Dreze, and Sen 1991): it may support it through the encouragement of risk taking, the choice of more productive technologies, and the way in which it deals with gender; but it may also hamper it through the elimination of risk and introduction of incentives to change individual behaviour. This renders the support of RM instruments by the government an important tool for economic development and may give rise to a trade-off between short-term effectiveness and long-term dynamic efficiency.

As discussed in the section on'Dynamic Economic Development and Growth Aspect', there are many arguments for the view that insufficient RM instruments impede efficient decisions and economic growth. The most important channels are likely to be too little risk taking, inefficient informal risk sharing mechanism, and sub-optimal choice of production technology by the poor and near poor, all of which contribute to too low growth and perpetuation of poverty. In turn, appropriate risk management instruments provided by markets or government compared to self insurance allow for higher risk taking by individuals. Risk taking is productive and risk can be seen as a factor for production with the same status as the better-known factor like capital and labour (Sinn 1998, quoting Pigou, 1932). Furthermore, the lack of appropriate RM instruments make countries more vulnerable to external shocks which can lead to breaks in the growth path of countries. Recent empirical evidence suggest that latent social conflicts and weak institutions of social conflict management (including low level of social safety nets) may explain why so many countries have experienced a growth collapse since the mid-1970s (Rodrik 1999).

On the other hand, however, the provision of RM instruments may also modify individual behaviour in ways that have detrimental effects on economic development. The public provision of insurance against income risk may improve the outcome in the face of a wide range of risks but may also reduce individual efforts (such as job search) or lead to taking too much or too little risk. This may be compounded by pervasive income redistribution that is often part of public welfare systems, and there is empirical evidence from OECD countries that an increase in social risk insurance in the welfare state reduces entrepreneurship (Ilmakunnas et al. 1999). In addition, welfare state interventions may imply a redistribution paradox where more redistribution results in more inequality of the pre- and/or post-tax income distribution (Sinn 1995 and 1998). This calls for a careful analytic and empirical assessment of publicly provided and managed risk management instruments.

Starting with informal SRM instruments in less developed economies, one can also be confronted with a trade-off between (short-term) distributive effectiveness versus (long-term) dynamic efficiency. A wide variety of informal arrangements may be effective in providing risk mitigation for the covered group, but it may come at high costs for current and future income, particularly for the poor. On the other hand, many publicly provided alternatives appear costly in the short run because additional budgetary resources have to be raised but may imply long-term efficiency gains if, for example, repressive informal institutional structures and low-level production technologies are removed. Therefore, there can be a trade-off between long-term economic gains and improvement in the inter-temporal budget constraint of government and the short-term cost of the new RM arrangement, which is likely to hit the short-term budget constraint in countries with low tax capacities especially hard.

(iii) Political sustainability issues

Discussions about the SP programmes (or more generally about the welfare state) have long been seen in terms of a simple trade-off between equality and efficiency once the social welfare function over individual income positions is defined. Yet the experience with public interventions and attempted reforms has shown that the best technical solution may not be politically sustainable.[9] As a result, the original, first-best design is blurred or totally reversed, while changes toward a potentially sustainable second-best solution prove politically difficult or even impossible. This suggests that considerations of political economy have to be part of system design and reform. And the simple trade-off has to be extended to a 'menage-à-trois': equality, efficiency, and political sustainability. The deterioration in system design and implementation of public SP programmes is the result of changes in voter coalitions as well as personal interests of politicians and bureaucrats. One method of protecting the original design consists of establishing an appropriate self-binding mechanism, enhanced transparency, and stricter accountability. Relatively successful examples of self-binding mechanisms include the long-term fiscal projections under the United States pension system, present value budgeting in New Zealand, and periodic evaluations of all existing programmes and of proposed changes in many industrialized countries.

Once political sustainability becomes a criterion for programme design, the resiliency toward political risk becomes an important element for programme selection. The conjectured trade-off between equality, efficiency, and sustainability suggests that an explicit second-best solution from an efficiency or equality point of view may be selected if it is considered more resilient to political risk. Examples include individual savings accounts to cope with income risk due to unemployment or health

[9]For example, the reserve funds in PAYG pension systems in developing countries have typically been depleted through increased benefits or outright theft. These funds should have allowed for a lower steady-state contribution rate. For a discussion, see Holzmann and Stiglitz, 2001.

compared to un-funded and publicly managed provisions.

Reforming public programmes of RM such as pensions, unemployment or sickness benefits, proves very difficult politically. Entrenched interests, acquired rights, or a lack of credibility of the proposed alternatives are among the most common obstacles. While resistance to reform is not specific to SP programmes, the problem is particularly prevalent and difficult to overcome.

4.4 New Guiding Principles for SP

For a conceptual framework to be operationally useful it must help in the derivation of policy recommendations. This section outlines some of the guiding principles suggested by the SRM framework, tempered by the experience with SP programmes.

(i) Espousing a holistic view

The complexity of the SRM framework demands a holistic view of the issues, options, and players:

a. At the level of issues and options SRM requires moving away from strict categorization of traditional programmes in cylinders (that is, public pensions, labour market interventions, and social safety nets) and seeing their interrelation, interaction with informal and market-based arrangements, and the (partial) substitutability or complementarity of the main strategies;

b. At the level of players, it calls for close interaction between the main stakeholders, those who govern them, and those from institutions who want to be helpful;

c. At the level of information, the new approach needs a new, or least different, data set for benchmarking and evaluation and improved analytical techniques. Data to measure and assess the effectiveness of alternative SRM instruments does not yet exist, and its future availability is likely to require a cooperative effort among countries, international institutions, and other national and international players.

(ii) Balancing coping, mitigation, and risk reduction strategies

On face value, the best SRM is to make sure that the (down-side) risk does not even occur. Risk mitigation comes next since the effects of risks are decreased ex-ante. Risk coping is essentially the residual strategy if everything else has failed. However, as each of these strategies have direct and opportunity costs, full reliance on risk reduction or mitigation may not be efficient or feasible. The experience of the formerly centrally planned economies has demonstrated that trying to eliminate all risks ex-ante through quantity planning, official price setting, and public ownership of productive means leads to serious costs in terms of slower economic development. Still, too much of current government intervention, particularly for the poor, is concentrating on risk coping. To increase effectiveness more effectively, more attention must be paid to risk mitigation and reduction. Promising areas where some experience and expertise exist include improved labour markets, skill enhancement of the labour force, participatory community projects, access to safe financial assets, and appropriate unemployment benefits.

(iii) Building on comparative advantage of actors

SRM has many actors; from individuals, households, communities, and NGOs to the government at various levels, bilateral and multilateral donors, international organizations, and the world community as a whole. They are characterized by different degrees of asymmetric information and instruments to overcome its effects. All have different advantages but none can provide perfect SRM instruments. Comparative advantages change over time as efficiency of information and markets develops. This suggests that no single actor or arrangement should dominate but that SRM should build on the comparative advantage of each with flexibility to allow for changes over time. Specifically, the new role of governments and international institutions in SRM could be to:

a. Strengthen their direct involvement in risk reduction, in particular in areas of disaster prevention and building the human capital base, including the fight against child labour and provision of equitable and inclusive labour markets, early childhood development and youth development services, etc.;

b. Reduce their direct involvement in risk mitigation while enhancing their role as regulator and supervisor of instruments provided by the private sector (for example, health insurance, pensions, etc.);

c. Focus their involvement in coping on the incapacitated, very vulnerable, and crisis situations.

(iv) Matching interventions and risks

There are certain types of risks that individuals, households, or communities are poorly equipped to handle, which include natural disasters, epidemics, and financial meltdowns. These risks call for government interventions and support from international institutions and the world community. Less catastrophic risks allow for informal and market-based SRM but in many instances it requires public interventions in the form of regulation, mandating, or provision. In order to be effective and dynamically efficient, however, the intervention must specifically address the type of risk and its environment. For example, unemployment insurance may not always be the best RM instrument when confronting repeated and large covariant unemployment risks in an economy with low administra-tive capacity and large informal sector. The experience with the difficult transition from plan to market in the 1990s and the most recent financial shock in East Asia have emphasized the need for tailored solutions profiting from world-wide experience.

5. Conclusions

The proposed new conceptual framework of SRM is intellectually appealing and may be productively applied in the developing and developed economies. The true value of any new concept, however, lies in its ability to help better understand and map reality and propose and implement better policies. The response of policy-makers and designers so far has been very encouraging.[10] The concept offers ministers for finance and policy-designers an integrated approach and suggests a broad range of RM mechanisms: It gives a strong role to well developed financial markets to supply RM instruments which go well beyond the demand for more fiscal resources and to price risks. It stresses the importance of functioning informal RM arrangements, most importantly the family and community. It provides a framework to rethink traditional SP programmes such as labour market interventions, pensions and unemployment insurance, and social safety nets. And draws to the attention of policy-makers and policy-analysts the importance of prevention and mitigation beside the mere coping strategies. In terms of further development of the framework and research, much more needs to be done, and the tasks include a better understanding of several topics: an analytically-sound but operational

[10]See Holzmann (2001) and visit the World Bank web-page for progress in the application and implementation of the SRM framework: http://www.worldbank.org/sp

definition of vulnerability; how government interventions can and should facilitate informal risk management arrangements; theoretical and empirical guidelines for the balance between risk prevention, mitigation, and coping; and the circumstances under which the various actors best perform their roles as providers of risk management and, conversely, serve as a source of risk.

References

Ahmad, E., J. Dreze, and A. K. Sen (1991) *Social Security in Developing Countries,* Oxford, Oxford University Press.

Alderman, H. and Ch. Paxson (1994) 'Do the poor insure? A Synthesis of the Literature on Risk and Consumption in Developing Countries', *International Economics Association Conference,* Moscow, 4.

——— (1992) 'Do the poor insure. A synthesis of the literature on risk and consumption in developing countries', *Policy Research Working Papers—Agricultural Policies,* WPS 1008, World Bank, October.

Badelt, Ch. (1999) *Social Risk Management and Social Inclusion,* World Bank, September (mimeo).

Barr, N. (1998) *The Economics of the Welfare State,* 3rd edition, Oxford, Oxford University Press.

Baulch, B. and J. Hoddinott (2000) Economic Mobility and Poverty Dynamics in Developing Countries, Journal of Development Studies 36 (6) pp. 1–24.

Bernstein, P. L. (1996) *Against the Gods—The Remarkable Story of Risk,* New York et al., John While & Sons.

Besley, T. (1995) *'Savings, credit, and insurance',* in J. Behrman and T.N. Srinivasan (eds), *Handbook of Development Economics,* Vol. III., Amsterdam (North Holland), pp. 2123–2207.

Binswanger, H. and M. Rosenzweig (1993) 'Wealth, weather risk and the composition and profitability of agricultural investments', *Economic Journal,* 103, pp. 56–78.

Coate, St. and M. Ravallion (1993) Reciprocity without commitment. Characterization and performance of informal arrangements, Journal of Development Economics 40, pp. 1–24.

Collier, P. and J.W. Gunning (1999) *'Why has Africa grown slowly', Journal of Political Perspectives* 13 (3) pp. 3–22.

Deacon, B., M. Hulse, and P. Stubbs (1997). *Global Social Policy— International Organizations and the Future of Welfare,* London et al., Sage Publications.

Deaton, A. (1997) *The Analysis of Household Surveys: A Microeconomic Approach to Development Policy,* Baltimore, Johns Hopkins University Press.

Eichberger, J. and I. Harper (1997). *Financial Economics,* New York et al., Oxford University Press.

Ellis, F. (1998) Household Strategies and Rural Livelihood Diversification, *Journal of Development Studies,* 35 (1), pp. 1–38.

Gerowitz, M. (1988) '*Saving and development*', in H. Chenery and T.N. Srinivasan (eds), *The Handbook of Development Economics*, Vol. I, Amsterdam, North Holland, pp. 382–424.

Gore, Ch. (1995) '*Introduction: Markets, Citizenship and Social Exclusion*', in G. Rodgers, Ch. Gore, and J.B. Figueiredo, (eds) *Social Exclusion: Rhetoric, Reality, Responses, Geneva,* IILS, pp. 1–42.

Hesse, P.J. (1997) '*Autour de l'histoire de la notion de risk*', in J. Van Langendonck (ed.) *The New Social Risk/Les Niveaux Risques Sociaux,* EISS Yearbook 1996, The Hage et al., Kluwer Law, pp. 5–52.

Holzmann, R. (2001) 'Risk and Vulnerability: The forward looking role of social protection in a globalizing world', paper presented at The Asia and Pacific Forum on Poverty—Policy and Institutional Reforms for Poverty Reduction, Asian Development Bank, Manila, 5–9 February 2001.

——— (1990) '*The welfare effects of public expenditure programs reconsidered*', IMF Staff Papers 37, pp. 338–59.

Holzmann, R. and S. Jorgensen (1999) 'Social Protection as Social Risk Management: Conceptual Underpinnings for the Social Protection Sector Strategy Paper', Journal of International Development, 11: pp. 1005–27.

Holzmann, R. and J. Stiglitz (2001) *New Ideas About Old Age Security,* Washington, D.C., World Bank.

Hoogeveen, H. (2000) 'Risk and insurance by the poor in developing countries', paper presented at the Microfinance for Disaster Risk Colloquium, sponsored by UNDP and the Disaster Management Facility, World Bank, Washington, D.C., 2 February.

International Federation of Red Cross and Red Crescent Societies (1999) *World Disasters Report,* Geneva, IFRC & RCS.

Ilmakunnas, P., V. Kanniainen, and U. Lmma (1999) *Entrepreneurship, Economic Risk, and Risk-Insurance in the Welfare State,* Helsinki School of Economics (mimeo).

Kanbur, R. and N. Lustig (1999). *Why is Inequality Back on the Agenda?,* World Bank (mimeo).

Ligon, E., J.P. Thomas, and T. Worrall (1997) *Informal Insurance Arrangements in Village Economies,* University of California, Berkeley, (mimeo).

Lipton, M. and M. Ravallion (1995) '*Poverty and Policy*', in J. Behrman and T.N. Srinivasan (eds) *The Handbook of Development Economics,* Vol. III, Amsterdam, North Holland, pp. 2551–657.

Morduch, J. (1994) (1999a) '*Between the State and the Market: Can informal insurance patch the safety net?*', The World Bank Research Observer, 14(2) pp. 187–207.

——— (1999b) '*The microfinance promise*', *Journal of Economic Literature* (forthcoming).

——— (1995) '*Income and consumption smoothing*', *Journal of Economic Perspectives,* 9 (3) pp. 103–14.

——— (1994) '*Poverty and Vulnerability*', *American Economic Review and Papers and Proceedings,* 84 (2) 221–5.

——— (1999) '*Assessing Performance and Policy—Implementing the OECD Jobs Strategy*', OECD Job Study, Paris, OECD.

OECD (1994), OECD Job Study, Paris, OECD.

Pigou, A. C. (1932) *The Economics of Welfare,* London, Macmillan.

——— (1999) '*Traditional sharing norms as an obstacle to economic growth in tribal society*', in J.P. Platteau (ed.), Institutions, Social Norms, and Economic Development, chapter 5, Chur, Harwood Academic Publisher.

Platteau, J. P. (1996) 'Mutual insurance as an elusive concept in traditional rural societies', *Journal of Development Studies* 23(4), pp. 461–90.

Ravallion, M. (1997) 'Famine and economics', *Journal of Economic Literature,* 35(3), pp. 1205–42.

Rodrik, D. (1999) 'Where did all the growth go? External shocks, social conflict, and growth collapses', *Journal of Economic Growth,* 4 December, pp. 385–412.

Sen, A. (1998) 'Economic policy and equity: An overview', in V. Tanzi, K. Chu, and S. Gupta (eds), *Economic Policy and Equity,* Washington, D.C., International Monetary Fund.

Sinha, S. and M. Lipton (1999) *Undesirable Fluctuations, Risk and Poverty: A Review,* Draft, World Bank (mimeo), October.

Siegel, P. and J. Alwang (1999) '*An Asset-based Approach to Social Risk Management—A Conceptual Framework*', Social Protection Discussion Paper No. 9926, World Bank, Washington, D.C..

Silver, H. (1995) '*Reconceptualizing social disadvantage: Three paradigms of social exclusion*', in G. Rodgers, Ch. Gore, and J. B. Figueiredo (eds), *Social Exclusion, Reality, Responses,* Geneva, IILS, pp. 57–80

Sinn, H. W. (1998) '*Social insurance, incentives and risk-taking*', in P. B. Sørensen (ed), *Public Finance in a Changing World,* London, Macmillan, pp. 73–100.

——— (1995) 'A theory of the welfare state', Scandinavian Journal of Economics 97, 495–526.

Stiglitz, J. E. (1988) '*Economic organization, information and development*', in H. Chenerey and T. N. Srinivasan (eds), *Handbook of Development Economics,* Vol. I, Amsterdam et al., North Holland, 94–160.

——— (1975) '*Information in economic analysis*', in M. Parkin and A.R. Nobay (eds), *Current Economic Problems,* Cambridge, Cambridge University Press.

Tanzi, V. (2000) '*Globalization and the Future of Social Protection*', *IMF Working Paper,* WP/00/12, January.

——— (1994) '*Risk and insurance in a rural credit market: An empirical investigation in northern Nigeria*', *Review of Economic Studies,* 63, 495–526.

Udry, C. (1990) '*Credit markets in northern Nigeria: Credit as insurance in a rural economy*', *The World Bank Economic Review,* 4, 251–69.

Vos, R. and E. de Labastida (1998) '*Economic and social effects of "el niño" in Ecuador, 1997–98,* First Workshop of the LACEA/IDB/World Bank Inequality and Poverty Network, Buenos Aires, 22–4 October 1998.

Walker, T. and J. Ryan (1990) '*Village and Household Economies in India's Semi-*

Arid Tropics', Baltimore, John Hopkins University Press.
World Bank (2001) '*Social Protection Sector Strategy—From Safety Net to Springboard*', Washington, D.C., World Bank.
——— (2000a) *World Development Report 2000/01—Attacking Poverty*, Washington, D.C., World Bank.
——— (2000b) *Dynamic Risk Management and the Poor—Developing a Social Protection Strategy for Africa*, revised draft, October.
——— (1994) '*Zambia Poverty Assessment*', Human Resource Division, Southern Africa Department, Africa Regional Office.

3

How to Reform Social Security and Why?

Estelle James

Over the next thirty-five years, the proportion of the world's population that is over age 60 will nearly double, from 9 per cent to 16 per cent. Due to rapid increase in life expectancy and decline in fertility rates, populations are aging much faster in developing countries than they did in industrial countries. As young working-age people approach retirement, around the year 2030, 80 per cent of the world's old people will live in what today are developing countries. These countries will be shifting from systems of informal to formal old age security and, given their rapid aging, it is essential that they get this right from the start. At the same time, industrialized countries are trying to reform their existing systems to make them more sustainable and less costly.

Cross-sectional analysis shows that public spending on formal pension plans increases exponentially as populations age. It now exceeds 15 per cent of Gross National Product (GNP) in some industrialized countries and will do so in many more countries as the demographic transition proceeds. With such large sums involved, how this money is generated and spent can affect the entire economy, by influencing factor supplies, productivity and, therefore, the size of the GNP pie. For example, high payroll taxes can lead to lower employment in the formal labour sector, while pre-funding pension expenditures can be part of a plan to increase national saving. As another example, countries with higher private pension spending and assets have lower public spending, and these two types of spending may have different effects on the broader economy. Therefore, two over-arching criteria should be used to shape and evaluate these programmes: they should protect the old (in an equitable way) and they should promote (or at least not hinder) economic growth, which is important both for the old and the young.

In the past, most old age security systems established by governments were PAYG systems, taxing workers today to pay pensions to old people today. This chapter argues that growing old is a predictable life experience that most of us will have with a high probability, so a large part of old age security can instead be provided by self-insurance, people saving for themselves, shifting consumption from their younger productive years to their older years when consumption exceeds income. Myopia among workers may require that retirement saving be mandatory. But relying, to some extent, on self-insurance and saving may reduce many of the incentive problems associated with tax and transfer PAYG systems, thereby having a positive impact on the overall economy.

Another part of old age security systems, however, requires pooling risks and insuring or redistributing across individuals—because some people, due to factors beyond their control, will retire early with disabilities, die young and leave dependents, live longer than average and run out of resources, or earn very low lifetime incomes which are insufficient to support them both for their working and non-working lives. This is the rationale for providing old age security through a combination of mandatory self-insurance and insurance across individuals, in a multi-pillar system that puts greater emphasis on saving, has separate financing and managerial mechanisms for redistribution and saving, and shares responsibility between the private and public sectors.

Over the past few years, many countries have indeed been adopting multi-pillar old age security systems. The experience of these countries shows that though structural change is difficult, it is possible, and that it takes somewhat different forms in different places and it usually involves transition costs that are spread over several generations. Preliminary empirical evidence suggests a positive impact on efficiency and growth. But it also brings to the fore new problems—concerning high administrative costs and regulatory regimes that distort investment decisions—that remain to be solved.

Section 1 of this chapter briefly describes the almost universal problems in traditional systems and sets forth a recommendation for tomorrow's systems. Section 2 contrasts three structural reform models that are now being implemented—the Latin American model in which workers decide how their savings will be invested, the OECD model in which employers and/or union representatives control the investment strategy for an entire enterprise or occupation, and the Swedish model in which workers have large notional accounts, possibly supplemented by small funded accounts with real savings and investments in them. Section 3 discusses methods that countries have used for covering transition costs. Sections 4 and 5 examine empirical evidence on the positive efficiency and growth impact of these reforms, as well as the major new problems that have emerged. The conclusion summarizes these recent policy and research developments.

1. Problems in Old Systems and Recommended New Systems

Most formal systems of old age security today are publicly managed, pay defined benefits according to a formula based on the worker's earnings and years of service, and are financed by payroll taxes on a PAYG basis, meaning that the contributions made by today's workers are used to pay the pensions of those who have already retired. However, it is now widely recognized that these systems generate many problems, that include:

- high and rising payroll tax rates that may increase unemployment;
- evasion and escape to the informal sector, where productivity is lower;
- early retirement, which reduces the supply of experienced labour;
- misallocation of public resources, as scarce tax revenues are used for pensions rather than for education, health, or infrastructure;
- lost opportunity to increase long term saving;
- failure to redistribute to low income groups;
- unintended inter-generational transfers (often to high income groups); and
- the growth of a large hidden implicit public pension debt, which makes the current system financially unbalanced.

As a result, existing systems have not always protected the old, will not protect especially those who grow old in the future, they often have not distributed their benefits in an equitable way, and have hindered economic growth. In addition, they are simply not sustainable in their present form.

Each of these problems are found in most countries, both developing and industrialized. This suggests that these problems are not accidental, but rather they are inherent in the economics and politics of PAYG DB schemes, which make it easy for politicians to promise short run benefits at the expense of large long run costs.

To avoid these dangers, the World Bank has been recommending and many countries have been moving toward a system that is partially defined contribution, funded and privately managed, rather than fully defined benefit, PAYG and publicly managed. Specifically, these new systems contain three pillars:

- a mandatory publicly-managed tax-financed pillar for redistribution,
- a mandatory privately-managed fully funded pillar for saving, and
- a voluntary pillar for people who want more protection for old age.

The first pillar resembles existing public pension plans but is smaller and focuses on redistribution, providing a social safety net for the old, particularly the old whose lifetime income was low. The benefit formula can be flat (uniform for everyone or related to years of covered employment, as in Argentina and the UK), means- and asset-tested (as in Australia) or provide a minimum pension guarantee, as in Chile. The last alternative is obviously cheaper while the first provides additional co-insurance and redistribution to lower middle class workers. In some cases (Australia, Chile) this pillar is financed out of general revenues rather than a payroll tax. Because of its limited scope and broad tax base, tax rates to support this pillar are much lower than the public system requires in most countries today.

The second pillar differs dramatically from traditional systems. It links benefits actuarially to contributions as in a defined contribution (DC) plan, it is fully funded and privately competitively managed. (In a DC plan the contribution rather than the benefit is defined and the future pension depends on accumulated contributions plus investment returns. In a fully funded system assets are always sufficient to cover future liabilities.) Essentially, people are required to save for their old age, and this pillar handles their savings.

A third pillar, voluntary saving and annuities, offers supplemental retirement income for people who want more consumption in their old age.

The second pillar is the most innovative and controversial of the three, so it is worth examining the rationale for its characteristics. This rationale takes into account the behavioural reactions of workers, savers, and politicians to incentives posed by alternative social security systems.

Why mandatory? The rationale here is myopia, a significant number of people may be shortsighted, may not save enough for their old age on a voluntary basis, and may become a burden on society at large in their old age.

Why DC? The close link between contributions and benefits in a DC plan should discourage evasion, escape to the informal sector, and other labour market distortions, since people are less likely to regard their contribution as a tax. And those who do evade bear the cost in the form of lower benefits rather than passing the costs on to others and undermining the financial viability of the scheme. Since the pension is acquired on actuarially fair terms given the age and accumulation of the worker, DC plans are likely to deter early retirement and to raise the normal retirement age automatically as longevity increases, without a collective decision that is often difficult for politicians to make.

Why fully funded? First, pre-funding makes costs clear up front so countries won't be tempted to make promises today that they will be unable to keep tomorrow. Second, it avoids large payroll tax increases that are needed in a PAYG system as populations age. Third, it prevents large inadvertent intergenerational transfers from young people to older workers. Once an unfunded system is set in motion, intergenerational transfers occur automatically as a result of the aging and maturation process, sometimes in ways that people did not expect and would not have chosen after an open discussion. For example, the early generations to be covered (including its rich members) gain, while later generations (including its poor members) lose, even though they did not even have a chance to participate in the political decision that produced this intergenerational contract. Full funding eliminates such undesirable transfers. Fourth, funding may be used to help build long-term national saving. These savings can enhance the productivity of future workers, they can be imbedded in consumer durables that provide a stream of future services, and they can be invested abroad, then redeemed to finance an inflow of consumer goods. Thus, saving can be an important ingredient of a long run strategy for providing additional domestic consumption when the dependency rate increases.

Why privately managed? This maximizes the likelihood that economic rather than political objectives will determine the investment strategy, thereby producing the best allocation of capital and the highest return on savings; and it helps countries (especially middle income countries) develop their financial markets. Empirical data show that publicly managed pension reserves typically earn low, even negative returns, largely because public managers are required to invest in government securities or loans to failing state enterprises, at low nominal interest rates that become negative real rates during inflationary periods. The hidden and exclusive access to these funds makes it easier for governments to run large deficits or to spend more wastefully than they could if they had to rely on a more accountable source of funds.

Competitively managed funded pension plans, in contrast, are more likely to be invested in a mixture of public and corporate bonds, equities and real estate, thereby earning a higher rate of return. Private pension funds can enjoy the benefits of investment diversification, including international diversification, that enables them to increase their yield and reduce their risk, by protecting them from inflation and other country-specific risks. They build constituencies that help them resist political manipulation. They spur financial market development, by creating a demand for new financial instruments and institutions. (But three caveats: countries must have at least rudimentary capital markets before they can put the funded pillar in place; considerable government regulation and regulatory capacity are needed in order to prevent fraud and excessive risk; and if this regulation is excessive or misdirected, financial markets and investment policies will not be optimal.)

All three pillars co-insure against the many risks that old people face, in particular, against the generalized risk stemming from uncertainty about the future economy or polity, such as breakdowns of the government or the market, changes in relative prices of labour and capital, deterioration in the position of a particular country, by diversifying across types of management (public and private), sources of finance (from labour and capital) and investment strategies (equities and bonds, domestic and international). Risk diversification is especially important given the long time periods and great uncertainty involved. Whatever unpredictable disasters occur in the future, as they surely will, this diversified system is most likely to continue providing protection for the old. (See World Bank 1994 for more details about the problems of old systems and the recommended new system. For a quantification of the welfare gains from diversification see Pujol 1996.)

2. How Have Countries Reformed?

During the past decade, with the pace accelerating during the last five years, several countries have adopted variations on this multi-pillar system. The three major variations are the Latin American (individual account) model, the OECD (employer sponsored) model and the Swedish (notional DC) model. We have learnt from this experience that pension reform is possible, even in democracies, but it takes somewhat different forms in different countries, as a result of different initial conditions and political economies.

For example, these different conditions led Argentina to choose a relatively large public pillar while in Peru there is no public pillar at all, at present. Chile and Australia both have a much larger private pillar than Mexico and Argentina, while the UK and Switzerland built upon a history of employer sponsored plans. Australia and Denmark built upon widespread union-negotiated plans, while Sweden and Italy adopted a DC plan in their structural reform, but to keep it largely PAYG.

One of the most important initial conditions that influences the shape of the reform is the implicit pension debt (IPD), the present value of the pension promises that are owed to current pensioners and to workers according to their years of participation in the old system. The IPD is inherent in PAYG systems, where workers expect to get a specified pension in return for their contributions, but assets are not accumulated to cover this; instead the obligation is covered by implicit IOUs of the government. The IPD exceeds the conventional explicit debt (backed by government bonds) in many countries and exceeds 200 per cent of GNP in some cases (Table 3.1). It is especially large in countries with high coverage, generous benefits, and older populations. Although this debt is not always legally binding, it tends to be socially

Table 3.1
Implicit Pension Debt (IPD)[a] and Pension Reform

Countries that have not reformed	IPD as % of GDP	Reforming countries[b]	IPD as % of GDP	Size of new public pillar[c]
Senegal	27	El Salvador	35	LO
Mali	26	Peru	37	LO
Burkina Faso	15	Colombia	40	LO
Venezuela	30	Mexico	42	LO
Cameroon	44	Bolivia	48	LO
Congo	30	Argentina	86	MED
Brazil	187	Kazakhstan	88	LO
Turkey	72	Chile	100	LO
Albania	67	Australia[d]	115	MED
China	63	United Kingdom[d]	184	MED
Ukraine	141	Netherlands[d]	188	MED
United States	113	Denmark[d]	189	MED
Japan	162	Switzerland	189	MED
Germany	157	Sweden	210	HI
France	216	Hungary	213	HI
Italy	242	Uruguay	214	HI
Canada	121	Poland	220	HI
		Croatia	350	HI

Notes: a: IPD is present value of accrued rights of pensioners and workers, under old system.

b: Estimated by author based on current public expenditure. Details available upon request.
Hungary, Uruguay, and Peru are taken from Kane and Palacios, *Finance and Development*, June 1996, p. 38.

c: LO: minimum pension guarantee, financed out of general revenues (except Bolivia).
HI: large earnings-related public pillar, financed out of payroll tax.
MED: flat (or compressed) public pillar and means-testing, usually financed out of general revenues.

d: Old system featured universal benefits financed out of general revenues not out of earmarked payroll taxes. Hence, the IPD owed as repayment of past contributions, is less applicable.

Sources: Kane and Palacios, *Finance and Development*, June 1996, p. 38; Robert Palacios for Albania; Cheikh Kane for Burkina Faso, Congo, Mali; Paul Van der Noord and Richard Herd, *Pension Liabilities in the Seven Major Economies*, OECD 1993, for OECD countries.

and politically binding; governments cannot easily renege on these obligations. Reform often converts (part of) the IPD into explicit debt, which creates a barrier to reform in countries that do not want to make their debt transparent. Most developing countries have small IPDs because of their low coverage rates, and are therefore in the enviable position of being able to change their systems to partial funding before the debt becomes unmanageable.

2.1 The Latin American versus the OECD Models

Choice of investment manager: individual choice versus group choice

The Latin American model was pioneered by Chile in 1980 and, bolstered by its initial success, was closely followed by Argentina, Peru, Colombia, Mexico, Uruguay, and Bolivia in the 1990s. It has just been adopted by the first countries outside the region, Hungary and Kazakhstan. It is now under consideration in Nicaragua and El Salvador and is one of the three options proposed by the Social Security Advisory Committee in the United States. In this model, each worker chooses the investment managers of their own individual DC retirement accounts.

By comparison, the OECD model built on the widespread existing employer-sponsored pension plans and made them the foundation for the second pillar. These plans simply became mandatory instead of voluntary in Australia, Switzerland, Denmark (and de facto by collective bargaining in the Netherlands), or an optional alternative to the state plan in the UK. In this model the employer or a combination of employer and union trustees choose the investment manager for each company or occupational group as a whole. This enables them to benefit from economies of scale and financial expertise, and possibly to minimize marketing costs (although this has yet to be proven). In DC plans, however, it introduces the principal–agent problem, where employer or union representatives choose the investment manager but workers bear the risk, the choice may not be in the workers' best interest and may not maximize net returns. For this reason, workers may ultimately demand more individual choice in OECD countries; they have already been given this choice in the UK and Australia.

Add-on versus diversion of contributions and size of the public pillar

As another important difference between the Latin American and

OECD models, most of the OECD countries cited earlier had a modest public pillar with a small IPD and with little or no payroll tax financing when they started their new system, so they could simply retain it, often as a flat benefit, and start the second pillar on top of that. They had no trouble financing the transition because accrued rights were small and/or contributions to the second pillar were added on, rather than being diverted from the first pillar.

For example, Australia had a means- and asset-tested first pillar, financed out of general revenues, to which it simply added a mandatory occupational funded pillar financed out of payroll contributions. Denmark's flat benefit in the public pillar (now being downsized) was also financed out of general revenues. In the UK the state earnings-related pension had just been started a few years earlier, when Thatcher, the then prime minister of the UK, decided to end it by encouraging employers and workers to opt out; the accumulated rights were still very small. Most workers in the UK are now simply eligible for the basic (flat) benefit. In Switzerland, employer-run plans that already existed in many firms became mandatory, on top of a compressed earnings-related public pillar which remained.

In contrast, the Latin American countries had bloated, and often regressive, benefit promises in public pillar to start out. Thus, to create space for the second pillar, the first pillar had to be greatly downsized and redesigned. In many cases (Chile, Bolivia, and Mexico) it was given a very subsidiary role—providing a minimum pension guarantee to low income workers whose personal accumulations fell below a specified amount.

When a worker switched to the new system, he was given credit for his past service under the old system, while part of his future contributions were diverted to the new second pillar. These countries had to find the money to continue paying the promised benefits to current pensioners and older workers (the IPD) under the old system, while part of the payroll tax flowing in was diverted to funded individual accounts—a problem that has become known as 'financing the transition'. Most countries that reform in the future will have to solve this problem. (For further details on the Latin American and OECD reforms, see Bateman and Piggott (forthcoming), Cerda and Grandolini 1997; Hepp (forthcoming), Johnson (forthcoming), Mitchell 1996a; Rofman and Bertin 1997; von Gersdorff 1997; Palacios and Rocha 1997; Valdes-Prieto (forthcoming), and Queisser 1998.)

2.2 The Swedish Model: Notional DC Plans

What is a notional defined contribution (NDC)? Many countries with large public pillars and implicit pension debts have found it exceedingly difficult to make the transition to a partially funded system with a mandatory private pillar, in part because of the financing problem but also because of the political interests associated with existing institutions. This explains the third group of reforming countries—those that feature NDC plans.

An NDC plan is one in which the worker has an individual account that is credited with his contributions plus interest. The accumulation, however, is notional rather than actual, since the money paid in by workers is immediately paid out to pensioners rather than being invested; that is, the system remains PAYG. Upon retirement, the notional accumulation is converted into a real annuity, supposedly on actuarially fair terms. Thus the NDC plan is essentially a reform of the first (PAYG public) pillar, although it is sometimes accompanied by a second (funded) pillar.

The notional account system was developed by Sweden, although it has not yet been implemented there. It was adopted shortly thereafter by Italy, but with a long transition period. In both these cases, the first pillar will be converted into an NDC plan, buttressed by a redistributive or guaranteed pension. This will be supplemented by a small (2.5 per cent) funded pillar in Sweden. The system is also being implemented by Latvia, which hopes to save enough money from reducing evasion and early retirement to eventually start a funded pillar. Poland plans to have a new system with a first pillar that is NDC and a second pillar that is funded, with investment managers chosen by the individual workers. Outside of Europe, China has an NDC system, de facto. While in principle China wants to start a second pillar made up of funded individual accounts, many cities thus far have been unable to finance the transition, so the individual accounts remain largely notional.

Labour market and equity effects: The NDC system was designed to capture some of the advantages described earlier of linking benefits closely to contributions within each cohort. Most important, it reduces idiosyncratic intra-cohort inequities and labour market distortions, including incentives to evade, provided the notional interest rate is close to the market interest rate. For example, early and late years of contributions receive the same rate of return and workers with flat and steep age-earnings profiles receive the same rate of return, while this is not true of most defined benefit systems. Most people would consider this more equitable. In addition, this pattern induces younger workers and workers with flat age-earnings profiles to remain within the system rather than try evasion. In addition, it makes the system more sustainable as it avoids the selection problem that occurs when low return people evade and high return people remain in the system.

Further, the NDC system discourages early retirement and avoids its negative impact on system sustainability, because workers automatically receive lower benefits if they choose to retire early; the costs are internalized rather than being passed on to others. For the same reason, it automatically adjusts the retirement age for increased longevity, thereby avoiding the difficult political decision to raise the retirement age that is periodically necessary in defined benefit plans.

However, the NDC system is not inherently redistributive, so it does not accomplish the crucial first pillar task of protecting low earners. For this purpose, a redistributive '0 pillar' must be added, creating a potential conflict with the NDC. If the redistributive component is large it may override the linkage between contributions and benefits that is responsible for these labour market improvements. In Sweden, for example, given the level of the guaranteed pension in the 0 pillar, the DC component will be irrelevant for many workers, including the majority of women.

Absence of funding and financial market effects: A bigger failing is that the NDC does not capture the benefits of funding, since there are no funds. That is, it serves as the first (PAYG) pillar, and may crowd out the opportunity for a large funded pillar. Intergenerational transfers remain, saving is not augmented, and financial markets do not develop. Most important, as the dependency rate increases, the contribution rate has to increase for newer cohorts, to keep the system solvent in the absence of pre-funding. These younger cohorts may have to 'save' for their old age a much larger amount than is optimal for them, in order to cover benefits promised to older cohorts. In that case, the incentives for evasion and escape to the informal sector would be strong.

Sweden plans to build a buffer fund to reduce the need for large tax increases as its population ages. But this buffer fund will be a publicly managed overlay, since the individual accounts remain notional. This raises all the problems (summarized earlier) concerning political manipulation and poor allocation of publicly managed funds.

Choosing the notional interest rate and conversion rate to annuities: A key factor in NDC plans is, how are the notional interest rate and the conversion rate of notional capital into annuities determined? If the notional interest rate is higher than the market rate, it will be a costly guarantee to the government. If it is less than the market rate, the contribution is more likely to be regarded as a tax so labour market distortions reappear and pressures may arise for an increase. Typically the interest rate is set equal to some exogenous rate, to insulate it from such political manipulation; nevertheless, the possibility remains that a future government will discard this connection and arbitrarily change the rate.

Most commonly, thus far, the notional rate has been tied to the growth in the per capita wage (possibly Poland), the total or covered wage bill (Sweden and Latvia) or GDP (Italy)—supposedly an equilibrating device. If the wage bill increases so too do contributions and therefore the ability to impute interest is high. However, this means that when the working age cohort is large and growing (the productive population) the imputed interest rate is high and the IPD increases rapidly, but when the working age cohort declines (the new generation) so too does the notional interest rate. This generation must then pay a high contribution rate to cover the IPD and will receive a low notional interest rate—fertile grounds for evasion and questionable from the viewpoint of intergenerational equity. Thus, using wage bill growth as the notional interest rate does not appear to be an equilibrating device as the dependency rate changes (Schwarz and Valdes 1998).

The conversion factor into annuities supposedly depends on expected longevity upon retirement. However, as the process is notional, it too is highly subject to political manipulation. For example, the government can decide to grant notional credit for non-contributing years (a common problem in old PAYG DB systems), it can impute a low or a high future interest rate into the calculation, and it can fail to adjust the conversion factor when life expectancy increases. In the absence of market discipline, implicit taxes or subsidies can creep into and interfere with the labour market efficiency effects of the new system. Since the conversion factor as well as the interest rate are set by the government, the NDC may be thought of as a PAYG DB in which the DB is defined in a new way.

In sum, the NDC system is attractive to countries that have very large implicit pension debts, especially those that are unwilling to incur an explicit fiscal deficit to finance the transition and will therefore end up with a large earnings related to the first pillar. In this context, it may be a politically convenient way to reduce benefits in inflated programmes and to equalize the retirement age for men and women. This may lay the groundwork for savings that eventually enable the growth of a funded second pillar; but until that happens it should be recognized as a reform of the first pillar rather than an introduction of a multi-pillar system. (For details on the Swedish reform see Sunden 1998; on Latvia see Fox 1998; on Poland see Rutkowski 1998; on Italy see Hamann 1997. For another comprehensive summary of recent structural and piecemeal reforms see Demurgic-Kunt and Schwarz 1997.)

3. Financing the Transition

If countries with a large PAYG pension debt shift to a multi-pillar system that includes a funded component, some of the contribution usually is shifted to the individual accounts. This creates a financing gap between the remaining PAYG revenues and the expenditures needed to cover the IPD; some other revenue source must be found to cover this gap. Countries following the Latin American model have faced this transition cost problem, while those following the OECD model have not (because they had small public pillars and did not divert contributions) nor did the NDC countries (because they remain largely PAYG). How did the Latin American countries finance the transition? Three types of basic methods have been used: reducing the value of the IPD and the financing gap, finding alternative revenue sources to pay it off, and, finally, resorting to the general borrowing and taxation powers of the treasury.

3.1 Reducing the Value of the IPD and the Financing Gap

1. Before making the transition, reform the old system by downsizing benefits, raising retirement age and penalties for early retirement, tightening eligibility for disability benefits, and changing the indexation method to price indexation, so the outstanding debt, whether implicit or explicit, will be smaller. Chile, Argentina, and Uruguay followed this strategy, which may be indispensable to a good pension reform. This cuts the benefits that must be paid to those who stay in the old system,

it also cuts the compensation owed to those who switch to the new system, and it increases the probability that they will switch. Otherwise, one runs the risk of casting in stone benefit promises that never should have been made in the first place, and making it more difficult for the government to escape from these promises.

2. Issue a recognition bond (as in Chile) or promise of a compensatory pension (as in Argentina) to each worker who switches to the new system, that acknowledges the value of the pension that he has earned thus far. This postpones the day when cash will be needed, as the recognition bond cannot be cashed until the worker retires and the compensatory pension is gradually paid off over the entire retirement period of the worker. Besides extending the pay-off period, the issuance of the recognition bond provides another opportunity to reduce the debt. As it is a legally binding piece of paper it gives the worker greater certainty that the pension debt will eventually be repaid, and in return for reducing uncertainty the government can downsize the face value of or interest rate on the bond (as in Peru). The face value can be further reduced if workers have much more faith in the new than the old system; they (especially young workers) will then be willing to switch even with little compensation for their past service. By choosing the minimum terms that are needed to convince the desired number of workers to switch, a government can substantially downsize the recognized debt and save considerable money in its transition costs (as in Hungary).

3. Keep some workers, and their contributions, in the old system. This may be accomplished by excluding some workers, such as the military or the police, from the new system (as in Chile), or by giving all workers a choice but making the new system attractive mainly to young workers (as in Argentina). Colombia has kept the old system operating side-by-side with the new and workers are permitted to switch back and forth. In Uruguay the new funded pillar is made compulsory only for rich and young workers, voluntary for the others. Since those remaining in the old system continue to contribute to it, this reduces the financing gap. The serious danger is that, in order to solve a short run cash-flow problem, these countries have increased their long term implicit debt by keeping participants in a financially unsound PAYG system; this solution may turn out to be non-sustainable.

4. Retain a large PAYG component in the new system, so that some of the revenue inflow continues to the public pillar. Argentina followed

this strategy, by utilizing a flat benefit in its new public pillar, rather than the narrower minimum pension guarantee as in Chile. In Argentina, about 60 per cent of the total contribution flows into the public pillar. In addition, workers can choose between a funded and a PAYG option for the second pillar. The inflow of funds to the first pillar and the PAYG second pillar helps to pay current pensioners and, eventually, the compensatory pension. But if the public pillar or PAYG second pillar offer benefits that are too generous (actuarially unsound), the reform will not be sustainable in the long run—a danger that Argentina faces.

3.2 Finding alternative revenue sources

5. Build a pre-existing primary surplus in the general treasury, that can be used to pay off part of the pension debt. Chile did this but most other countries are burdened with fiscal deficits rather than surpluses.
6. If there is a pre-existing surplus in the social security system, use it to pay off part of the debt. While the Latin systems generally did not have a surplus, the United States social security trust fund could be used in this way, if the United States were to make a transition.
7. If public enterprises are being privatized, use some of the proceeds to pay off the pension debt—a cancellation of long term assets against long term liabilities. This strategy is being followed by Peru, considered by Poland, and Bolivia is also using privatization assets for pension reform. An existing unfunded pension debt generates uncertainty that reduces the market value of enterprises in the process of privatization, so paying off the pension debt may enable a higher price as public enterprises are privatized.
8. Reduce evasion and increase coverage, thereby increasing system revenues. This was part of Argentina's plan; however, the reduced evasion has not yet materialized. China is considering financing the transition by bringing all workers at township and village enterprises, a rapidly growing group, into the new partially funded system. Such coverage expansion would help to pay off the old IPD but simultaneously would create a new IPD, as the newly covered workers will eventually demand their pensions. If future benefits are generous, the short run gain comes at a high long run cost while the promised benefits are low and the cross-subsidy is high, evasion will be encouraged among the newly covered workers. Thus, this strategy is most useful as a temporary financing device if the PAYG part of the

new system is small and the newly covered workers will be making most of their contributions to and getting most of their pension from their individual accounts.

3.3 Using General Borrowing and Taxation

9. Issue general treasury debt to cover the remaining cash gap in the short run. Because of the fungibility of money we do not know to what extent resources for pension reform have come from debt versus other general revenue sources, but government borrowing has usually increased in the early years of the reform. In countries with a large IPD, use of temporary debt finance is almost inevitable so that a heavy double burden of taxation is not imposed on the transition generation of workers. Since young and future workers will benefit most from the reform, it is appropriate that they should also pay part of the cost.

Some of this debt may be sold to the pension funds in the new second pillar; government debt and bank deposits have been the largest initial investments of the new pension funds. An important proviso is that the pension funds should not be compelled to purchase government bonds; bond sales should be open, transparent, and should pay the market interest rate. However, all Latin American countries limit international diversification of pension fund investments, which virtually ensures large investments in government bonds.

Is this temporary debt finance problematic? Financial markets might react negatively if they were not previously aware of the size of the implicit pension debt, if they believed the obligation to repay it was 'soft' and has now become 'hard', and if this increases the expected default risk on regular bonds. Two pieces of evidence suggest that, so far, the financial market response has been positive. First, the IMF recently adopted the position that debt finance earmarked for a pension transition should be allowed beyond the permissible ceiling for other debt, because it is a swap of implicit for explicit debt in the short run and is intended to reduce the over-all debt, hence to improve fiscal solvency, in the long run. Second, Hungary's credit rating from Moody's improved after it adopted its pension reform, even though this required an increase in the explicit debt, for much the same reasons.

10. Eventually pay off this debt through taxation, or the object of increasing national saving will not be achieved (additional private saving will be offset by additional public dissaving if the implicit debt

is simply changed to an on-going explicit debt). The redemption of the debt through tax revenues can be spread over a long period of time—but the longer the pay-off the slower the country will receive the benefits of increased national saving for productive investment.

The kind of tax that is used can greately affect the benefits of the transition (Kotlikoff 1996). In general, a consumptin or value-added tax will be least distortionary and most growth-enhancing; but it may also be the most difficult to implement in developing countries and is problematic from an equity point of view if coverage is incomplete. As discussed earlier, frequently, the payroll tax paid to the public pillar is used to finance part of the transition. It is estimated that if half the current PAYG system were converted to a funded system the financing gap would be paid off by a payroll tax rate of about 1.5 per cent for 70 years in the US (Gramlich 1996) and a roughly similar amount in China (Friedman et al. 1996).

Some of these measures have also been used to mitigate political opposition to reform. Bureaucrats and unions that helped to run the old system often do not want to phase it out. Maintaining a large PAYG pillar in the new system not only reduces transition costs but also serves to palliate opponents of pension reform and therefore may facilitate passage of reform legislation. Borrowing to finance the transition reduces the costs to, and therefore the opposition of, middle-age workers. But a consequence is that the benefits of a full reform are not received and sustainability of the new system may be undermined. This conflict between pragmatism and principle, short run and long run, has been faced in almost all the reforming countries.

4. Efficiency and Growth Effects of Reform: How Large Are They?

The chief theoretical argument for the recommended multi-pillar system is that it will have a positive effect on efficiency and growth, because the old system introduced or failed to remove distortions that will be eliminated by the reforms. A secondary argument is that it will enhance the financial sustainability of the old age system and thereby provide better protection for the old in the long run. And yet, a third argument is its better distributional effects, especially on intergenerational equity.

Efficiency and growth effects are notoriously difficult to quantify and prove, partly because relatively little experience and data are available and partly because, even if we had the data, it would be difficult to build models that capture all the complex dynamic interactions; that is, it is difficult to specify the counter factual. Pension reform has several different potential efficiency effects; usually studies focus on one of these while ignoring or holding the others constant. For example, general equilibrium models that analyse labour supply effects often assume perfect capital markets and thereby limit the predicted increases in saving, and vice versa. In this section I summarize the limited empirical research that has been done on these topics, concentrating on the simulated effects in countries that have been considering structural reforms and econometric estimation of the actual effects in Chile, the main country that already has a track record. In general, the beneficial labour market effects come from the shift from defined benefit to defined contribution, the beneficial impact on saving comes from the shift from PAYG to funding and the financial market impact comes from private management of these funds.

First a brief comment on the distinction between efficiency and growth. Greater efficiency, for example, due to a reduction in labour market distortions, increases the level of output. If some of the increased output is ploughed back into investment, as would often be the case, it also increases growth. Growth can also be increased without an increase in efficiency. For example, an increase in saving (and consequently growth) may simply indicate an intergenerational or life cycle redistribution that does not increase efficiency because it does not make (or have the potential to make) everyone better off. However, such an increase is efficiency-enhancing if the initial saving rate was sub-optimal due to public or private myopia or to a tax wedge between private and social returns to investment. Both of these conditions are usually alleged as a justification for mandatory retirement saving plans, in which case they would expand both efficiency and growth. In the following pages both efficiency and growth effects are discussed, focusing on the former in the case of labour markets and the latter in the case of saving and financial markets. While measuring these effects is problematic, the available evidence indicates that they are positive, possibly large, and undoubtedly the financial sustainability of the system has improved.

4.1 Reduced Labour Market Distortions: Early Retirement and Informal Sector

One problem in PAYG defined benefit (DB) systems is the possibility that the high payroll tax will lead to labour market inefficiencies (stemming from distorted decisions about labour force participation, hours worked, age of retirement, choice of job and location, degree of effort, form of compensation, etc.), while in a DC system the contribution may be regarded as saving rather than as a tax. We have only fragmentary evidence about the effect of pension reform on most of these actions.

Perhaps most important, Wise shows that the age of retirement is very sensitive to the implicit social security tax on labour, stemming from the absence of actuarial penalties on early retirement. The loss of generous DB benefits during years when older men continue working induces most men to stop working before the age of 60 (Wise 1997). Countries that have a larger actuarial adjustment in their systems, hence a lower implicit tax on labour, have higher labour force participation rates of older men. Funded DC plans automatically build in this actuarial adjustment, so, by extension, should deter early retirement and its negative impact on GNP and financial solvency of the scheme.

The distortionary labour market effects of traditional systems on younger workers may be larger in developing than in industrialized countries because escape to the informal sector is easier there, for workers as well as employers. Productivity in the informal sector may be lower as firms have less access to product and credit markets, or because technological change is embodied in capital in the formal sector and has an external effect on labour productivity throughout the economy (as in the endogenous growth literature). In addition, regulations that set a minimum wage and other benefits in the covered sector may lead to a wedge between wages and productivity in the formal versus the informal sectors. In simulations for a representative economy, Corsetti and Schmidt-Hebbel (1997) show that a payroll tax rate of 20 per cent could cause a massive (47 per cent) shift to the informal sector, thereby reducing the economy-wide growth rate by over 1 per cent annually. In many Latin American countries the informal sector, and small firms in the quasi-informal sector do indeed absorb more than half of the labour force (ILO 1996). Although many other forces are of course at work, a shift to a DC system might reduce these incentives for informality, because it closely links benefits to contributions.

What light is thrown on this issue by actual experience in Chile? Between 1980 and 1990, a period when the average share of informal employment in Latin America increased from 26 per cent to 31 per cent, this share dropped from 36 per cent to 31 per cent in Chile. Unemployment fell and wages rose. Edwards (1997) shows that, given reasonable assumptions about the elasticity of labour demand in the two sectors, the pension reform was responsible for a decline of 2.2 per cent–3.6 per cent in unemployment and a 5–8 per cent increase in wages.

In evaluating these numbers and their applicability to other countries, it is important to realize that a shift to DC may not always have this salutary effect. For example, myopic workers may continue to evade contributions because they will not be able to access their mandatory savings for many years. In periods when investment returns are low, workers may be especially tempted to evade, preferring to consume or to invest in education, housing or consumer durables. In Chile, returns have been high (over 12 per cent real during the first 15 years), encouraging compliance.

As another example, if the payroll tax for pensions is only a minor part of a large total payroll tax, the incentive to escape to the informal sector may remain strong. Indeed, this seems to be the case in Argentina, where the overall payroll tax is high (Valdes-Prieto, forthcoming). In contrast, a careful study in Chile, where the total payroll tax is relatively small, found that evasion had dropped to only 5 per cent of potential contributors (Chamorro, 1992; Schmidt-Hebbell, 1997). (Chile does not even attempt to cover the self-employed, who are the biggest evaders in other countries.) It is difficult to be conclusive about this, because it is hard to separate evasion from normal labour force withdrawals and exogenous shifts into self-employment.

If escape to the informal sector occurs in a funded DC plan it does not have the same negative effects on system sustainability that it does in a PAYG DB plan, as the costs are simply borne by the evader in the form of lower benefits, rather than being passed on to others in the form of a higher contribution rate. This is a big plus. Nevertheless, it still creates the same problem for labour allocation and productivity and an even greater problem for the financial security of the evading workers who may not have an adequate pension and may become a charge on the public treasury when they grow old. So, while the initial evidence is encouraging, we need to analyse the data on evasion, wages, and employment carefully, as other countries reform their systems, to determine how robust and generalizable are these results.

4.2 Increased Long Term National Saving

A major rationale for pension reform that emphasizes fully funded plans is that it will increase long term national saving. This is important because empirically we observe that most savings stay in the country of origin and most of the productive investment of a country comes from its own saving, despite the global capital markets that supposedly prevail.

When a country without a prior PAYG system institutes a multi-pillar system, consumption will decrease and saving will increase if the mandatory saving rate exceeds the voluntary rate. When a country with an existing PAYG system replaces it with a multi-pillar system, national saving increases if benefits are cut or taxes are increased, usually to cover transition costs. In both cases, putting part of the contribution into the worker's own mandatory saving account may be more politically acceptable and less economically distortionary than increasing saving through a high tax rate that goes into the general treasury. As mentioned earlier, this increase in saving is likely to enhance both efficiency and growth in many cases.

But again, there are reasons why this increased saving might not materialize. For example, mandatory saving may not increase total private saving if individuals find ways to offset them against other voluntary saving or accumulated assets. In that case, capital may accumulate and returns increase in the mandatory pillar, but they may commensurably decrease in the voluntary pillar. With perfect capital markets, private saving will not increase at all, since people will simply borrow against their mandatory pension saving. A positive saving effect ultimately depends on the assumption that voluntary long term saving and assets are small and borrowing opportunities limited for substantial groups within the population. The low asset condition probably holds for most slow-growing economies; the limited borrowing condition for most developing countries; and both hold for low income households in most countries.

Public as well as private saving matter. On the one hand, pension reform may decrease public dissaving as governments no longer need to borrow to cover escalating pension costs, but on the other hand, it may increase public dissaving if the build-up of pension reserves relaxes fiscal discipline and makes it easier for governments to run large deficits. If the transition is fully financed by borrowing, government dissaving will offset private saving, and the expected increase in national saving will simply not transpire. But if it is financed through taxes or cutbacks in other government expenditures, public saving increases national saving further. Estimating the impact on public saving therefore requires modelling government behaviour—how governments will behave after pension reform and how they might have behaved in the absence of reform.

A number of simulations have been run projecting the impact on saving of a shift to a fully funded scheme. Not surprisingly, the results turn out to be highly dependent on the assumptions, especially the assumptions about the crowd-out of voluntary by mandatory saving and the method of financing the transition. Underlining the importance of the former, simulations of a 'representative economy' indicate that a tax-financed transition to a fully funded system in the presence of credit constraints (implying low crowd-out) will increase output by 22 per cent and welfare by 16 per cent in the long run, while the gain is only 2 per cent without credit constraints (Cifuentes and Valdes-Prieto, 1997).

In planning its mandatory occupation scheme, Australia assumed 50 per cent crowd-out and higher for workers who already were covered by voluntary occupational plans. This implied that, in the long run, when the contribution rate reached 12 per cent, national saving would increase by 1.5 per cent of GDP, thereby almost doubling the current net national saving rate which is 2.2 per cent of GDP. (The gross national saving rate is about 15 per cent of GDP.) Australia, of course, had the advantage that the government did not have to borrow to pay off a pension debt since the second pillar was an add-on rather than a diversion of previous contributions. Although initially the tax-deductibility of contributions was projected to cause some government dissaving, in the long run the decreased burden on the means-tested public pension is expected to reduce government dissaving. One of the main effects of the reform may be to shift the allocation of private saving away from home ownership, which is now the predominant form because of investment, and toward other more productive forms (Bateman and Piggott, forthcoming).

In his simulations for Mexico, Ayala (1996) assumes a 30–40 per cent rate of crowd-out. If the transition is tax-financed or if it is debt-financed and Ricardian equivalence holds (so that private saving goes up to offset public dissaving), total saving goes up to 0.4 per cent–2.1 per cent of GDP, a similar magnitude to that expected in Australia. But if the transition is debt-financed and Ricardian equivalence does not hold, the impact on total saving is much smaller, even negative in some years, although positive overall during the next 30 years.

The only country that has had a mandatory saving plan long enough for saving effects to be estimated is Chile. Data from Chile are problematic and the savings ratio is erratic, complicating this analysis and making the results highly sensitive to the starting date for comparisons. According to Corsetti and Schmidt-Hebbel (1997), private sector saving as a percentage of GDP increased from almost zero in 1979–81 to 17 per cent in 1990–2 while private consumption decreased commensurably. Their reduced-form two-stage-least-squares regressions attribute half of the decline in the private consumption ratio to the growth of Chile's funded pension plans and correlated developments such as capital market deepening. Time series regression analyses by Haindl Rondonelli (1996) indicate that pension reform accounts for 6.6 of the 9.9 percentage point increase in the national saving rate in Chile (from 16.7 per cent of GDP 1976–80 to 26.6 per cent 1990–4). Of the 6.6 per cent increase, 3.1 per cent was due to the direct impact of pension saving, 4.2 per cent was due to the financial market deepening impact of pension fund size on other private saving, and a crowd-out effect of –0.7 per cent was due to borrowing constraints. Using an error correction model, Morande (1996) also finds a significant positive effect of a pension fund dummy on private saving, 1960–95. He speculates that the financial market deepening caused by pension reform may have made voluntary saving less likely to be crowded out by, and therefore less sensitive, to fluctuations in foreign saving; and made the country's supply of investible resources less dependent on foreign capital.

Agosin, Crespi, and Letelier (1996) are more sceptical because they find that the main source of increased private saving was private corporations, whose saving gradually jumped from 6 per cent of GDP in 1978–85 to 23 per cent in 1994—a response, they believe, to the non-availability of foreign credit and the privatization of public enterprises. (Of course, privatization was itself facilitated by the pension reform, illustrating the complex interactions among these variables.) Voluntary saving of households was negative (about 4 per cent of GDP) throughout this entire period, indicating consumer dissaving or borrowing. However, forced saving through the new pension system gradually grew to almost 4 per cent of GDP, and this was not offset by greater voluntary dissaving (presumably because credit constraints had already been exhausted). This 4 per cent magnitude is roughly consistent with the findings of Bosworth and Marfan (1994), that the pension reform increased saving by 3 per cent of GDP. The risk remains that the growth of consumer credit, possibly fuelled by the pension reform, could increase consumer dissaving and offset some of these gains in the future (Holzmann 1996).

While these analyses focus on enhanced private saving, other studies emphasize the impact of pension reform on public saving and dissaving. Chile had to finance a pension transition, in part through deficit finance, which decreased national saving. The fiscal costs of the transition may have cancelled out the positive effect on private saving initially (Agosin et al. 1996). Observing that the pension-related deficits of the government (payments to pensioners left over from the old system plus redemptions of recognition bonds for new pensioners who had switched) were larger than the inflows to the new pension funds until 1989, Holzmann concludes that during the 1980s the new pension system had a negative effect on national saving. He, however, appears to overlook the fact that redeemed recognition bonds became part of private pension saving and were not immediately consumed. Correcting for this point alone generates a positive savings effect as early as 1985.

More important, a simple accounting exercise neglects the disciplining impact that pension reform might have had on government behaviour, particularly other taxes and expenditures. Chile ran an increasing surplus over this period, possibly to help cover the transition costs. Since 1987 the consolidated government budget has been in surplus, which quickly exceeded 5 per cent of GDP. In addition, Chile accumulated a large budgetary surplus ex ante in preparation for the reform, thereby reducing its need for deficit finance. While we do not know how large the current or past surplus would have been otherwise, to the degree that the pension reform was financed by increasing general taxes, cutting other public spending or accumulating a prior surplus, transition costs did not decrease public saving. Moreover, the transition costs are short run while the increased private saving may persist in the long run. As a result of all these factors, total national saving in Chile is currently much higher than it was pre-reform.

Thus, preliminary evidence indicates that pension reform can have beneficial effects on long term national saving and capital formation, increasing it by 10 to 30 per cent of the ex ante gross rate and even more of the ex ante net rate, especially if it is accompanied by a broader set of policies designed to constrain consumer and government borrowing.

4.3 Financial Market Development

One reason for favouring private management of pension funds is that this will develop a set of financial institutions—investment managers, insurance companies, and banks—that are essential for economic development. On the one hand, a funded pillar cannot get started without some minimum financial market capacity, but on the other hand, the funded pillar, if competitively managed and well regulated, can be instrumental in enabling the financial market to grow in safety, size, depth, and complexity. In developing countries, where private saving is already high, one of the main effects of a funded pillar may be to shift these savings out of land and jewellery and into long term financial market investments that are better for the broader economy, because of the development of these financial institutions.

Even in Australia it is expected that the financial market will grow as a result of the mandatory second pillar. For example, as noted earlier, some private saving may be redirected out of owner-occupied housing into the financial markets. Insurance companies are expanding, developing a new line of products, including annuity products, to meet the anticipated demand stemming from pension funds (Bateman and Piggott, forthcoming). In Switzerland also, growth of the life insurance industry, investment companies, and mutual funds has been spurred by mandatory funded pension plans. And corporate governance has been gradually changing, as institutional investors have demanded disclosure and better performance (Hepp, forthcoming). All these changes are efficiency enhancing.

But the strongest evidence for this expected growth effect comes from Chile. During the five years preceding the adoption of its new system, Chile prepared the groundwork by organizing a primary market for treasury bonds, reforming its laws governing mutual funds, corporations, and securities, privatizing banks, authorizing a price-indexed mortgage bond market, and liberalizing the provision of insurance and reinsurance (Valdes-Prieto 1997). After the new system was introduced, this process continued. Financial markets became more liquid as the number of traded shares on the stock market and their turnover increased; demand was created for the equities of newly privatized state enterprises; information disclosure and credit-rating institutions developed; the variety of financial instruments including indexed annuities, mortgage, and corporate bonds grew; and asset pricing improved. In several of the studies summarized earlier, financial market deepening, associated with pension reform was given credit for the observed increase in private saving. Econometric analysis suggests that financial market efficiency induced by the reformed pension system (and other factors with which this was closely correlated) increased total factor productivity by 1 per cent per year, or half of the increase in total factor productivity, in Chile (Holzmann, 1996).

Summary

In sum, a small but growing body of empirical evidence indicates that pension reform has produced positive efficiency and growth effects. That is, the impact on saving, productivity, output, and welfare may be high relative to exogenous sources of growth and other policies available to increase growth.

Several caveats are essential in interpreting this evidence. First, given the high correlation between pension reform and other reforms that are often simultaneous, the controversy surrounding the determinants of private saving and labour supply (for example, which variables are endogenous?), the even greater uncertainty about the determinants of public saving (for example, what is the counter-factual?), and the difficulties in modelling feedback effects, all these econometric and simulation results are highly sensitive to model specification and the topic clearly requires additional evidence and research. In particular, the econometric analyses for Chile are subject to omitted variable bias and the simulation results depend heavily on assumptions about crowd-out, transition costs, and rates of return. Second, the growth impact also depends on key policy decisions in setting up the new system, such as the question of how high the required contribution rate will be, what proportion of the multi-pillar system should be funded and DC, and how the transition will be financed. While debt finance may be necessary for political purposes, partial tax finance may be necessary to meet the economic objective of increased saving, and of course some taxes have better efficiency properties than others. Third, it is important to remember that, even if it claims to use a general equilibrium model, each study typically deals with only one possible source of growth, so, many of these results are partially additive—the total growth effect is the sum of the separate effects on labour market distortions, early retirement, escape to the informal sector, capital accumulation, financial market development, and other sources of growth. So if each separate effect increases GNP in amounts ranging from 1–10 per cent, their sum may increase GNP much more.

5. New Problems and Issues for Further Research

While many efficiency gains seem to have been achieved, the new systems have also created new problems that remain to be solved and related research that needs to be done. The major problems that have surfaced so far concern high administrative costs and financial market distortions due to regulations. A third area needing further study involves the distributional effects of pension reform. Finally, the analysis of annuities markets will become increasingly important as workers begin to retire under the new systems.

5.1 Administrative Costs

The big advantage of private over public investment is the likelihood that it will produce a better allocation of capital, therefore higher returns for the fund and growth for the economy. However, decentralized systems also may charge high administrative fees, partly due to high marketing costs in competitive industries. In some cases marketing costs produce important side-benefits of consumer information and increased compliance, but this does not appear to be the case in most countries that have recently reformed.

Preliminary evidence indicates that workers are ill informed, do not make decisions based on investment returns, and pension funds incur high sales commissions and other marketing costs to attract them. In Chile and most other Latin American countries fees are front-loaded, meaning that workers pay a one-time fee on new contributions rather than an annual fee based on assets. (This system was probably adopted because the new system had no assets initially.) Specifically, this one-time fee is about 2 per cent of wages, or 15–25 per cent of new contributions, in virtually all cases, and about one-third of this is for marketing.

These numbers appear very high. To understand their impact on net returns, it is necessary to convert these one-time charges on contributions into their equivalents in terms of annual charges on assets, a conversion which depends on how large the assets are, relative to the contributions. Obviously, for accounts that have small accumulated assets (young workers with few years of contributions), this fee will be high relative to assets. However, for accounts that have built up substantial assets over the years, the fee will be small relative to assets.

Simulations show that if the current fee schedule is maintained, the average Chilean worker who contributes for 40 years will pay the equivalent of less than 1 per cent of assets per year. This is approximately the same amount that mutual funds charge for voluntary retirement savings accounts in the United States; it is not excessive from the lifetime point of view, in comparison to a competitive market retail price for individuals. Moreover, it is not excessive in comparison to a less expensive system that produces much lower gross and net returns (for example, publicly managed reserves in Singapore and the United States social security trust fund). Competition may bring costs down further in the long run.

However, this fee structure is an apparent problem in the early years of a new system, when all accounts are small. It is a real problem for workers who will be in the system for only 20–30 years, such as workers who were relatively old upon the date of reform; simulations show that these workers pay a much higher lifetime fee as a percentage of assets. It is a problem for transient workers who move in and out of the labour force, such as women, especially if their contributions are concentrated in their later years. The higher lifetime fee as a percentage of assets and hence the lower net return received by these groups is a matter of concern on equity grounds in a mandatory system. In addition, for workers who are very risk-averse, it is questionable whether to compel them to incur these costs with certainty while the benefits are uncertain. Besides the equity consideration is the practical consideration that high costs may lead these groups to evade. Moreover, it would be desirable to find ways to increase administrative efficiency for all workers, since this would increase their rates of return and replacement rates.

Some analysts believe that administrative costs would be lower under a group plan and hence favour choice by the employer or union. Such group plans may be better positioned to benefit from economies of scale in decision-making, greater financial expertise, and lower marketing costs. (On the existence of scale economies see James and Palacios 1995; Mitchell 1996b.) This is one rationale given for employer and/or union choice of the investment manager in OECD countries. However, because employers or union representatives make the investment decision while workers bear the risk, such plans can also open the door to financial abuse and principal–agent problems—employers might choose investment managers or strategies that benefit them even if this implies lower returns for their workers.

For example, lower wholesale changes appear to be available for large group [402(k)] plans in the US, but not all employers have gone through the effort of obtaining these rates. In Switzerland, employers tend to place retirement funds at banks with which they have had long-standing financial relationships, without exploring other options carefully (Hepp, forthcoming). One of the worst cases of employer abuse of worker retirement funds was the Maxwell scandal in the UK, but individual choice also led to a scandal in that same countryy, as uninformed workers were induced to abandon their employer's plans and purchase financially disastrous policies by unscruplous insurance company salesmen (Johnson 1997). Basing the second pillar on occupational plans is especially a problem for mobile workers, who may end up with many small costly accounts unless these can be consolidated in one personal account—problems which weighed heavily in Australia and the new Hong Kong scheme.

Thus we have anecdotal evidence about costs and returns to group choice versus individual choice and a careful empirical study has yet to be done. Meanwhile, the principal–agent problem makes it likely that political pressures will develop to give workers the right to opt out of employer pension plans into their own personal retirement savings plan in most mandatory systems, and this has already happened in the UK and Australia.

A third alternative may be desirable in small countries whose markets cannot support many pension companies efficiently due to economies of scale, countries with undeveloped financial markets that want to attract investment expertise and minimize start-up costs, and countries with low contribution rates to the second pillar. Instead of open entry, the government might auction off operating rights to a limited number of investment companies, among whom workers then choose. The contract could specify the maximum risk, offer a reward for high returns, and choose the winners based on who charges the lowest administrative fees.

The voluntary Thrift Saving Plan for the United States federal employees uses a competitive bidding process to choose its money managers, at a total cost of less than 10 basis points (0.1 per cent). An auction process was recently used in Bolivia, which expects to have much lower administrative costs than Chile as a result. Or instead of letting the fee be determined in an auction for a pre-specified number of winners, an alternative is to set a low fee ceiling and open entry to all qualified pension fund managers willing to abide by that limit. Sweden will use a variation on this theme for its new second pillar—centralized collection and record-keeping, while workers choose among mutual funds that have reached an agreement on fees with the central agency.

The dangers here are the difficulties in insulating the auction and investment process from political manipulation, corruption, and collusion, and the importance of incorporating incentives for good performance, when entry and price are limited. Otherwise, while these mechanisms may feature lower marketing expenditures, they may also feature lower investment returns, less consumer education and service. The advantages are that much lower costs, allowing substantial increase in rates of return and replacement rates, can be achieved if the process is well-handled.

Summing up, one could construct a continuum with considerable choice, competition, political insulation, and relatively high administrative cost on one end (Chilean pension funds (AFPs), the UK, Australia, voluntary IRAs in the United States), with limited choice, competition, and lower costs on the other end (Bolivia, Sweden, the United States federal employees Thrift Saving Plan), each arrangement having different implications for political insulation, rates of return, and other kinds of service. Countries could then choose which mix of costs and benefits they prefer. Many additional measures can be and are being considered to economize on costs and their effects should appear over the next decade.

5.2 Financial market distortions

Multi-pillar systems have justifiably been given credit for stimulating the growth of financial markets in middle income countries where this is an important ingredient of the recipe for economic growth. However, as these systems have been implemented, we also observe ways in which they have distorted the operations of financial markets.

This problem stems from the fact that policy-makers want workers to make investment decisions and bear the corresponding risk, but they also want to limit this risk to avoid a disaster. Relatedly, the government must set certain investment constraints and offer guarantees in order to overcome political opposition to reform. The contradiction here can potentially lead to malfunctioning markets, particularly if the pension funds are relatively large players in the market.

As examples of this ambivalence, in Chile and several other Latin American countries pension funds (AFPs) are heavily penalized if they deviate more than 2 percentage points from the group mean. This practice has been accused of leading to herding behaviour, as each AFP tries to look very much like the other. Rather than having a choice of different points on the risk-return frontier stemming from differing asset allocations, as would be the case in a well-functioning financial market, workers have the much less meaningful choice among companies that provide the same asset allocation and risk-return mix. Also, workers are required to invest in one AFP instead of diversifying among several and thereby reducing their risk; of course, given the lack of meaningful portfolio differences among the AFP, the gains from diversification would be small in any event.

In Mexico all workers are required to enter the new system but those currently in the labour force are given the right to return to the old PAYG system upon retirement if this allows them to fare better. This insurance scheme was included to acknowledge the 'acquired rights' of workers and therefore avoid a legal challenge to the reform efforts. However, it creates an obvious moral hazard problem—workers have an incentive to gamble with their pension funds, accepting too much risk, since they are substantially protected from loss. The Mexican authorities have avoided the moral hazard problem by greatly limiting the AFORES choice of investment strategies: at least 65 per cent of all assets must be invested in government bonds (currently the AFORES are 99 per cent in bonds) and international investments are proscribed. Since workers have no real choice of portfolios, moral hazard is avoided; but the flow of funds through the AFORES to the financial market and the private sector is also avoided.

Bolivia initially intended to invest most of its revenues from privatization (targeted for pension reform) abroad, to protect it from excess government borrowing and other country-specific risks. However, in order to overcome union opposition to these reforms, the government had to take on the responsibility of paying off the implicit debt of the complementary pensions that unions had negotiated in the past. To cover these and other expenditures, the final arrangements decreed that initially almost all of the privatization assets would be invested domestically, in government bonds. In Uruguay, to help cover transition costs, AFPs are required to put at least 80 per cent of their assets into special issue government bonds, while the risk-reducing benefits of international diversification and diversification into private sector securities is one of the rationales for pension reforms. In fact, most Latin Americans require or strongly encourage almost exclusive domestic investments with a heavy concentration on government bonds. Regulations in Switzerland require a 4 per cent nominal guaranteed rate of return in their second pillars, thereby leading to a very conservative investment strategy, consisting largely of bonds. Until recently, providers of second pillar pensions for civil servants in the Netherlands faced little competition, again leading to low rates of return that might have been off or at a corner of the risk-return frontier.

These distortions should not be exaggerated, because the guarantees and limits on competition and portfolio diversification are likely to fall through time, as the schemes mature. Chile started with rigid restrictions but has gradually opened up the system to greater diversification, including international investment. Mexico is now considering allowing each AFORES to offer more than one type of portfolio, together with worker diversification among different portfolios. Along similar lines, pension funds might be allowed to differentiate their asset allocation strategies and corresponding benchmarks (if available), applying different risk limits depending on type of portfolio chosen. For example, portfolios might be offered that concentrate in bonds, stocks, and international investments, with different degrees of risk implied by each (as in the United States federal employees Thrift Saving Plan). This would allow workers to choose their preferred point on the risk-return frontier and should help the financial markets to operate better, but it also requires substantial worker education as well as greater diversity of financial instruments than exists presently in many developing countries.

5.3 The Distributional Impact of Pension Reform

Although this chapter has focused on the efficiency and growth impact of pension reform, an equally important topic is the impact of reform on equity. Because traditional pension systems are typically both inefficient and inequitable, they offer an opportunity to improve both. However, it is not known whether—or the extent to which—multi-pillar system has actually succeeded in achieving a better distributional outcome. Closer examination suggests that the devil is in the details and some of the results may be surprising.

For example, in Chile's public pillar, workers are eligible for a minimum pension guarantee of about 27 per cent of the average wage after 20 years of contributions, meaning that the government tops up the benefits of these workers to the guaranteed point if their own accumulation does not suffice. The main beneficiaries here will be low earners who worked only 20 years, disproportionately females, who have limited labour market attachment, while workers who remain in the formal sector for a full career are unlikely to receive this subsidy. In contrast, in Argentina a flat benefit of about 28 per cent of the average wage is paid to all workers who have at least 30 years of contributions (plus an additional 1 per cent for every year above 30, up to 45). The main recipients will be workers who spent most of their adult lives in the formal labour sector and (in sharp contrast to Chile) women are unlikely to qualify. In the UK, which pays a flat benefit that is about half the size of Argentina's (as a proportion of the average wage) but does not set a required number of contributory years, the big gainers are people who work a few years and live long lives, such as women. Switzerland's public pillar is earning-related and hence appears less redistributive than that in Argentina, but the payroll tax which finances it is levied on all earnings (that is, there is no ceiling on taxable earnings as there is in Argentina), which works in the opposite direction.

The setup of the second pillar also has distributional consequences. If flat fees per account are permitted, this reduces net returns for low earners more than for high earners. Flat fees were charged by Chilean AFPs initially but the unfavourable publicity they encountered was one factor leading them to drop this practice; it is now used by some AFORES in Mexico. If low income workers tend to choose more risk-averse investment strategies than high income workers, this will lead them to have lower replacement rates in the future. The distributional issue is explored further in a separate paper (James, 1997) and certainly merits additional empirical research.

6. Conclusion

Averting the Old Age Crisis (World Bank, 1994), argued that old age security systems with a large funded defined contribution component, decentralized competitive management of these funds, and a social safety net, are most likely to promote economic growth, provide acceptable income to the old, and reduce risk by diversification. During the past five years, the move toward multi-pillar systems has accelerated. With the aging of the global population, it has become increasingly important to choose a reliable and cost effective method of old-age support. As economic growth slows and financial markets open, it has become increasingly important to raise productivity through improved incentives in the labour market and through the accumulation of capital which is then allocated to its most efficient uses. As income disparities have widened, it has become increasingly important to provide additional protection to low wage earners who have grown old. A multi-pillar system that includes a mandatory publicly managed tax-financed defined benefit pillar for redistribution, a mandatory privately managed funded defined contribution pillar to manage peoples' retirement savings, and a voluntary pillar for people who are willing to pay for more security, has seemed to many countries most likely to accomplish these objectives.

Thus several Latin American, OECD, and transition countries have already adopted multi-pillar systems, and they are under serious consideration in many more. Preliminary evidence from Chile, the only country that has had this system for long enough for empirical studies to be conducted, supports the existence of a positive growth effect, stemming from increased labour market efficiency, mobilization of long term saving, and financial market development. This suggests that the reward may be worth the effort of a carefully planned reform that takes into account its impact on the broader economy.

It may be surprising to find so much variety among the countries that have adopted multi-pillar systems of old age security, indicating substantial room for country-specific conditions. It should not be surprising to find that the new solutions have created new problems, in this case high administrative costs and restrictions on financial market flexibility. Countries that are on the verge of reforming their social security systems can learn from the experience of the first-movers and make the late reforms even better.

References

Agosin, Manuel R., Crespi T. Gustavo, and S. Leonardo Letelier (1996) 'Explicaciones del Aumento del Ahorro en Chile,' Centros de Investigacion Economica, Santiago, Chile: Banco Interamericano de Desarrollo.

Ayala, Ulpiano (1996) 'The Savings Impact of the Mexican Pension Reform,' *Green Cover Report 16373ME*, Mexico Country Dept., World Bank.

Bateman, Hazel and John Piggott (forthcoming) 'Mandatory Occupational Pensions in Australia' *Annals of Public and Cooperative Economics.*

Bosworth, Barry and Manuel Marfan (1994) 'Saving, Investment, and Economic Growth', in Barry Bosworth, Rudiger Dornbusch, and R. Laban, (eds.), *The Chilean Economy: Political Lessons and Challenges,* Washington D.C., Brookings Institution.

Cerda, Luis and Gloria Grandolini (1997) 'Mexico: The 1997 Pension Reform', EDI Conference volume.

Chamorro, C. (1992) 'La Cobertura del Sistema Chilean de Pension', Ph.D. Dissertation, Catholic University, Santiago, Chile.

Cifuentes Rodrigo and Salvador Valdes-Prieto (1997) 'Transitions in the Presence of Credit Constraints', in Salvador Valdes-Prieto (ed.) *The Economics of Pensions: Principles, Policies, and International Experience,* Cambridge: Cambridge University Press.

Corsetti, Giancarlo (1994) 'An Endogenous Growth Model of Social Security and the Size of the Informal Sector', *Revista de Analisis Economico,* 9(1) pp. 57–76.

Corsetti, Giancarlo and Klaus Schmidt-Hebbel (1997) 'Pension Reform and Growth', in Salvador Valdes-Prieto (ed.), *The Economics of Pensions: Principles, Policies, and International Experience,* Cambridge, Cambridge University Press.

Demurgic-Kunt, Asli and Anita Schwarz (1997) 'Taking Stock of Pension Reforms Around the World', EDI Conference volume.

Edwards, Sebastian (1997) 'Chile: Radical Change Toward a Funded Pension System', paper presented at Kiel Week Conference, University of Kiel, Germany, UCLA and NBER, processed.

Fox, Louise, (1998) 'The Latvian Pension Reform', World Bank, Washington, D.C.

Friedman, Barry, Estelle James, Cheikh Kane and Monika Queisser (1996) 'How Will China Care for Its Aging Population?', World Bank PRD Discussion Paper.

Gramlich, Edward (1996) 'Different Approaches for Dealing with Social Security', *Journal of Economic Perspectives*, 10(3), pp. 55–66.

Haindl Rondanelli, Erik (1996) 'Chilean Pension Fund Reform and its Impact on Saving', IBC Discussion Paper 96-2. University of Miami, International Business Center, Coral Gables, Florida, (processed).

Hamann, A. Javier (1997) 'The Reform of the Pension System in Italy', IMF Working Paper WP/97/18.

Hepp, Stefan (forthcoming) 'The Swiss Multi-Pillar System', *Annals of Public and Cooperative Economics*.

Holzmann, Robert (1996) 'On Economic Usefulness and Fiscal Requirements of Moving from Unfunded to Funded Pensions', University of Saarland Working Paper, Saarbrucken, Germany.

ILO (International Labour Organization) (1996) PANORAMA, Geneva.

James, Estelle and Robert Palacios (1995) 'Costs of Administering Public and Private Pension Plans', *Finance and Development* 32, 12–15.

James, Estelle (1997) 'Pension Reform in Latin America: Is There an Efficiency-Equity Trade-off?', in Nancy Birdsall, Carol Graham and Richard Sabot (eds.), *Beyond Trade-offs: Market Reforms and Equitable Growth in Latin America*, Inter-american Development Bank and Brookings Institution, Washington, D.C.

Johnson, Paul (forthcoming) 'Pension Reform in the United Kingdom', *Annals of Public and Cooperative Economics*.

Kane, Cheikh and Robert Palacios (1996) 'The Implicit Pension Debt', *Finance and Development*, 33, 38–41.

Kotlikoff, Larry (1996) 'Privatizing Social Security At Home and Abroad', Discussion Paper.

Mitchell, Olivia (1996a) 'Social Security Reform in Uruguay', Pension Research Council WP, University of Pennsylvania, pp. 96–20.

—— (1996b) 'Administrative Costs in Public and Private Pension Systems', NBER Working Paper.

Mitchell, Olivia and Annika Sunden (1994) 'An Examination of Social Security Administration Costs in the United States', Pension Research Council WP, University of Pennsylvania, pp. 94–7.

Morande, Felipe G. (1996) 'Savings in Chile: What Went Right?', Inter-American Bank Working Paper Series 322a.

Office of the Government Plenipotentiary for Social Security Reform (1997) 'Security through Diversity: Reform of the Pension System in Poland', Warsaw.

Palacios, Robert and Roberto Rocha (1997) 'The Hungarian Pension System in Transition', EDI Conference Volume.

Pujol, Thierry (1996) 'Some Considerations on Pay-As-You-Go vs. Fully-Funded Schemes', World Bank.

Queisser, Monika (1998) *The Second-Generation Pension Reforms in Latin*

America, OECD Development Centre Studies, Paris.

Reid, Gary and Olivia Mitchell (1995) 'Social Security Administration in Latin America and the Caribbean', World Bank Working Paper.

Rofman, Rafael and H. Bertin (1997) 'Lessons From Pension Reform: The Argentine Case', EDI Conference Volume.

Rutkonski, M. (1988) 'A new generation of Pension Reform Conquers the East: A Taxonomy in Transition Economies', *Transition,* 9(4).

Schmidt-Hebbell, Klaus (1997) 'Pension Systems: From Crisis to Reform', EDI Conference Volume.

Schwarz, Anita and Salvadore Valdes (1998) 'Notional Accounts: An Analytic Framework', World Bank, Washington, D.C..

Sunden, Annika (1998) 'The Swedish Notional Account System', Working Paper, World Bank, Washington, D.C..

Von Gersdorff, Hermann (1997) 'The Bolivian Pension Reform: Innovative Solutions to Common Problems', World Bank Working Paper.

Valdes-Preito, Salvador (forthcoming) 'Pension Reform in Latin America: Transition and Implementation Problems', *Annals of Public and Cooperative Economics.*

——— (ed.) (1997) *The Economics of Pensions,* Cambridge University Press.

Whitehouse, Edward (1998) 'Pension Reform in Britain', Social Protection Discussion Paper 9810, World Bank, Washington, D.C..

Wise, David (1997) 'Retirement Across Decades, Across Nations (using HRS data)', presented at Conference on Economics of Aging, International Health and Retirement Surveys Conference, Amsterdam, (processed).

World Bank (1994) *Averting the Old Age Crisis: Policies to Protect the Old and Promote Growth.* Washington, D.C., World Bank, and Oxford University Press.

4

Issues in Reforming Retirement Income Provisions*

Nishan de Mel

INTRODUCTION

This chapter takes a look at the issues surrounding design specifications of retirement income-security provisions (RIPs). The central purpose of the chapter is to enumerate the basic underlying elements in designing RIPs and discusses the relative merits of transitioning from one form of design to another.

The section on 'Theoretical Framework' first, introduces a conceptual framework for evaluating the design of RIPs with respect to how the underlying functions relate to the principal targets and measures, and second, it outlines the theory of RIP and demonstrates that all the various forms of RIP design can be categorised into three main types. This section also introduces the terminology and the variables that are of interest in assessing performance and sustainability.

*This paper was originally presented at the international conference on Social Security and Policy: Lessons for India and South Asia, New Delhi (1999). Another version of this paper along with specific applications to Sri Lanka was published by the Institute of Policy Studies, Sri Lanka (de Mel 2000). This version includes revisions and corrections that were made in August 2002.

The section on 'Issues of Transition and Reform' looks at specific elements of design and how they affect the underlying functions and particularly at the effect of transitioning from one form of design to another. Specifically it looks at transitioning from: (1) unfunded to funded systems, (2) payments linked to incomes, payments linked to contributions, (3) PAYG to Provident Fund-type systems, and (4) public centralized management to private competitive management. It evaluates these transitions in terms of the underlying functions of: (i) improving the distribution of risk, and (ii) increasing the efficiency of savings markets, for the (a) welfare of individuals selected (perhaps due to vulnerability), and (b) welfare of society as a whole. It concludes by describing a general framework for framing and implementing the reform of RIPs. The framework consists of four broad policy goals and several contextual instruments which are appropriately sequenced.

This chapter is restricted to a discussion of formal RIPs. That is, where the retirement income is secured through an explicit mechanism of transfers which are financed by specific contributions or taxes. This is distinct from informal sources of retirement income such as family support and rents from private wealth. It must be noted that formal RIPs are not always mandated. Participation in retirement-income-security schemes can also be voluntary. In this case the scheme would act as a specialized savings instrument that assists a person to optimize her consumption stream over the lifetime. There is also a third method by which governments can provide income-security to the elderly. This can be called the involuntary method. That is, simply to make an income transfer based on an assessment of the need of the retired person. This manner of providing income security is a form of welfare scheme for the elderly poor.

Some people find themselves in such dire poverty that their marginal propensity to save is close to zero. Such individuals are potentially well served by embedding the elements of a welfare scheme into the design of formal RIP (for instance, by using a method of means testing within the retirement provision to provide supplementary benefits to those with low capacity to save/contribute). It is, however, difficult to have significant involuntary provisions within voluntary RIPs because of adverse selection.

It is important to note that the poor are not necessarily better served by embedding welfare scheme within schemes of RIP. Due to the particular incentive structure there exists in financing RIPs the objectives of RIPs, and the objectives of welfare schemes can both be adversely affected by trying to marry the objectives of the two.

Failure to separate the discussion of welfare schemes from RIP often leads to confusion in theory and thinking on the subject. Whether or not RIPs should have welfare schemes embedded is a question that needs to be evaluated based on the specific economic conditions and objectives a policy-maker faces. This chapter introduces a generalized theoretical structure by which such an evaluation may be attempted.

1. Theoretical Framework

A formal RIP is a method of explicit (or implicit) savings (or taxes) from incomes (or consumption) during the productive working years, designed to provide a secure and adequate transfer of income for those who are in retirement years (when consumption is greater than income).

It is not always obvious, especially from the perspective of economic theory why saving for a retirement income provision cannot be a concern left entirely to the voluntary choice of each individual. The rational choice assumption of individual utility maximization might be interpreted as suggesting that, given freedom and information to choose, the choices that individuals actually make about their consumption and savings are the most efficient.

There is, however, a growing volume of literature demonstrating that when people actually make choices under uncertainty and over time, these do not seem to operate according to the set of consistency conditions implied by rational choice. This is most starkly seen in the phenomena of preference reversals. That is, even with no change in the external environment except for the passing of time, the intentions that people claim for themselves and the actions that they carry out, are often at odds with each other. This paradoxical behaviour is particularly evident in savings markets.

Many attempts have been made to explain preference reversals. Tversky et al. (1990) describe the attempts to demonstrate that preference reversal is consistent with the economic model of choice by relaxing the independence axiom and the reduction axiom. Extensive experiments, however, demonstrate that the phenomenon is attributable rather to violations of transitivity and invariance which are integral to the standard models of choice. This is substantiated by the theory of hyperbolic discounting which has been recently developed by economists to give formal structure to the concept of myopia in life-cycle savings.[1]

The failure of the rational choice assumption in the context of probability weighting and time discounting has significant implications for planning RIP. It means that people could often fail to save optimally for retirement and regret their decisions later. An important implication derived from describing this myopia through hyperbolic discounting is that certain commitment devices that restrict choice can actually increase welfare.[2] Therefore, the commitment to save engendered by RIPs can be a vital aspect of their function and design.

A second reason that formal RIPs are often designed to alter incentives and interfere with voluntary choices in savings stems from moral hazard.[3] In terms of political economy, savings which lead to old age poverty burdens not only the individual but also the welfare system of a society. But the fact that there is recourse to the welfare system can in turn create a perverse incentive for lower savings. Formal RIPs can be designed to mitigate this hazard.

A third reason for interfering with choices is asymmetric information. In insurance markets for annuities the providers of insurance cannot observe the risks of longevity. This can lead to adverse selection of the insurance aspect of RIPs, causing the markets to unravel. Therefore, formal RIPs can be a mechanism for improving the efficiency of these markets.

[1]At a much simpler level of conceptualization economists have attempted to explain such choice as deriving from the inadequacy of information. This approach attributes preference-reversal type behaviour to a chronic lack of information with regard to probabilities and the future, rather than a failure to synthesize that information according to the conventional theory of rational maximization. Becker and Murphy (1990) is an example. While this simpler conceptualization is useful in considering risks and uncertainty in the future state of the world, the lack of information would apply not only to the future states of the external world but also the future state of internal preferences—an issue that proponents of this approach fail to address. Hyperbolic discounting theory provides a structure by which the future state of internal preferences may be factored in to current decision-making.

[2]Laibson (1998) summarizes the implication of hyperbolic discounting for life-cycle savings behaviour.

[3]Moral hazard occurs when an intervention that is designed to protect people from a certain risk results in the alteration of behaviour in such a manner as to redefine the risk that the intervention seeks to protect against.

In summary, the most observable function of a formal RIP is that of providing individuals with an income transfer during retirement years. The reasons for doing so (or the underlying functions of RIPs) are two fold: first, to help individuals and society manage various types of uncertainty and risks and, second, to improve overall economic efficiency. Therefore, the design of a RIP is best described and evaluated in the conceptual framework of targets and measures. From the discussion so far it is possible to distinguish two types of targets and two types of measures.

The targets are:

(1) Welfare of selected individuals,

(2) Total social welfare.

The measures are:

(a) Improving the intertemporal and interpersonal distribution of risk,

(b) Increasing the efficiency of savings markets.

In the rest of this chapter this conceptual framework will be laid out in a targets–measure matrix such as in Table 4.1, and will be used to evaluate the elements of RIP design.

Table 4.1
Matrix of Targets and Measures for RIP

	Improving the distribution of interpersonal and intertemporal risk	Increasing the efficiency of savings behaviour and markets
Selected (individual) welfare improvements	Example: Redistributing income to reduce the risk of poverty among the elderly	Example: Partial cure for the tendency of myopia in individual saving habits
General (social) welfare improvements	Example: Providing insurance against risk factors that may affect incomes of the elderly	Example: Pareto improving effects on the functioning of insurance and capital markets

1.1 Formal Definitions

A formal RIP usually depends on a financial contribution made during the working lives in order to secure the entitlement for an adequate income transfer during retirement. This contribution, however, need not be necessarily explicit or directly related to the retirement income payment made to any particular worker.

The retirement benefit can either be pre-determined or (as is more usual) be linked directly to (1) contributions made, (2) wages, (3) years of work (4) age of retirement, or some combination of these variables. When the payment amount is linked directly to contributions and the contribution is determined (in terms of wage or a fixed amount) then the RIP is classified as being a DC scheme. When the contributions are not determined and the retirement benefit is determined in terms of the other variables listed above, then the RIP is known as a DB scheme.

The contribution towards the retirement benefit can be made by one of three parties: (1) the worker, (2) the employer, (3) the government, or any combination of them. The retirement benefit can be financed from: (1) an accrued fund made up of explicit past contributions, or (2) current contributions being made on behalf of current workers, or (3) an implicit liability (generated by promises that are tantamount implicit past contributions) being made explicit.

When the financing is from an accrued fund that is backed by some form of assets, it is a funded scheme. When the financing is from current contributions (and not from accrued funds), it is an unfunded scheme and is also referred to as a PAYG scheme. Unfunded schemes can sometimes have notional funds. Notional funds are ghost funds which are maintained only on ledger accounts and not backed by assets. DC plans when unfunded tend to maintain notional funds, since it is necessary to track contributions in order to calculate future payments. But DB plans, when the benefit calculation is not dependent on contributions, tend to dismiss with this bit of additional accounting.

The nature of funding describes the way in which the discounted value of expected future payments are accounted for in the present. Funded schemes maintain a designated asset base from which to finance future liabilities. Fully funded schemes, maintain the full present discounted value of expected future payments in a fund.[4] Partially funded schemes maintain less than the full present discounted value of such liabilities. Unfunded schemes do not maintain a separate designated fund but can keep an account of future liabilities through a notional fund. In the absence of a notional fund any liability accrued in the present is concealed from the accounts. While

[4]This describes the simplest form of full funding.

governments often resort to unfunded PAYG mechanisms as a method of financing, commercial institutions by statutes of accounting practice are required to account for retirement-income-security liabilities at least through notional funds (Mosich and Larsen 1986).

The retirement benefit can also be either fixed or indexed. When indexed, the payment amount is allowed to increase with variables such as inflation and/or wage growth in the economy. The replacement rate is the proportion of wages that is replaced by the retirement benefit.[5] Whenever a DC type scheme is funded the retirement benefit can depend on the rate of return which is the return on investment of the capital accrued in the fund. Further, when it is a DB scheme (where the replacement rate is defined by the rules of the scheme) the expected rate of return will determine the required contribution rate, which is the ratio of current wages that is channelled into the scheme in the form of contributions.

Therefore, if payment is to be made in the form of a pension (that is, a monthly payment from retirement to mortality) computing the exact monthly payment (in a DC scheme) or the required monthly contribution (in a DB scheme) can involve complex actuarial work. It would depend on assumptions about the life expectancy, choice of work and retirement timing of the participants, and several macroeconomic variables such as wages and inflation. The replacement ratio, which is the ratio of the replacement rate to the contribution rate, is a convenient benchmark for evaluating the generosity of a scheme. The passivity ratio, which is the ratio of years worked (making contributions) to the years spent in retirement (drawing benefits), is a reflection of the burden placed on the scheme.

1.2 Elements of Design

The simplest and broadest conceptualization of a formal RIP is to see it as a series of contributions made on behalf of workers that is used to finance payments to the retired. Therefore, all formal RIPs boil down to a general form that can be represented as follows:[6]

[5]The effective wage can be estimated in numerous ways. Some schemes use the final wage, others use the average wage over the full period, and others use calculations that result in values in between these two.

[6]Simple mathematical notation is used because this book is meant for a wide readership.

Contributions on behalf of workers = Payments to those in retirement

$$\int_{\tau=0}^{T} \sum_{i=1}^{N_C} \left(Contributions_{(i,\tau)}\right) \times (1+r)^{(t-\tau)} = \int_{\tau=0}^{T} \sum_{i=1}^{N_B} \frac{\left(Payments_{(i,\tau)}\right)}{(1+r_t)^{(\tau-t)}} \tag{4.1}$$

Where:
The scheme is implemented over the time horizon (0, T)

N_C = Number of participants contributing

N_B = Number of participants benefiting[7]

r = Economic rate of return/discounting for a unit of time, in the units of τ

t = the point in time for which the contribution and payment is measured.

$Contributions_{(i,\tau)}$ = Contributions[8] made on behalf of the participant i at time τ.

$Payments_{(i,\tau)}$ = payments received by participant i at time τ

The manner in which the contributions are equated to the payments can change depending on the design of a particular RIP. The predominant schemes fall into three specific types of design. They are labelled A, B, and C, for ease of reference.

1.2.1 Type A: Today's workers pay for today's retired

Contributions on behalf of today's workers = payments made to those in retirement today

Then applying equation (4.1) it is true at any given time that:

$$\sum_{i=1}^{N_C} Contributions_i = \sum_{i=1}^{N_B} Payments_i \tag{4.2}$$

This design which is being labelled as 'Type A', describes a typical PAYG scheme. As today's payments are instantly converted to

[7]Note that the number of contributors could differ from the number of beneficiaries because of the possibility of death prior to retirement.

[8]The contributions do not have to be made by the individual alone, it could be made on behalf of the individual by their spouse, their employer, or by the government.

payments, it is by the nature of design an unfunded scheme. Current payments depend on current contributions rather than on an accrued source of funding. This type of RIP is sustained by a form of social contract between generations.[9] Each generation contracts to finance the payments for the previous generation on the understanding that the next generation will do the same. Therefore in Type A Retirement income security design, the retirement income is generated from current contributions and the security is based on a 'tacit' intergenerational social contract, that is sustained by the government.[10]

1.2.2 Type B: Each generation of workers funds their future benefits

Future value of accumulated contributions on behalf of today's workers = payments made to today's workers when they are in retirement (in the future)

Then applying equation (4.1) it is true for every generation that:

$$\int_{\tau=0}^{T_1} \sum_{i=1}^{N_C} \left(\text{Contributions}_{(i,\tau)}\right) \times (1+r)^{(t-\tau)} = \int_{\tau=0}^{T_2} \sum_{i=1}^{N_B} \frac{\left(\text{Payments}_{(i,\tau)}\right)}{(1+r_t)^{(\tau-t)}} \tag{4.3}$$

where T_1 and T_2 refer respectively to the times at which the last person in the generation retires and the last person faces mortality.

This Type B design refers to a RIP that is fully funded. All contributions are accumulated and invested in some asset that is later depleted to finance the payments that are made when current contributors are in retirement. This represents a form of intragenerational agreement where each generation supports itself through every person in that generation entering into social agreement on a mechanism of pooling their investments with others and sharing the

[9]The word 'generation' is used here and in the rest of the chapter in a very particular manner. In this particular understanding, at any given point in time, society consists of two generations. The first generation: those who are in retirement; and the second generation: those who are in the labour force. People become 'visible' to the system by entering into one of these two groups. When a person goes from being in the labour force to being retired, she ceases to be a part of the second generation and begins to be a part of the first.

[10]The contract is 'tacit' because the contract inevitably involves future generations that are yet to be born and have not been explicitly consulted.

resulting risks and benefits. Therefore, in Type B retirement income security design, the retirement income is generated from past contributions and the security is based on an intragenerational agreement that is sustained by the managers of the scheme. This type of scheme is substantively no different from a classic insurance scheme.

1.2.3 Type C: Each individual funds his/her future benefits

Future value of accumulated contributions on behalf of each worker = payments made to that worker in retirement (in the future)

Then applying equation (4.1) it is true for every person that:

$$\int_{\tau=0}^{T} (\text{Contributions}_{\tau}) \times (1+r)^{(t-\tau)} = \int_{\tau=0}^{T} \frac{(\text{Payments}_{\tau})}{(1+r_t)^{(\tau-t)}} \qquad (4.4)$$

The design described as Type C, also refers to a fully funded RIP as in Type B. In terms of funding it is in fact a derivative form of Type B. However, unlike Type B, this design does not require any form of, even tacit, social agreement. In this design, the contributions of each individual is separately accounted and the payments are based on the accrued values of the 'individual accounts'. Therefore, in this design each person supports herself, without any direct reference to other generations or even the others of her own generation. When it is mandated the government prescribes the share of income to be saved in order to generate an endowment that adequately finances retirement payments. The government also either manages or underwrites the management (and investment) of these funds. This then is basically a personal savings account which is regulated and treated more formally than others. In this form of retirement income-security design, the retirement income is generated from mandated savings and investments during employment and the security is based on the period of employment being substantial and the investment being in the hands of dependable managers, and the underwriting of the government.

1.2.4 Flexibility within different types of design

Type A schemes, though typically unfunded can sometimes be partially funded by an addition of a buffer fund that allows the smooth maintenance of the payment expectations given the stickiness of contributions in the short run. Type B and C schemes can go from full to partial funding if the scheme is subsidized. In this partial funding case a part of the contribution on behalf of workers would be made only retrospectively at the time of making retirement income payments. Such a subsidy is tantamount to a welfare component. Type B and C cannot be completely unfunded without ceasing to be a RIP and becoming a welfare scheme for the elderly.

All three types, technically, can be designed as DB or DC schemes. But, in practice, due to the complexities of the calculations and adjustments involved in setting contribution rates and calculating sustained payments these schemes fall into a particular side of the DB/DC spectrum. Type A schemes tend to fall on the DB side of the spectrum, and Type C tends to be on the DC side of the spectrum with Type B falling somewhere in between.

1.3 Factors that Affect the Rate of Replacement

In funded as well as unfunded provisions, when equating payments to contributions is considered, it is clear that one simple way of increasing the replacement rate is to increase the rate of contribution. But for any given rate of contribution, the factors that affect the replacement rate can be different for funded and unfunded provisions.[11]

Unfunded Provisions

When current contributions are set to equal current payments as in a typical unfunded DB, PAYG scheme, and the contribution rate is fixed then the replacement rate is proportional to two factors:

(1) System wage growth—directly proportional. The system wage growth is the real wage growth between the current beneficiaries (those who are retired) and the current contributors (those who are working) in the scheme.

(2) System dependency ratio—inversely proportional. The system dependency ratio is the ratio of current beneficiaries to the current contributors in the scheme.

The system wage growth in turn is correlated positively with growth in productivity. The system dependency ratio is correlated positively with the life expectancy of those in retirement and negatively with

[11]This section deals algebraically with the basic identities and scenarios. For a simple algebraic exploration of scenarios not discussed in this chapter see Vittas (1993).

years of participation as contributors (or years of work) as well as the age of retirement.

Funded Provisions

Likewise it can also be deduced as in unfunded provisions, that when the system is fully funded the replacement rate depends on two apparently different factors:

(1) It is directly proportional to the real rate of return (on the investments of accumulated contributions).

(2) It is inversely proportional to the passivity ratio (that is, the number of months spent in retirement vs the number of months spent as a worker)

The real rate of return is in turn correlated positively with GDP growth. The passivity ratio is correlated positively with life expectancy for those in retirement, and negatively on the years of participation as contributors as well as on the age of retirement.

Therefore, the replacement rate of funded as well as unfunded schemes depends on: (a) life expectancy of the older population, (b) age of retirement, and (c) years of financial contributions made to the system. In addition the replacement rate depends on wage growth in an unfunded scheme; and on the rate of economic return in a funded scheme.[12]

[12]This is an alternative (and more standard) depiction of the difference in replacement rates between funded and unfunded arrangements. Consider an unfunded arrangement where population is constant, dependency ratio is in steady state, the contribution rate is c, and average lifetime wages while benefits are being accrued is W. Then a worker contributes cW during his working life towards the RIP.

The benefits that the worker receives are equal to the contribution of a worker in the next generation. If, in a generation productivity grows at the rate of g (and wage growth reflects productivity growth) then the benefits that the worker receives is $cW(1+g)$. When the population is not constant and grows at the rate of n, the benefits increase to $cW(1+g)(1+n)$. In a funded arrangement, if the economic rate of return over a generation is r, the same worker would receive a benefit equal to $cW(1+r)$.

The replacement rate in a funded vis-à-vis the replacement rate in an unfunded system would depend on whether r is more (equal to or less) than g (if population is growing g would be replaced by $g+n+gn$). See Kotlikoff (1989).

1.4 Additional Notes on Terminology and Theory

1.4.1 Pension Plans vs Provident Funds

The RIPs, as they work in practice, can be approximately divided into two broad categories; Provident Funds and Pensions Plans.

The principal difference between a provident fund and a pension plan, is that the former makes a lump sum payment at retirement while a pension plan makes a stream of regular payments from retirement to the end of life.[13]

A pension plan can either have a DB or DC method of calculating retirement benefits and can either be funded or unfunded. Provident funds on the other hand, by design, follow a DC method of calculating the retirement benefits and are fully funded. They fit the description of Type C plans. Government pension plans, as they have evolved in the world are usually of the DB type and are often not fully funded. They tend to follow the Type A design.

A provident fund benefit can be converted to a pension plan by annuitizing the accrued capital.[14] Converting an unfunded pension plan into a provident fund can be a little more complicated. When funded, however, the accrued capital of a pension plan can be paid out as a lump sum making it equivalent to a provident fund.

Therefore, the important distinction between provident funds and pension plans as they have evolved, is not the payment of a lump sum vs a stream of payments but the DC vs the DB nature of determining the retirement benefit, and the funded vs PAYG nature of financing the payments.

[13]As an aside, it is important to point out that a provident fund is different from a gratuity in that a provident fund is explicitly financed and funded, while a gratuity payment usually is not.

[14]For instance, consider annuitizing a capital of Rs Y (accrued through a provident fund) at an expected long term monthly interest rate of r_m number of months N (which is the age specific mortality at the point of purchasing the annuity). The fixed payment F can then be worked out as:

$$F = Y \times \frac{\left[(1+r_m)^N - r_m\right] \times r_m}{\left[(1+r_m)^N - 1\right]}$$

1.4.2 Demographic Transitions

A demographic transition is fuelled by two factors: one, a decrease in the total fertility rate and two, the increase in the longevity of life. Together these two factors result in a period during which the population growth in the lower age groups is less than the population growth in the higher age groups. This has implications for RIPs because it means that the share of the employed people will decrease and the share of the retired people will increase in the total population of the country. In other words the system dependency ratio will increase.[15]

Therefore, for the purpose of this discussion, a demographic transition is a period during which the system dependency ratio increases from one steady state level to another. Such transitions as they have been experienced in the world have often resulted in the doubling of the system dependency ratio from around 10 per cent to around 20 per cent. This generally happens in the course of many decades, but sometimes (as it is tipped to be in the case of Sri Lanka) in just under two decades.[16]

The impact of demographic transitions on RIPs depends on the nature of funding and the rules of the RIP.

Unfunded (Type A) PAYG Provisions

It can be shown that in an unfunded provision, *ceteris paribus* the replacement rate would fall if the system dependency ratio were to increase. But if such provision is of DB type (and this is generally the case) then the replacement rate is fixed by the rules of the scheme. Therefore, the increase in the system dependency ratio has to be offset either by an increase in the system wage growth or by the increase of the contribution rate by the current workforce.

It must be noted that the system wage growth serves as a means to offset the demographic transition only if the benefits are not indexed to wage growth, but only to inflation. Therefore, when the pension payments are indexed to wages, if system dependency doubles, then the contribution (tax) rate has to be doubled to honour the rules of the RIP. Suppose that such a RIP had a tax rate of 20 per cent (this is the

[15]For a fuller discussion on aging and dependency ratios see Clark (1989).

[16]See James (1997a) p. 32, for a country comparison of time taken for the share of population above 60 to double from 9 per cent to 18 per cent.

very low end of tax rates for such schemes in the world) then the demographic transition would result in increasing the tax rate to 40 per cent. Most countries in the world with such schemes would end up with tax rates of over 50 per cent.

Taxation invariably affects labour supply decisions and is considered distortive because it can cause the labour market to move away from the non-tax equilibrium. While the actual effect of taxes depends on the elasticity of labour supply and demand, the distortive effects of taxation increases with size of the tax.[17]

The tax rate affects not only the decisions about how much labour to supply but also decisions about what labour to supply and how to avoid and evade taxes.[18] Empirically it is found that as the tax rate increases there is an increased tendency for workers to avoid and evade taxes as well as for such activity to seem acceptable, which in turn increases the rate of avoidance and evasion. Workers can avoid and evade taxes in three ways: (1) migrating to the informal sector, (2) converting wages to modes of non-taxable compensation, and (3) non-reporting of income. Avoidance and evasion in any of these ways will give rise to a vicious cycle where, as workers avoid and evade taxation, system dependency ratio will increase (or wage growth will decrease) causing the required contribution rate to rise further, causing further avoidance and evasion of tax contributions, etc. If the cycle continues, there will come a point at which the retirement scheme becomes unsustainable.[19]

[17]From basic tax theory: the distortion (dead-weigh-loss) increases with the square of the increase in the tax rate. Therefore a tax of 40 per cent would be 4 times as distortive as a tax of 20 per cent $\{(0.4)^2/(0.2)^2 = 4\}$. In other words, the growth of the distortion would be the square of the growth of the tax rate.

[18]Tax avoidance is the re-organization of economic activity to pay lower taxes, this is not illegal. But tax evasion, the non-reporting or non-payment of tax liability is illegal.

[19]The vicious cycle can be modelled as follows:

$$\frac{r}{c} = \frac{w_1(1-e_1)}{w_2} \times \frac{n_1(1-e_2)}{n_2}$$

c is the contribution rate and r is the replacement rate. w_1 w_2 are the average real wages of those making contributions, and those receiving benefits, respectively. n_1 and n_2 are the number of contributors and beneficiaries, respectively. Here, e_1 and e_2

Funded (Type B and Type C) schemes

The first causal factor of the demographic transition (namely increase in the longevity of life), would, *ceteris paribus*, result in the increase of the passivity ratio. It can be shown that in funded schemes the replacement rate would fall when the passivity ratio increases.

Funded retirement income payments can be either of DB type (Type B) or DC type (Type C). When the payments are of DB type the replacement rate is fixed by the rules of the scheme. Therefore, the increase in the passivity ratio has to be offset either through earning higher rates of return on the accrued funds or by increasing the contribution rate. Two points must be noted:

(1) The increase in the passivity ratio is not as drastic as the increase in the system dependency ratio. Passivity ratio would increase by the same percentage as the percentage increase of the time spent in retirement. This would generally be around 30 per cent during a typical demographic transition. The system dependency ratio, however, would double (that is, increase by a 100 per cent). Therefore in funded schemes the contribution rate would have to increase by only around 30 per cent as opposed to a 100 per cent in unfunded schemes.

(2) In funded schemes, there is no difference between those who make the higher contributions and those who require a larger quantum of funds to finance their retirement benefits. Therefore, the consequences of evasion are different from an unfunded scheme. If current contributions are reduced through evasion then the payments that need to be made from the current contributions will also be equally reduced. In unfunded schemes when evasion increases (that is, current tax contribution decreases) the payments that need to be made from current taxes remain the same (only the payments that need to be made from future taxes will decrease).

When the funded system is of DC type, then the replacement rate is not set by the rules of the scheme. That is, the replacement rate is determined by the existing annuity market and the accumulated capital in the fund. In this scenario there is no necessary obligation on the part of the pension fund managers or the government to ensure that

are functions of c. Therefore if r is held constant, then, *ceteris paribus*, increases in e_1 and e_2 have to be compensated for by increases in c which in turn leads to increases in e_1 and e_2 so on and so forth.

the replacement rate remains constant. There is, however, an incentive for people to change their work and retirement duration in order to reduce the passivity ratio in order to receive a higher replacement rate.

Therefore, in terms of maintaining an existing pension system, honouring the rules and meeting the accrued liabilities, a demographic transition poses the most problems for pension systems that are unfunded and of DB type (Type A). And the least problems for pension systems that are funded and of DC type (Type C).

2. Issues of Transition and Reform

2.1 Background to Reforming Retirement Provisions

The current wave to reform RIPs can be traced back to the pension reform in Chile in 1980 (Piñera 1997).[20] The World Bank and the IMF have invested significant resources in research and project assistance to facilitate these reforms, and the discussion has shifted to the centre stage of policy-making in many countries. Since these reforms are really about moving from certain forms of RIP design to others it can sometimes be more appropriate to use the word 'transition' rather than the word 'reform' to describe this process. Therefore, this chapter will speak of transitions rather than reforms.

The impetus for transitions has come not only from the perceived success of the Chilean transition but more so from the perceived problem posed by demographic aging on the sustainable financing of existing types of RIP designs (Daykin and Lewis 1998). The effect of demographic transitions has been discussed under the section 'Theoretical Framework'.

Today, the World Bank is the principal promoter of pension reform in the world. It has promoted a multipillar RIP consisting of segments that are voluntary and mandatory, fully funded and unfunded, DC and DB, privately managed and publicly managed—in other words, a little bit of everything. The voluntary segment (or, pillar, in the terminology of the Bank) is basically the duplication of a mandatory pillar, but on a voluntary basis for those who want extra retirement income. Therefore, in effect, the proposed multipillar RIP boils down to just two types of provisions. One, a tax financed (unfunded) DB provision

[20]The new system came into operation on 1 May 1981.

(designed to guarantee a minimum pension) which is publicly managed, and the other, a payroll financed (fully funded) DC/DB provision, which is privately managed.

This essentially two-pronged (pillar) approach to RIPs is justified by the World Bank on the basis of hedging against the potential risks of having any single approach.[21] It has also been prompted by the difficulty in making a full transition from publicly managed PAYG (tax financed) DB provisions to privately managed, fully funded, DC provisions (James 1997a). In countries with such existing provisions, the two-pronged approach enables a gradual reduction in the tax financed benefits and a transition towards dependence on fully funded benefits, easing the process of reform.

When considering the adoption of this multipillar approach, it is important to remember that the starting point matters. Because the multipillar approach emerges out of the need to make changes in conventional PAYG pension schemes, it is easier to justify this approach for a country which has an entrenched PAYG scheme as the principal RIP, than for a country which has provident funds (or other fully funded schemes) as the principal RIP.

It must also be borne in mind that to bring about a change from a pre-existing system into a new one has different consequences to that of adopting a totally new system from scratch. When deciding about RIP reform countries are not starting from scratch. Rather, each country is faced with the issues of modifying or changing pre-existing pension systems and making a transition to a new system. In cases where the issue of reform arises there are four possible transitions that deserve close scrutiny.

1. Transitions from PAYG provisions to funded provisions; that is, transitions from Type A provisions to Type B and Type C provisions.

2. Transition from DB provisions to DC provisions with individual accounts; that is, transitions from Type B to Type C provisions.

3. Transition from unfunded DB provisions to funded DB provisions. That is, the double transitions from Type A provisions to Type C provisions.

4. Transition from mandated centralized public management to mandated decentralized private management of RIP assets.

[21]Potential risks of each type of arrangement are discussed in sections 2.2 to 2.5 of this chapter.

Each of these transitions has implications on individual and social welfare, risk distribution, and economic efficiency. Each of them is described and discussed in turn in the ensuing sections because a comprehensive understanding of the associated trade-offs is important for good policy-making in this arena.

2.2 Transition from Unfunded to Funded Schemes

(Type A to Type B)

Funded systems, whereby each generation (Type B) and even each individual (Type C) funds its own retirement income benefit, are being increasingly resorted to as a sustainable alternative to the current PAYG (Type A) schemes.

The advantages and disadvantages of funded RIP designs over unfunded designs can be evaluated on the targets-measure matrix introduced in part one of this chapter.

Table 4.2
Analysis of Funded RIPs vis-à-vis Unfunded RIPs

	Improving the distribution of risk	Increasing efficiency of savings markets
Welfare of selected	(weaker) Introducing an investment risk to the financing of retirement incomes	(stronger) Reducing the cost of financing future retirement incomes of current contributors
General social welfare	(weaker) Reducing the capacity to redistribute income risks from one generation to another	(stronger) Stimulating savings and capital markets, reducing distortions, promoting a more democratic approach to decision-making

When a RIP is not funded it does not require any outlay of funds during the initial stages when a worker is accruing pension rights, but has not reached the age of retirement. A worker becomes a cost to the system only after retirement when she becomes eligible to receive payments.

A funded RIP works in exactly the reverse. It becomes a cost to the system at the moment that a worker begins to accrue retirement benefits. But when the same worker retires and becomes eligible to receive payments, she stops being a cost to the system, and the retirement benefit is paid out of the accrued fund.

Figure 4.1 depicts the difference in magnitude and timing of costs for funded and unfunded systems when the size of the labour force participating in the RIP remains constant.

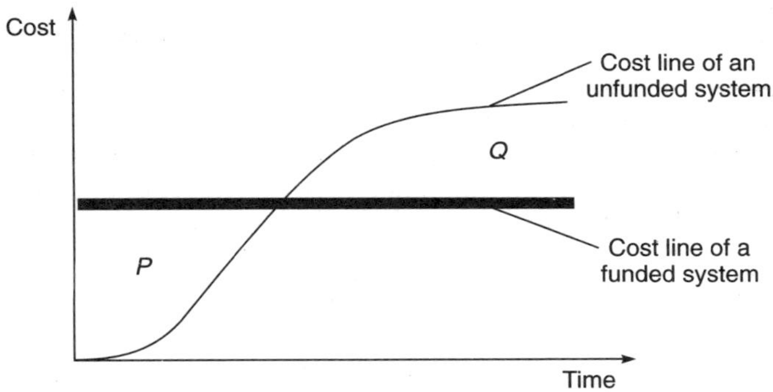

Fig. 4.1: Intertemporal Costs under Different Financing Options[22]

Due to the different timing of costs of the two different systems, they affect government budgeting and economic planning in different ways. An unfunded system is very cheap to run in the initial stages and gradually becomes more expensive as the system matures. Eventually when the system has accrued a whole generation of retirees (usually after about 30 years) the cost will approach its upper limit. However, in an aging population where the percentage of retirees in the population is also increasing the cost of the system will continue to increase until the demographic transition is complete. A funded system is more costly to operate in the initial stages. But demographic aging has no impact on the cost of such a system.

It must, however, be remembered that this insulation from demographic changes comes at the expense of the capacity to redistribute income risks from one generation to another. This can be

[22]See Hemming (1998) for further discussion and detail on cost models.

an important consideration for a low income country or a transition economy that has low capacity to generate financing in the present, but expects its prospects to improve substantially in the future. From a fiscal standpoint therefore, if a country is in a situation where it can expect to have high rates of economic growth in the future but is experiencing tight budgetary constraints at present, an unfunded system can make economic sense. But if the current budgetary situation and growth prospects cannot be expected to change significantly in the future, the failure to fund a system, prior to a demographic transition can be equivalent to starting off an economic time bomb.

The higher long run cost of an unfunded system (the area Q in Figure 4.1) as opposed to the lower short run cost (the area P in Figure 4.1), is due to the debt accrued by the system during the initial stages. Whether the costs of an unfunded system stabilize at a permanently higher rate depends on the difference between the economic rate of return and the rate of productivity and population growth.[23]

However, when dealing with a system that is currently unfunded, the system cannot be made cheaper by just making the transition to a funded system. This is because the transition to a funded system will include the cost of funding plus the cost of financing the accrued debt of the unfunded system. This aspect is discussed later. It turn out that, in theory, the cost of financing the accrued debt can be shown to be exactly equal to the cost saving from switching to a funded system, that is, if the past promises are fully honoured. In practice, however, this rarely happens—transitions to full funding are usually exploited as opportunities to reduce the implicit pension debt by increasing retirement age and under-valuing the pension claims that have accrued. While this involves at the very least subtle deceptions of the beneficiaries, it is sometimes justified on the grounds of overgenerous promises made in the past, which need to be re-aligned in order to be sustainable. Clearly, weighing theoretical strengths and weaknesses

[23]Let r, g, and n be defined as in footnote 12. Let c_u be the contribution rate of the worker from the unfunded RIP and c_f be the contribution rate from the worker in the funded RIP. When both workers are given the same replacement rate with respect to wages, then c_f would be less (equal to or more) than c_u depending on whether r is more (equal to or less) than $g+n+ng$. Therefore, the funded system would cost less than the unfunded system when r is more than $g+n+ng$. The converse is also true.

alone may not be enough to make a decisive case for transitioning from unfunded provisions to funded provisions. The preferences of a society in what values should prevail in how risk and income is redistributed is particularly important in making this decision.

Perhaps the strongest reason for a country to make the transition to a fully funded pension scheme should be that funded schemes ensure more democratic political decision-making with regard to RIPs. Unfunded schemes, that are susceptible to political manoeuvring, insulate politicians against the cost of financing the pension commitments made today as well as the true democratic response to those decisions. In an unfunded scheme, increased pension commitments made today are of benefit to those who can vote today and the cost of financing has to be borne by those who are not old enough to vote and those who are not yet born. In short, an unfunded pension scheme creates the avenue for a political decision in which a large part of the constituent parties are unable to indicate their response.

The problem of unfunded schemes, therefore, has some parallels to the moral hazard problem in insurance markets, but with applications in the realm of political decision-making. Just as in insurance markets, where an insulation from the true price causes changes in behaviour patterns that lead to over consumption,[24] here the insulation from the true democratic response can lead to over-commitment in terms of pension promises. Therefore, such schemes run a significant risk of today's commitments becoming unsustainable in the future. Funding makes pension commitments visible in the government budget and thereby automatically (unlike unfunded systems) creates pressure for greater fiscal discipline and cost cutting.

It must, however, be noted that transitioning to funded systems may replace the 'political risk'—that politicians will promise more than what future generations will be able to sustain—with the 'market risk'—that investments will behave in ways that could not have been anticipated.[25]

[24]For instance, the over consumption of health care in health insurance.

[25]These would be situations where the expectation of risk suddenly changes in a particular market, leading to a dramatic change in the nature of returns. The capital markets in East Asian countries during the crisis would be an example of such a situation. This can happen due to the imperfections in the investment market as well as weakness in the associated situations.

In summary, there may be instrumental, intrinsic, and constructive efficiency gains from the transition to a funded scheme. First, instrumentally, the transition can be used to restructure overgenerous existing promises, thereby reducing the accrued pension debt and making future benefits cheaper to finance. Second, intrinsically funded schemes tend to have less distortionary effects on economic activity. This is mainly due to them being perceived as a savings plan rather than a tax. Third, constructively, funded schemes may help to increase national savings, promote deeper capital markets, and further the principles of democracy in decision-making. These efficiency gains, however, come at the expense of lower capacity to redistribute income risks across generations, and the introduction of market risks to the financing of retirement provisions.[26]

2.3 Transition from DB to DC Schemes

(Type B to Type C)

In DB plans benefits are defined as a ratio of earnings (during a certain period of life) rather than contributions. In DC plans benefits are defined with direct reference to contributions. The advantages and disadvantages of RIPs with DC designs over DB designs are described in Table 4.3 targets-measure matrix.

Table 4.3
Analysis of RIPs with DC designs vis-à-vis DB

	Improving the distribution of risk	Increasing efficiency of savings markets
Welfare of selected	(weaker) Reduces the capacity to redistribute income even among individuals of one generation	(stronger) Increases ownership over contributions and ease of transferability
General social welfare	(weaker) Diminishes risk pooling capacity and reduces the potential insurance provided	(stronger) Increases the link between contributions and benefits and reduces labour market distortions

[26]A further discussion on objections that have been raised with regard to the benefits of funding and a response to those objections can be found in de Mel, 2000.

When it comes to income redistribution and risk sharing either across generation or across individuals of the same generation DB plans offer more flexibility than do DC plans.

DB provisions, by design, involve a form of risk and resource pooling among the participants. Therefore, DB provisions can engage in redistribution by defining the rules in a manner that favours the low income earners in the pool over the high income earners. It must, however, be noted as a caveat that DB plans do not always yield the desired kind of redistribution through the insurance, which it provides participants. For instance, when the risk pool is common and average life expectancy is used to calculate the monthly benefits payable after retirement, those who live longer will invariably receive more benefits from the DB provisions than those who do not. This on one hand may be seen as a means of redistributing the risk of an unexpectedly long life. On the other hand, when those who tend to live longer are the more affluent and those who do not, tend to be the poor, the redistribution can be seen as being somewhat perverse (James 1997b).

But the principal problem with DB systems is that they can contribute to several inefficiencies. The lack of linkage between contributions and benefits in DB systems can result in them being perceived as a tax rather than a saving by the labour market (Sachs 1997). Consequently, DB systems can result in a tendency of labour to escape into the informal sector. Labour market inefficiencies of DB systems also include a reduction in job mobility especially in the years close to retirement. This is due to the fact that contribution rates are usually kept constant and as income increases (usually with tenure) the present value of the benefits that are accrued exceed the contributions. Furthermore, DB systems are administratively harder to manage, requiring constant adjustments to contribution rates, and management decisions based on the projection and estimation of several imponderables such as long term interest rates and future wage growth.

Therefore, while the principal criticism of a DB to DC transition is that it would reduce welfare by reducing the capacity to redistribute risk between individuals and generations, the principal argument for promoting a DB to DC transition is that of improving the efficiency of the labour market as well as the management of the RIPs.

2.4 Transition from PAYG Pensions to Provident Funds

(Type A to Type C)

The transition from pension type schemes to provident fund type schemes involve compounding the two transitions described earlier.[27] Therefore, the preceding discussion applies in addition to the following:

The transition from an unfunded DB system to a funded DC system requires a funding and phasing out of the DB liabilities that have already been accrued. This involves: (1) for current pensioners, to find an alternative mechanism of financing the pensions they were receiving under the DB system, since the intergenerational contract is being dismantled; and (2) for the current participants, to calculate the accrued value of their implicit or explicit past-contributions and to cred them to individual accounts.

There is, therefore, a certain explicit cost to this double transition.[28] It is the cost of financing all the implicitly accrued debt under the unfunded DB system. Financing this debt has been handled in many different ways by different countries, and is an area that requires much thought and consideration in making such a transition.[29] The DB debt can be financed by: (1) increasing government debt (for example, issuing zero coupon bonds), and/or (2) increasing the current rate of taxation. The combination of instruments used will affect the nature in which this debt gets distributed across generations.

A generationally neutral way of financing the DB debt would be to let each generation pay just enough of the debt so that the next generation inherits exactly the same debt, measured as a percentage of GDP. This would involve: (1) converting the implicit present and future liabilities into explicit current debt and assessing this debt as a percentage of current GDP; (2) floating a zero-coupon bond where the

[27]An elaboration of the terms 'pension' and 'provident fund' was given in an earlier section 'Pension Plans vs Provident Fund' of this chapter.

[28]This explicit cost exists in any transition from unfunded to funded arrangements. But when the transition does not include a move from DB to DC the cost can remain implicit. A transition to a DC arrangement makes the cost explicit.

[29]Chile, for instance, handled the cost of reform by issuing government bonds to the value of the accrued benefits. These were paid as indexed long term bonds with a 4 per cent real rate of return, maturing at the time the recipient would have been eligible for his/her pension under the previous system.

face value on maturity is equal, as a percentage of GDP at maturity, to the current debt as a percentage of current GDP; (3) introducing taxes to cover the gap between the market value of the bond and the current debt, and (4) repeating steps two and three at the point whenever the bond has to be redeemed.

There is much discussion in the literature on whether or not this type of transition will reduce the tax burden (contribution rate) on the future population of a country for a given replacement rate. The discussion is based on the observation that market rates of return (even when adjusted for risk) are often greater than the implicit rate of return (Feldstein 1997). Recall that the implicit rate of return (which is derived from the replacement ratio) increases with the system wage growth and decreases with the system dependency ratio. The simple argument is that if market rates of return are higher than the implicit rate of return then the same replacement rate as is derived under the unfunded provisions can be derived under the funded provisions at a lower cost (that is, lower tax rate or contribution rate).

This argument, however, is overly simplistic. Given that a transition from Type A to Type C needs to finance the commitments that have already been accrued under the Type A system, the cost of financing those accrued rights will exactly offset the cost saving from making the transition (Sachs 1997). This is because the same market rate of return which works to reduce the cost of Type C systems will also work to increase the cost of servicing the debt that has been accrued under the Type A systems.

It has already been noted that defined contribution plans (Type C) have less manoeuvrability in terms of redistribution of income between generations. Also the value of pensions received under a DC funded approach depends on the savings instruments available and the return obtained. In many countries, which have instituted funded systems, the choice of savings instruments is limited. If small accounts are confined to, safe, bank instruments, the rate of return can be lower than that which is obtained through PAYG schemes.

2.5 Transition from Centralized Public to Decentralized Private Schemes

Perhaps the most controversial transition for low income countries is the transition from centralized publicly managed systems to decentralized privately managed systems. The advantages and

Table 4.4
Analysis of RIPs with Public Centralized Management vis-à-vis Private Decentralized Management

	Improving the distribution of risk	Increasing efficiency of savings markets
Welfare of selected	(weaker) Reduces protection from risk pooling and increases information requirements	(stronger) Allows for more variation and choice in risk exposure
General social welfare	(weaker) Increases adverse selection in risk markets and reduces insurance to high risk groups	(stronger) Promotes competition to deliver higher returns and better management

disadvantages of public centralized RIP designs over private decentralized designs are summarized in the following targets-measure matrix.

Chile is regarded as a prototype in this form of transition as well. In 1981 a government-run pension system was replaced with a privately administered national system of pension saving accounts. The apparent success of the Chilean pension reform has led to it being hailed as a model for other countries, and has been emulated by several Latin American countries in recent years. However, the reasons for the 'success' of the Chilean reform are mixed and some very real problems persist. The most significant problem that has arisen with regard to decentralization is that administrative costs are invariably higher when the fund size is smaller (Diamond 1994). When the decentralized system is competitively managed by the private sector this problem is compounded by the fact that marketing and advertising increase the administrative costs by a substantial percentage.

It is worth noting that the so-called success in Chile's private fund management was sustained by the less publicized fact that the government issued pension fund managers with bonds and treasury bills at high rates of real interest. This is financially no different from a direct government subsidy.

After the transition, in order to function effectively competitive private management depends on the availability of sophisticated capital markets (Kotlikoff 1996). In the absence of such markets within the country the options are to: (1) invest in capital markets outside the country, or (2) invest much of the assets in government debt. The first option invariably denies capital to local investors and the government for initiating development programmes within the country. The second option may result in a mediocre investment performance which fails to justify the higher administrative costs of private competitive management.

The chief objection to government management is derived from an empirical extrapolation. It springs from the observation that in such situations much of the fund is absorbed into financing government debt and therefore results in a lower-than-market rates of return. When this is true, another way to look at the lower rate of return is to see it as having a hidden tax. That is, the identical result could be achieved if the market rate of return was realized and the government introduced a higher tax on the earnings. The rate of the implicit tax then is the difference between the market rate of return and the lower rate of return.

Therefore, making the transition from government management to private management has the same effect as reducing the government tax revenue (as a ratio of debt). This is another way of expressing the fact that cost of government debt would increase after the transition. This revenue gap poses the same financing problem posed by the conversion of implicit debt under a DB provision into explicit debt. (See discussion about transition from Type B to Type C.) It results in the conversion of an implicit tax into an explicit tax, and the higher rates of return do not directly result in a net economic gain. Therefore the vital questions, again, are about the incidence of these taxes, and the resulting efficiency of the system.

It must be noted that the implicit tax falls on the wage earners—those participating in the retirement scheme—and not on the unemployed, or those in the informal sector. The tax (as a percentage of monthly income) also falls more heavily on those who have been in employment longer over those who have been in employment for a shorter time period. This is because the base of the implicit tax is the accrued savings in the scheme. If the revenue gap is going to be bridged by a tax on pension assets, then the participants can be no better off under private management than under public management. If the gap is going to be bridged by a tax on wage income then those who have been in the system longer will benefit at the expense of those who have been in the system for less time. If the tax is on consumption, then all the wage earners will benefit at the expense of the unemployed and those in the informal sector.

The efficiency gain would result from the manner in which this transition affected perceptions and behaviour. If the lower rates of return under government management are not perceived as a tax, then the increase in explicit taxation would introduce a new distortion into the labour market. This would be a loss of efficiency. But if the transition created a greater sense of ownership and control over the contributions it could lead to people being drawn from the informal sector into the formal sector and result in improving the efficiency of the labour market.[30]

In addition to the functioning of the labour market, the functioning of the financial market is also a factor in the designing of RIP. There is much evidence to show that the proliferation of fund managers (often driven by the introduction of private pension funds) helps to improve the efficiency of the financial markets (Vittas 1998). The expectation of making labour and financial markets more efficient could then be the primary reason for promoting this transition.

2.6 Targets and Instruments for Policy Reform

What the preceding sections have demonstrated is that when evaluating the designs of retirement income provisions for policy reform, attention must be paid not only to the consequences of new designs which are mooted but also the consequences of making the transition from the existing types of design to the designs mooted under reforms.

This section will consider a framework for applying the insights from the preceding discussion to the formulation of policy. It is useful from a perspective of policy-making to frame the problem of finding the right sort of RIP design in terms of achieving four distinct policy goals: 1. maintaining adequate replacement rates, 2. ensuring sustainability and enhancing coverage, 3. improving management and increasing competition, and 4. mitigating labour market distortions.

[30]This was done in Chile by issuing little red books that reflected the balance on retirement accounts and were regularly updated. Note, however, that building a sense of ownership in this way can be done even outside the context of such a transition.

All activities to improve the distribution of risk and increase the efficiency of economic activity with regard to pensions feed into one or more of these goals. These policy goals too can be mapped (approximately) into the conceptual framework of the targets-measure matrix.

Table 4.5
Mapping of Policy Goals for RIPs

	Improving the distribution of interpersonal and intertemporal risk	Increasing the efficiency of savings behaviour and markets
Targeted (individual) welfare improvements	Maintain adequate replacement rates (1)	Promote efficient and competitive management (3)
General (social) welfare improvements	Set up sustainable mechanisms of financing and increase participation (2)	Mitigate labour market distortion (4)

There are many different policy instruments that can be used to achieve these four policy goals. Table 4.6 provides examples of policy instruments that could be applicable for each policy target.[31]

In addition to matching instruments to goals a policy-maker must also consider how to sequence the particular instruments that are chosen. As in the choice of instruments, what the appropriate sequence is will depend on the context. For instance, in a country where the retirement age is very low and the replacement rate is high, instrument 'a' would need to precede instrument 'b'.

Conclusion

To provide individuals with an income transfer during retirement years is the most tangible function of formal RIPs. The underlying functions are to improve the distribution of various risks and increase overall economic efficiency for both individuals and society.

People could often fail to save optimally for retirement and regret their decisions later. For this reason as well as the problems of moral hazard that arise from welfare for the elderly poor and for the problems

[31]It must be understood that there would be overlap in the effect of policy instruments on policy targets and that which instrument suited which target can depend on the existing context. In Table 4.6, the Sri Lankan context is used as a backdrop for matching instruments with targets.

Table 4.6
Pivotal Policy Instruments to Improve the Functioning of RIPs in Sri Lanka

Policy targets	Policy instruments
1. Maintain adequate replacement rates	(a) Increase the statutory age of retirement (b) Provide indexed benefits
2. Ensure sustainability and enhance coverage	(c) Convert unfunded RIPs to funded RIPs (d) Create tax incentives for retirement savings
3. Improve management and increase competition	(e) Adopt professional and independent management of government RIPs (f) Introduce regulated, market driven mechanisms to allocate pension funds for private management
4. Mitigate labour market distortions	(g) Foster of annuity markets and enable the convertability of DB schemes to DC schemes (h) Phase out existing DB RIPs in favour of DC RIPs

of asymmetric information in insurance markets, formal RIPs need to be either mandated or designed to alter the incentives of voluntary savings choices.

Formal RIPs can be conceptualized as a series of contributions that are used to finance income provisions for retirement. There are at least three broad approaches to the design of RIP. One is where current workers finance the retirement income provision of the current retirees. The second is where the contribution of each generation of workers is collected and used to finance the retirement income provision of that generation. The third is where the contribution of each individual worker is used to finance her individual retirement income provision plus an insurance premium. Retirement income payments are usually based on some function of contributions, or incomes, or both.

The method of deriving contribution rates and replacement rates of a RIP depends on the details of the design. For a given contribution rate the factors that affect the replacement rate depends particularly on whether or not the RIP is funded. Higher rates of wage growth improve the replacement rate of unfunded schemes and higher real rates of return on investments improve the replacement rate of funded schemes. But the replacement rate can be increased in either type of scheme by increasing the age of retirement and thereby reducing either the dependency ratio or the passivity ratio.

A demographic transition is a period during which the proportion of elderly in a population increases from one steady state level to another (higher level). Demographic transitions tend to pose several problems for RIPs. The nature of the problems depends on the details of the design. The necessary elements of a funded design tend to lead towards automatic internal adjustments in contribution and replacement rates in response to demographic changes. But when the RIP makes payments based on incomes (DB type) rather than on contributions (DC type) the lack of good technical supervision can lead to poor adjustment. Unfunded RIP designs do not share this element of self adjustment. Rather, the adjustment to contribution and replacement rates necessitated by a demographic transition need to be made purposefully. As the required horizon of planning is long, and the adjustments required invariably unpopular, unfunded RIPs can become severely destabilized during demographic transitions. Therefore, during a demographic transition RIPs that have the least difficulties are the funded DC schemes. RIPs that are most susceptible to crisis are the unfunded DB schemes.

The reform of RIPs is really a discussion about the efficacy of four kinds of transitions: (1) transitions from PAYG schemes to funded schemes; (2) transition from defined benefit schemes to defined contribution schemes with individual accounts; (3) double transition from unfunded defined benefit schemes to funded defined contribution schemes; and (4) transition from centralized public management to decentralized private management. Each of these transitions has implications on individual and social welfare, risk distribution, and economic efficiency.

Contrary to the expectations that have been expressed in some quarters, a transition from unfunded to funded systems does not necessarily lead to a reduction in costs. This is because the lower cost of the funded provision gets offset by the added cost of making such a transition. There are, however, instrumental, intrinsic, and constructive efficiency gains that can result from a transition to funded provisions. First, instrumentally, the transition can be used to restructure over generous existing promises, thereby reducing the accrued pension debt and making future benefits cheaper to finance. Second, intrinsically, funded provisions tend to have less distortionary effects on economic activity. This is mainly because they are perceived as a savings rather than as a tax. Third, constructively, funded schemes may help to increase national savings, promote deeper capital markets, and further the principles of democracy in decision, making. These efficiency gains, however, come at the expense of lower capacity to redistribute income risks across generations, and the introduction of market risks to the financing retirement incomes.

The principal argument for promoting a DB to DC transition is that of improving the efficiency of both the labour market and the management of RIPs. But these benefits once again come at the expense of reducing the capacity to redistribute risk between individuals and generations.

Because the inefficiencies of government management are a form of hidden tax, making the transition from government management to private management has the same effect as reducing the tax revenue of the government (by increasing the cost of government debt after the transition). This revenue gap poses the same financing problem as the conversion of implicit debt under an unfunded provision to explicit debt under a funded provision. It results in the conversion of an implicit tax into an explicit tax, and the higher rates of return do not necessarily result in a net economic gain. Therefore, the vital questions, again, are about the incidence of these taxes, and the resulting distribution of risk and efficiency of the provisions. In this efficiency assessment, the cost of management, the response of the labour market to taxes, as well as the impact on financial markets must be considered. There is much evidence to show that the proliferation of fund managers (often driven by the introduction of private pension funds) helps to improve the efficiency of the financial markets. The expectation of generating greater deeper financial markets, with consequent positive externalities on other economic activity could be the primary reason for promoting this transition.

Each of the transitions involved in RIP must be evaluated in their particular country context in terms of how they would function in: (i) improving the distribution of risk and (ii) increasing the efficiency of savings markets for the (a) welfare of individuals selected groups and (b) welfare of society as a whole. Much of these functions can be broadly captured in four policy targets: (1) maintaining adequate replacement rates ;(2) ensuring sustainability and enhancing coverage; (3) improving management and increasing competition; and (4) mitigating labour market distortions.

The challenge for India and South Asia then, is not to simply adopt a particular form of retirement income package but to identify the design specifications based on the consequences of transition and the instruments that would enable each country to achieve the functions and policy goals that have been cited. The nature of appropriate policy reform will depend on the existing mechanisms of retirement income provision, the structure of labour and financial institutions in the country as well as the capacity for professional fiscal management and the socio-political priorities in reducing risks and enhancing welfare of vulnerable groups. It is important that governments reevaluate existing systems of retirement income provision. But it would be a mistake to believe that the appropriate reforms must conform to one particular mould.

References

Becker, G. S. and K. M. Murphy (1990) 'A Theory of Rational Addiction', *Journal of Political Economy,* 96, pp. 675–700.

Clark, R. L. (1989) 'Ageing Populations', in J. Eatwell, M. Milgate, and P. Newman (eds), *The New Palgrave: Social Economics,* UK, Macmillan Press Ltd.

Daykin, C. D. and K. Lewis (1998) 'A Crisis of Longer Life: Reforming Pension Systems', (mimeo) presented to the Institute of Actuaries and to the Society of Actuaries in Ireland, Dublin, 18 September 1998.

de Mel, N. (2000) *Designing Retirement Income-Security Arrangements: theory, issues and applications to Sri Lanka,* Research Studies, Human Resource Development Series No. 3, Institute of Policy Studies, Sri Lanka, Colombo.

Diamond, P. (1994) 'Privatization of Social Security: Lessons from Chile', in *Revista de Ana álisis Económico,* 9 (1) pp. 21–33.

Feldstein, M. (1997) 'Supporting Retirees I: The Case for Privatization', in Foreign Affairs, 76 (4) pp. 24–38.

Hemming, R. (1998) *Should Public Pensions be Funded,* Working Paper WP/98/35, Washington, D.C., International Monetary Fund.

James, E. (1997a) *New Systems for Old Age Security: Theory Practice and Empirical Evidence,* Policy Research Working Paper No. 1766, Department Poverty and Human Resources Division, Washington, D.C., World Bank.

——— (1997b) *Is there a Tradeoff between Efficiency and Equity?* Policy Research Working Paper No. 1767, Department Poverty and Human Resources Division, Washington, D.C., World Bank.

Kotlikoff, L. J. (1996) 'Privatizing Social Security at Home and Abroad', *American Economic Association papers and proceedings*, 86 (2).

——— (1989) 'Social Security', in J. Eatwell, M. Milgate, and P. Newman (eds) (1989), *The New Palgrave: Social Economics*, UK., Macmillan Press Ltd., pp. 231–42.

Laibson, David (1998) 'Life-cycle consumption and hyperbolic discount functions', *European Economic Review*, 42, pp. 861–71.

Mosich and Larsen (1986) 'Employers Accounting for Pensions', revised chapter 19, *Intermediate Accounting*, sixth edition, USA, McGraw Hill.

Piñera, José (1997) *Empowering People*, Testimony of José Piñera, president of the International Centre for Pension Reform, co-chairman of the Cato Project on Social Security Privatisation, before the Senate Committee on Banking, Housing, and Urban Affairs, Subcommittee on Securities, (mimeo), 25 June 1997.

Sachs, J. (1997) 'Notes on the Transition to a Privatised Pension System', The Global Social Security Crisis Workshop, Economic Development Institute of the World Bank and the Harvard Institute for International Development, (mimeo).

Tversky, A., P. Slovic, and K. Dhaneman (1990) 'The Causes of Preference Reversal', *American Economic Review*, 80, pp. 204–17.

Vittas, D. (1998) *Institutional Investors and Securities Markets: Which Comes First?*, Policy Research Working Paper No. 2032, Development Research Group, Finance, Washington, D.C., World Bank.

——— (1993) *The Simple(r) Algebra of Pension Plans*, Policy Research Working Paper No. 1145, Financial Sector Development, Washington, D.C., World Bank.

World Bank (1994) *Averting the Old Age Crisis: Policies to Protect the Old and Promote Growth*, A World Bank Policy Research Report, New York, Oxford University Press.

PART II

Labour Markets and Social Security Reforms in India

5

Economic Reforms and Implications for Labour Markets

V. R. Panchamukhi, Nagesh Kumar, and Ram Upendra Das

Introduction

With the globalization of different markets most of the developing countries have been prompted in recent times to effect wide-ranging economic reforms aimed at liberalization. Economic reforms and increasing global integration of the Indian economy have important implications for their respective labour markets. Reforms in trade and industrial policies, among other policy regimes, tend to influence the structural traits of production process in different sectors of the economy. These structural shifts in turn could influence various dimensions of the labour markets such as employment levels, wage rates, labour productivity, intersectoral labour flows, labour-demand structure, and so on. These would have implications for evolving adequate social safety nets in these countries so as to maximize the benefits of economic reforms and minimize the associated costs whatsoever. These concerns are further highlighted if one takes into consideration the immiserization thesis as referred to in this paper.

The chapter is divided into four sections. In the first section, the broad contours of recent economic reforms in the spheres of trade and industry in India have been laid down. Some of the important conceptual issues in terms of the implications of economic reforms for the labour markets have been dealt with in the second section. This section also explores the linkages between the labour market consequences of economic reforms and social security issues. The third section reports some of the empirical findings suggesting the nature of structural transformation that the manufacturing sector in India has been undergoing in the recent past. Employment policy imperatives in India have been highlighted in the fourth section by referring to various recent Planning Commission reports on labour and employment. Finally, the policy implications of the analysis presented in the earlier sections are summarized in the fifth section and their implications for social security measures as part of the overall development strategy have been highlighted.

1. Dimensions of Economic Reforms

Although the process of the internal liberalization and external liberalization began in India during the 1970s and 1980s it was in the 1990s that it was given a considerable thrust. Internal liberalization essentially meant delicensing, debureaucratization and rationalization of different procedures especially in the spheres of trade and industrial policies. On the other hand, external liberalization entailed trade and industrial policy reforms with a thrust on outward orientation. Most of these reforms aim at assigning greater weightage to market forces and reduce the role of the state to one of a facilitator.

Economic reforms in India have covered different sectors such as trade, industry, finance, and capital market. In this chapter the focus is mainly on the trade and industrial policy liberalization as these are relatively more relevant for labour market consequences. Trade liberalization in India has entailed the following: (i) reduction in tariff barriers, (ii) scaling down of quantitative restrictions, (iii) decontrol of the exchange rate regime and devaluation, (iv) reduction in fiscal subsidies, and (v) dismantling of export subsidies, etc. The liberalization of the investment regime has focused on creating an investment-friendly environment and attracting foreign direct investment (FDI) by undertaking the following measures: (i) increasing fiscal incentives such as providing tax holidays for different companies, tax exemption on royalties, devising mechanisms for avoiding double taxation, etc.,

(ii) offering investment guarantees, (iii) raising equity participation limits for foreign investors, (iv) enhancing the coverage of automatic approvals, (v) liberalization of measures relating to repatriation and hiring of foreign technicians, and (vi) providing provisions for setting up units in export processing zones (EPZs), etc. Some of the recent notable trade and investment policy changes are documented here.

Trade Liberalization

Liberalization of the trade regimes has served as an important component of the overall economic reforms in India. The trade policy regime has been transformed beyond recognition. The peak tariff rates have been reduced from 300 per cent in 1990 to 30 per cent in 2002 while the average applied MFN (most favoured nation) rates to 29 per cent (WTO 2002). All quantitative restrictions on imports maintained for balance of payment reasons were eliminated by April 2001. In 1993, the exchange rate was unified and in 1994 full current account convertibility was achieved.

Liberalization of Investment Policy Regime

After pursuing a somewhat restrictive policy towards FDI over the four decades with a varying degree of selectivity, India changed track in 1990s and embarked on a process of reforms designed to increase her integration with the global economy. The New Industrial Policy (NIP), announced on 24 July 1991, marked this departure. The NIP and subsequent policy amendments have liberalized the industrial policy regime in the country especially as it applies to FDIs beyond recognition. The industrial approval system in all industries has been abolished except where it is required for strategic or environmental grounds. In order to bring greater transparency in the FDI approval system and expedite their clearance, a system of automatic clearance was put into practice for FDI proposals fulfilling the conditions laid down, such as the ownership levels of 50 per cent, 51 per cent, 74 per cent, and 100 per cent. The cases other than those following these norms are subject to normal approval procedures. A new package for enterprises in EPZs and 100 per cent export oriented units was announced including automatic clearance for proposals fulfilling specified parameters on capital goods imports, location, and value addition, etc. The guidelines have been laid down for this approval process as well. The Foreign Exchange Regulation Act (FERA) of 1973 has been amended and restrictions placed on foreign companies by the FERA have been lifted. New sectors such as mining, banking, insurance, telecommunications, construction and management of ports, harbours, roads and highways, airlines, and defence equipment have been thrown open to private including foreign-owned, companies.

Privatization

Disinvestment in the public sector has been an integral part of the Industrial Policy Statement of 1991. The main goals of the disinvestments programme have been to restructure and revive potentially viable companies and to close down those that are no longer viable, to reduce government equity in all non-strategic companies to 26 per cent or below; and to use the receipts of disinvestments for meeting expenditure in social and infrastructure sectors, closing down public sector enterprises or retire public debt.

Regional Trade Liberalization

India has been engaged in progressive liberalization of its intraregional trade under SAPTA which has concluded three rounds of exchange of preference with the fourth one in progress. Steps have also been taken to sign bilateral free trade arrangements (FTAs) between India and Sri Lanka (1998), with India–Nepal and India–Bhutan FTAs already in place. There have also been unilateral offers to liberalize intraregional trade such as the announcement by India to remove all the non-tariff barriers on her imports from the SAARC countries. The region is also moving forward to sign a treaty establishing a South Asian Free Trade Area (SAFTA) in the near future (see RIS 2002, for more details).

The mapping of different trade and industrial policies suggests that India has significantly liberalized its trade and industrial policy regimes in the recent past. The implications of these for the labour markets at the analytical level are discussed subsequently.

2. Implications of Economic Reforms for Labour Markets: Some Conceptual Issues

The description of economic reforms in the trade and industrial sectors in the Indian economy needs to be analysed in terms of the structural transformation that they would bring in the trade and industrial sectors. First, the trade liberalization measures would increase competition between imported and locally produced goods in the domestic market. Second, they could provide a thrust to production activities in the exports sector with greater availability of cheaper imported inputs. Third, competition also becomes intense due to increased FDI inflows. Thus some of these major instruments of reforms would induct structural shifts in the very manufacturing process by increasing competition in the domestic market from three main sources viz. competition from imports, competition in the export sector, and competition emanating from the FDI inflows. This would influence the labour markets in a variety of ways. In this context, changes in some of the important labour market characteristics such as employment levels, labour productivity gains, wage rates, labour-demand structure, choice of technique are discussed here (Panchamukhi and Das 1999).

Mismatch Between Demand for and Supply of Labour

With the growing competition, enterprises tend to focus more on the productivity of labour by using modern technologies. Handling of new technologies requires different types of skilled labour that might not be readily available in the labour market. The mismatch between the demand for and supply of labour could be aggravated further by the tendencies to shift from the Taylorist form of industrial organization to the flexible form.

Furthermore, workers would move away from less competitive enterprises to more competitive ones. The relocation of economic activities within a country would make labour engaged in some activities redundant. The changes in the pattern in demand for labour might not be matched by the nature of changes in the pattern of supply of labour. Since the supply of labour has a long gestation lag in the short and medium term, a shift in the demand pattern could aggravate the nature of the mismatch between the supply and demand. To correct the mismatch through appropriate training and retraining of workers and to facilitate the intersectoral mobility of workers, some rethinking would be required on the policy front.

Adoption of labour displacing technologies

The surge in competitive pressures prompts enterprises to focus more and more on efficiency considerations which forces them to cut their overall costs of production. Minimization of labour costs is often a natural response in such a situation. Consequently, adoption of labour displacing technologies becomes an obvious choice made by the entrepreneurs. If FDI inflows assume more importance, there could be an intensification of this tendency as multinationals would generally bring in technologies of this nature. Therefore, in the age of heightened consciousness for quality and competitiveness, a rise in unemployment becomes a misgiving of the modernization process.

Pressures on Wage Levels

With increasing global integration and liberalization measures, new pressures are felt on the levels and the spreads of wage rates for different categories of labour. With the increasing number of multinational enterprises in the domestic manufacturing space there is likely to be a ratchet effect of increasing the overall wage level in the economy. This may happen because of the ability of multinationals to pay higher wages than their local counterparts. Due to a shift in the demand for labour from unskilled to skilled and to trainable labour also, pressure on wage levels increase. The speed at which wage rates rise compared to the speed at which changes in output take place would determine an entrepreneur's competitive strength. Our hypothesis is that enterprises would be prompted to adopt labour saving techniques to regain their comparative advantage if wages rise faster than rate of increase in output.

The Immiserization Thesis

In this context reference may be made to the immiserization thesis as proposed by Panchamukhi (2000). In the era of economic reforms, structural changes in production and trade envisage that if a country vacates an industrial production activity after losing its comparative advantages, then the same industry could be shifted to some other country, where it can acquire competitive advantage for production and trade. Evidently, the speed at which a country would lose its comparative advantage in a labour intensive industry would depend upon the speed at which wage rates will increase. However, the ability of the country to introduce the 'compensatory structural adjustment' may be limited, in terms of moving on to some higher value added products in the same sector or by introducing more sophisticated technology or significant product diversification. Thus, maintaining the trend in the growth rate of GDP and employment would be possible only when the vacation of one industry is more than counterbalanced by the induction of new production activities or shifts in technological horizons. The limitation on this kind of compensated structural adjustment may be imposed by the non-availability of the institutional infrastructure of safety nets and labour redeployment and also by the lack of adequate capability for technological innovation and product diversification.

It is possible to introduce the compensable restructuring in production provided the period over which an industry loses its comparative advantage is reasonably long enough and during the period of gradual loss of comparative advantage the economy is to introduce product diversification, product upgradation and/or technological innovations. During the recent process of global integration, however, wage rates have shown a tendency of increasing at a pace which is much faster than that at which wage rates had increased in the East Asian or South East Asian economies when they were engaged in structural adjustment. The limited capabilities of the South Asian countries such as India to bring about compensatory adjustment for acquiring new comparative advantage and also for providing safety nets and social protection system need to be taken note of. This implies that the period over which they lose their comparative advantage has been shortened to such an extent that it is not enough to acquire new comparative advantage and also to make the transition process smooth and sustainable. When this happens, a country, especially of the South Asia region would experience a kind of immiserization due to global integration.

Openness, Labour Productivity, and Employment

As mentioned earlier, in a globalized and open economic environment, competitive pressures force enterprises to focus on modernization efforts and efficiency gains. Efforts are geared towards raising the labour productivity levels. Labour productivity becomes a key issue for an enterprise to survive in the domestic and global markets. However, labour productivity gains could have two potential conflicting effects on employment levels: (i) employment expansion and (ii) employment contraction. Given that openness provides opportunity for scale expansion, labour productivity gains could lead to higher scale of operation. This could result in a rise in employment levels. If scale expansion is not possible due to protectionist tendencies in the destination countries or due to global demand constraints, labour productivity gains could result in lower demand for labour per unit of output, consequently employment might fall.

Labour Market Consequences of Privatization

Privatization entails different effects on the labour markets. Conceptual clarity about the economic effects of privatization would help devising policies to minimize the labour market costs and maximize the social gains. During the privatization process workers' redundancy is often solved by workers' retrenchment. These trends also result in the stagnation of employment at the aggregate level in the organized sector. The process is also characterized by growing casualization of labour (Joshi 2000). The aspects of redundancy, retrenchment, employment stagnation, and casualization, together call for a comprehensive policy package which sets in place adequate safety nets.

Influence of Trade Liberalization, Exports, and FDI on Employment

Tariff liberalization has the potential for enhancing competition between imports and indigenously produced goods. Increase in competition through this route could have important implications for employment prospects, as several domestic companies might not be able to withstand competitive pressures.

Furthermore, exports expansion and increase in FDI have been heralded as two major positive outcomes of the development strategy based on outward-orientation. However, they need to be regarded as instruments of development and not an end in themselves. Unless these instruments bring in employment and income effects, an economy's growth process would not pick up as desired. The increasing tendency to adopt labour displacing technologies to achieve product competitiveness is expected to alter the factor intensity of exports. Exports, especially from the South Asian countries such as India have traditionally been labour intensive. With the structural shifts in the production process exports tend to become more technology and capital intensive. This could happen due to a more than proportionate increase in wage rates as compared to the rate of output growth, as highlighted earlier. In such a situation employment levels may be influenced adversely.

Access to foreign financial resources in the form of FDI inflows is another advantage of global integration process. However, the influence of FDI inflows on labour market need to be assessed in terms of its ultimate effect on an economy's growth. The effect of FDI on the overall employment situation in a country would depend on the kind of production technique foreign enterprises adopt. There is a possibility that FDI inflows move towards less labour intensive sectors affecting employment levels adversely. The unemployment situation gets aggravated especially when FDI crowds out local investment. Recent studies have shown that FDI could crowd out FDI in a number of situations (see Kumar and Pradhan, 2002 for a discussion). FDI inflows could affect employment and labour in the host countries in a number of other ways as well. These include their possible tendency to adopt more capital intensive technique of production than their local enterprises, the relative extent of vertical interfirm linkages generated by foreign affiliates, their relative tendency to pay higher wages and salaries and spend on training. FDI could also have indirect effects on employment and labour through relative scales of operation, trends in their restructuring, their competitive effects on local industry among others. This once again brings to the fore the imperatives of creating adequate social safety nets so as to facilitate intersectoral mobility of workers and their adequate training.

3. Empirical Evidence

Labour Market Consequences of Economic Reforms

Empirical results of a study conducted by Panchamukhi and Das (1999) on some of the issues highlighted earlier are presented here. It was found in this study that there has been a tendency to adopt labour displacing production techniques in the manufacturing sector. Between 1980s and 1990s labour intensity (defined as ratio of wages and salaries to output minus wages and salaries) declined in India. Such a shift is not evident at the aggregate level in the manufacturing sector, however, a more disaggregated level investigation reveals that there are many sectors in which labour intensity has declined in India.

On the other hand, the rank correlation coefficient between changes in labour intensity and export–output ratio was found to be negative with very low magnitudes, that is, –0.02. This implies that exports have become less labour intensive during the period under consideration (Panchamukhi and Das, 1999).

These trends together have influenced the employment levels adversely in India. The total number of persons employed increased by just 7 per cent in the manufacturing sector as a whole to 102 per cent increase in output in this period. Further evidence to this phenomenon is given in Sharma (this volume) whereby employment elasticity has declined from 0.50 (1983–94) to 0.00 (1994–2000) in the agriculture sector; from 0.33 to 0.26 in the manufacturing sector, and from 0.41 to 0.15 for the economy as a whole during the same period. In a nutshell, shift in choice of technique has adversely impacted the employment levels.

The Indian economy is also found to have experienced labour productivity (defined as output per worker) gains during the period under consideration. Interestingly enough, the two conflicting effects of labour productivity gains in terms of employment expansion and contraction too, were found to be present when the analysis was undertaken at the sectoral level. There is also evidence of a shift in the demand for more skilled type of labour as wage rate increases have been accompanied with falling employment levels (Panchamukhi and Das, 1999). As also highlighted by Dev (2000), the share of highly skilled sub-sectors in manufacturing employment has increased in India.

It is noted in Panchamukhi (2000) that for low technology industries, India can claim to have a revealed comparative advantage (RCA). One observes that there has been a very high wage growth in 1985–90 and this has implied loss in the RCA level (Table 5.1). Though there seems to be some gain in the RCA for medium technology industries during 1985–90; the period, 1990–4, seems to have experienced a persistent increase in growth rate and wage rates and sharp fall in the RCA. This inverse relationship of wage growth and RCA has also been seen in the case of high technology industries. Thus, for India the hypothesis of immiserization implicit in rapid global integration seems to be holding good in the sense that India has been losing its comparative advantage in the low technology industries due to wage rate increases while at the same time it has not been gaining significant comparative advantages in the other industrial categories. These trends call for setting in place adequate social safety nets and other related mechanisms as highlighted earlier.

Table 5.1
Growth in Revealed Comparative Advantage (RCA) and Wage Rate across Industries in India between 1980 and 1994

(per cent)

Industry specification	RCA and wage growth	1980–85	1985–90	1990–94
Low technology	RCA growth	8.8	–9.2	0.0
	Wage growth	7.4	30.5	6.3
Medium technology	RCA growth	–43.1	145.9	10.9
	Wage growth	20.0	17.3	22.1
High technology	RCA growth	–30.0	–19.4	–2.1
	Wage growth	11.4	18.3	11.1

Source: Panchamukhi (2000).

An important indicator of economic reforms is reduction in tariff levels. As observed in Table 5.2, in the case of India, tariff liberalization committed in the Uruguay Round suggests that sectors marked with declining labour intensity between 1980s and 1990s are subjected to high tariff reduction rates.

The privatization process has had significant consequences on the labour market in the form of redundancies and contractualization of jobs. A recent analysis of privatization programme in India suggests that 23 per cent of jobs in public sector enterprises had been made redundant under voluntary retirement schemes following privatization (Joshi 2000: 4). Furthermore, it has been estimated that 20,000 jobs have been contractualized in nine top performing public sector enterprises called Navratnas (Joshi, ibid: 3). Therefore, the trend of privatization has significant labour market consequences.

It also needs to be highlighted that the distribution of employment by category of employment has also undergone perceptible changes between 1972–3 and 1993–4. The trends reveal an increase in the share of casual workers. This fact needs to be taken note of as casual workers face maximum poverty especially in the rural areas (Table 5.3).

Yet another indicator of economic reforms is volume and direction of FDI inflows. In the case of India, it has been found that both domestic investments as well as FDIs have favoured those sectors that are characterized by low labour intensity or sectors that have experienced declining labour intensity over the period under consideration. Since these sectors are given major thrust in the investment policy as evident from Table 5.4, such trends might not be

Table 5.2
Tariff Liberalization and Trends in Labour Intensity in India

Summary product category	Labour intensity movement between 1980s and 1990s	Percentage of imports GATT bound		Levels and changes weighted by imports from the world exc. FTA[a]		
		Total Pre-UR	Total Post-UR rate	Post-UR applied	Tariff reduction[b] rate	Post-UR bound
Wood, pulp, paper, and furniture	D[c]	22.3	98.2	14.9	29.2	27.9
Textiles and clothing	D	30.8	74.7	42.4	20.0	33.8
Leather and footwear	D	0.2	76.9	39.9	23.1	32.3
Metals	D	0.5	52.7	38.3	19.5	38.8
Chemicals & photographic supply	R	2.6	83.7	36.4	20.0	38.7
Transport equipment	R	35.5	89.6	30.9	15.4	22.3
Non-electric machinery	R	22.7	99.8	31.0	9.2	32.3
Electric machinery	R	8.9	72.1	48.5	17.4	36.3
Mineral prod., prec. stones & metal	D	9.3	26.8	5.5	23.2	25.6
Manufactured articles nes.	D	15.7	82.3	43.4	16.3	48.8

Notes: a=Value of imports from the partner countries that do not participate in Free Trade Agreement with India; b=weighted average tariff reduction measured by dT/(1+7) in percentage; c=of which furniture has shown a rising trend in labour intensity; D = Declining, UR = Uruguay Round.
Source: Panchamukhi and Das (1999).

consistent with the employment objectives. Further empirical investigation is also necessary to find out whether such investments have been able to meet their employment targets.

Table 5.3
Percentage Distribution of Workers by Category of Employment in India

	Rural	Urban	Total
Self Employment			
1972–3	65.3	41.2	61.4
1977–8	62.6	42.4	58.9
1983	61.0	41.8	57.3
1987–8	59.4	42.8	56.0
1993–4	58.0	42.3	54.8
Regular Salaried Employment			
1972–3	9.3	46.3	15.4
1977–8	7.7	41.8	13.9
1983	7.5	40.0	13.8
1987–8	7.7	40.3	14.4
1993–4	6.4	39.4	13.2
Casual Wage Employment			
1972–3	25.4	12.5	23.2
1977–8	29.7	15.8	27.2
1983	31.5	18.2	28.6
1987–8	32.9	16.9	29.6
1993–4	35.6	18.3	32.0

Source: Planning Commission (2001).

Table 5.4
Investment Profile of Sectors Grouped by Labour Intensity in India: 1991–7

	Domestic investment scenario				Foreign investment scenario
	Share in domestic investment		Share in proposed employment		
Sectors* with	Delicensed (%)	Licensed (%)	Delicensed (%)	Licensed (%)	Share in FDI (%)
Declining LI	58	29	62	66	27
High LI	19	10	24	24	10
Medium LI	43	24	49	48	52
Low LI	34	66	20	28	38

Note: LI = Labour Intensity, * Decline over 1980–90 and high, medium and low status in the 1990s.
Source: Panchamukhi and Das (1999).

FDI and Labour Markets : Some More Evidence

Partly as a result of the liberalization of FDI regime and partly because of continuing expansion of global magnitudes of FDI inflows, the overall scale of FDI inflows in India, as well as their relative dependence on it as a proportion of gross capital formation has increased in the recent years. FDI inflows to India increased from US$574 million (Rs 57.4 crores) in 1993 to US$2315 million (Rs 231.5 crores) in 2000. Similarly, the relative importance of FDI in gross fixed capital formation in India increased from 1.0 (1993) to 2.4 (1999) (UNCTAD 2001). Implications of this higher exposure of India to FDI on its labour markets could be analysed in the light of some evidence that is available, as discussed here.

The empirical evidence available for different developing countries including India suggests that foreign affiliates generally employ techniques that are relatively more capital intensive than those used by local firms. Very often, however, the differences in the choice of techniques could be explained in terms of their relative scales of operations, technological rigidities, and relative factor prices facing them rather than the foreign ownership per se (Caves 1996). On account of the generation of vertical interfirm linkages, there are two streams of literature. One stream that is highly investigated for different developing countries including India suggests that foreign affiliates are more heavily dependent upon imported inputs than their local counterparts. Hence, their operations generate fewer vertical interfirm linkages compared to their local counterparts (Caves ibid; Kumar and Siddharthan 1997). The other stream has examined the relative extent of vertical integration of operations of foreign and local enterprises. A study in India has reported that foreign affiliates had significantly greater extent of vertical integration compared to local firms. The difference persisted even after controlling for sectoral composition, scale of operations, profitability and other extraneous influences (Kumar 1994). The two streams of literature together imply that operations of FDI may generate fewer interfirm linkages than domestic investments. This in turn would imply that indirect employment generation by per unit of FDI is lower than that by domestic investments. Some literature in the context of East and South East Asia has raised concern about the 'enclave' nature of FDIs especially that in EPZs which generated little linkages with the rest of the host economy. This concern has pushed the host governments in developed as well as developing countries to impose a variety of regulations on foreign enterprises such as local content regulations or screwdriver regulations, etc. (Kumar 2002).

Foreign affiliates have been found to have a distinct preference to operate at a much larger scale than local enterprise in India. The differences persisted even after controlling for extraneous influences (Kumar 1994). In so far as larger enterprises tend to adopt more capital intensive techniques, larger scale of foreign enterprises may imply a higher capital intensity. Foreign affiliates also tended to pay higher wages than local firms but the difference seems to be more on account of the skill differences and scales of operations. In particular, foreign affiliates were found to reveal a tendency to employ more qualified employees. Furthermore, some limited evidence that is available suggests that foreign affiliates offer more training to their employees than local firms. Outward mobility of their personnel, however, seemed lower than that of other private enterprises (Kumar and Siddharthan 1997). Furthermore, an increasing proportion of recent FDI flows has been accounted for by mergers and acquisitions (M&As), globally as well as in India (Kumar 2000a). M&As are used by multinational enterprises to restructure and consolidate their operations worldwide. One of the major motivations for M&As is to improve their efficiency, productivity, and competitiveness by reducing the duplication in their activities. Hence, an immediate consequence is job losses. UNCTAD (1999) reports a loss of 75,000 jobs worldwide resulting from M&As in 1998 alone. Since M&As lead to restructuring and consolidation of merged corporations in their host countries, a large number of jobs are lost there as well. For instance, following the merger of Ciba-Geigy and Sandoz to form Novartis in Switzerland, their Indian subsidiaries have also merged to form Novartis, India. Furthermore, with liberalization of takeover codes in India and other countries, the entry of multinational enterprises often takes the form of a direct acquisition of an existing enterprise. It could also indirectly crowd out local enterprises through competitive pressures. A recent study found that FDI crowds out domestic investment in net terms in 29 countries out of a sample of 52 developing countries. In India's case too the crowding out appears to prevail in net terms although the relationship was not significant in statistical terms (Kumar and Pradhan 2002). Therefore, the quality of FDI inflows is an important issue as far as its effects are concerned (Kumar 2002, for a discussion of quality of FDI). In recent years, examples of both have multiplied although it would be difficult to arrive at a precise number on proportion.

Thus, an increasing exposure of South Asian countries such as India to FDI inflows is likely to bring about a number of changes in the labour market. The labour market is expected to favour highly skilled personnel and higher average wages, although the number of jobs created per unit of capital may actually decline. Yet another effect of FDI on employment creation could be through its contribution to the growth in the host countries. The evidence on FDI inflows and growth is ambiguous because of the simultaneity problem. A recent study conducting the tests of causality finds that in majority of sample countries studied, including India, the direction of causation was not pronounced and in a substantial proportion of cases the direction of causation actually runs from growth to FDI rather than from FDI to growth (Kumar and Pradhan 2002). Therefore, the indirect effect of FDI on employment generation through growth seems to be insignificant too, if at all positive.

4. Employment Policy Imperatives in India

The discussion so far has shown that the Indian labour market has been characterized by slow labour absorption due to increased usage of labour displacing technologies which has manifested itself in declining labour intensities. The labour market has also witnessed a structural change in the demand for labour and wage rigidities. Recent Planning Commission reports on labour and employment (July 2001, December 2001, and May 2002) have also acknowledged that the rate of job creation has been much slower than the requirements despite the fact that in recent times the economy has been growing at a relatively faster rate. The reports also refer to the problems of underemployment, casual employment as well as unorganized sector employment and take cognizance of the economic, social, and political implications that such a trend has.

While the Planning Commission reports differ in terms of emphasis on acceleration of economic growth vis-à-vis special programmes for creating jobs it is essential to emphasize that high economic growth could be a necessary but not a sufficient condition for job creation as our empirical analysis also suggests. Unless due emphasis is placed on the choice of an appropriate technology which is conducive to the demographic and skill profiles of the country and special employment as well as social security programmes are given further impetus, mere high growth strategy might not be sufficient to meet the employment objectives. It is in this background that it may be suggested that a detailed exercise to identify medium labour intensive sectors for giving them a place of primacy in the overall development and industrialization strategy needs to be undertaken. The merit of the medium labour-intensive sectors is that they offer an opportunity to the policy-makers to strike a balance between the employment and technological modernization objectives.

5. Conclusion

To sum up, economic reforms have entailed adoption of labour displacing technologies, labour productivity gains, wage rigidity, and structural change in the demand for labour. Reforms reflected in terms of tariff reductions and change in investment policies to engender FDI inflows have so far not been able to target the objective of employment augmentation to the extent necessary. The labour market is expected to favour highly skilled personnel and higher average wages with declining employment per unit of capital invested. If economic reforms broadly are not employment friendly they will influence adversely the income levels, purchasing power and, in turn, the aggregate demand in the economy. Hence, these observations call for evolving afresh a development paradigm so as to strike a balance between reforms aiming at supply side improvements and those tackling demand generation. It is in this context that labour and social policies have to play a crucial role.

The labour market consequences of economic reforms have engendered job and income insecurities. These highlight the imperatives of devising adequate social security policies. These insecurities themselves have the potential for inducting uncertainty in the savings behaviour of employees and households which is an important determinant of pension benefits providing old age security. This is a possible factor explaining the volatile savings behaviour observed in the Indian economy.

The need for devising adequate social safety nets in the wake of labour market consequences of privatization and industrial restructuring is also clear. Efforts would have to be made on the dimensions of retraining, reskilling, and redeployment of workers. This might also mean creating more effective mechanisms for interindustrial labour mobility. Setting in place social security policies to take care of such workers is another area which needs to be addressed. Overall, employment generation must remain a crucial policy objective.

References

Caves, Richard (1996) *Multinational Enterprise and Economic Analysis*, Cambridge University Press.

Dev, S. Mahendra (2000) 'Economic Liberalisation and Employment in South Asia—II', *Economic and Political Weekly*, 15 January.

Dreze, Jean and Amartya Sen (1995) *India: Economic Development and Social Opportunity*, New Delhi, Oxford University Press.

Government of India (2001–2) *Economic Survey*.

Joshi, Gopal (2000) (ed.), *Privatization in South Asia*, ILO-SAAT, New Delhi.

Kumar, Nagesh (2002) *Globalization and the Quality of Foreign Direct Investment*, Oxford University Press.

——— (2000) 'Mergers and Acquisitions by MNEs: Patterns and Implications', *Economic and Political Weekly*, 35(32), 5 August, pp. 2851–8.

——— (1994) *Multinational Enterprises and Industrial Organization: The Case of India*, Sage.

Kumar, Nagesh and N. S. Siddharthan (1997) *Technology, Market Structure and Internationalization*, Routledge.

Kumar, Nagesh and Jaya Prakash Pradhan (2002) *Foreign Direct Investment, Externalities and Economic Growth in Developing Countries: Some Empirical Explorations and Implications for WTO Negotiations on Investment*, RIS Discussion Paper, No. 27.

Panchamukhi, V. R. and Ram Upendra Das (1999) *Economic Reforms, Regional Integration and Labour Markets in the SAARC Region*, ILO–SAAT, New Delhi.

Panchamukhi, V.R. (2000) 'Trade, Technology and Employment: A profile of Systemic Dilemmas and Paradoxes', *The Indian Journal of Labour Economics*, 43 (1).

Planning Commission (2002) *Report of the Special Group on Targeting Ten Million Employment Opportunities per year over the Tenth Plan Period*, Government of India, May.

——— (2001a) *Report of the Task Force on Employment Opportunities*, Government of India, July.

——— (2001b) *Report of the Steering Committee on Labour and Employment for the Tenth Five Year Plan*, Government of India, December.

RIS (2002) *South Asia Development and Cooperation Report 2001/02*, New Delhi: Research and Information System.

UNCTAD (2001) *World Investment Report*.

——— (1999) *World Investment Report*.

WTO (2002) *Trade Policy Review: India*, Geneva, World Trade Organization.

6

Pension System Reform in India
Turning a Crisis into an Opportunity

Ramgopal Agarwala and
*Rajendra K. Sharma**

History will record that Lee Kuan Yew got it right in Singapore with his Provident Fund (self-financed social welfare benefits) while Bismarck got it wrong in Germany with his social welfare system of intergenerational transfers.

Lester Thurow, (1997), *The Future of Capitalism*; p. 108

1. Evolution of the Indian Pension System

Since independence, the Indian socio-economic system, including the pension system, has been guided largely by the notion of welfare state, popular among the Fabian socialists in the UK in the 1940s and 1950s, without considering the fact that the economic, and administrative conditions in India were vastly different from those in the UK at that time. These ideas were applied only to the organized sector and the implicit notion was that over time, the unorganized sector will shrink and the modern organized sector will dominate the economy. In reality, however, even after 50 years of development, about 90 per cent

*assisted by Gauri Modwel.

of the workforce is in the unorganized sector and it is the share of the organized sector that is shrinking.

Institutionalized pension/provident fund system in India covers about 10 per cent of the workforce and, as of March 1998, the number of workers covered under such systems was as follows:

Government employees	
Central government employees	4.176 million
State government employees	6.8 million
Union territory employees	0.163 million
Total	11.11 million
Other categories	
EPF members	21.44 million
Coal Mines (PF) members	0.806 million
Assam Tea Plantation PF members	0.75 million
Seamen's PF members	30,000
Jammu & Kashmir PF members	0.145 million
Total	23.1 million

Note: PF = Provident Fund

Source: Paper presented by A.N. Roy at Asian Sub-regional seminar on Social Security for the Elderly, Social Security Association of India, New Delhi, 2000.

1.1 Pension system for the Civil Service

Government employees are eligible for a non-contributory, DB pension (50 per cent of the salary for the last ten months of service for a worker with 33 years of service) funded by the state. In addition, most civil servants enjoy coverage under a government provident fund with employee contributions ranging from 6 to 8.33 per cent of their salaries.

Contribution by government servants to the state pension funds are part of the public accounts and are used solely to finance the deficit of the government and, therefore, constitute a contingent liability of the state. Since April 1986, these funds carry an interest of 12 per cent per annum. The system for state government employees is exactly analogous to that for the centre, that is, the contributions are part of the consolidated fund. Pension benefits (of which the latter are provided under the government employees pension scheme for retired government servants) are paid out from tax and non-tax revenues of the government.

1.2 Employees Provident Fund Organization

The earliest legislation for old age security in India was the Employees Provident Fund (EPF) Act of 1952. This is the largest and most important of the schemes. The EPF Act initially applied to factories and establishments falling within specified industries which had completed three years of existence and employed 50 or more workers. The Act is now applicable to factories and establishments engaged in 177 industries employing 20 or more persons and functioning for a period of three years from the date of establishment. The wage ceiling for coverage under EPF scheme has been enhanced from time to time and stands at Rs 5000 per month with effect from 1 October 1994. The basic mode of its operation requires that contributions be credited to personal accounts of the members and the benefits available in old age defined on the contribution plus interest (or return) thereon. The EPF is administered by the Central Board of Trustees comprising a chairman and representatives of the state and central governments and employers' and employees' representatives of the organizations appointed by the central government. The EPF scheme is, therefore, a fully funded contribution plan with benefits equalling total contributions from employees and employers, plus accrued interest.

The scheme aims at making provision for the future of the covered employees after they retire and also for their dependents, in case a worker meets an early death. In terms of benefits, apart from terminal benefits, generous withdrawals to fund marriages, treatment of illnesses, housing, purchase of life insurance policies, and education, etc. can also be provided under the scheme. The normal rate of contributions by the employers and employees was, for a long time, 8.33 per cent of the wage of the employees. This has been raised to 10 per cent, effective from 1 May 1997.

Under the EPF Act 1952, two choices are available to employers: (a) either use the scheme run under the aegis of the Central Provident Fund Commission (CPFC); or (b) seek an exemption and manage their own provident fund trust. At the end of 31 March 1996–7, 2970 establishments were in the exempted sector, covering 43.3 lakh workers. Although the return or benefit to individuals under either route is stipulated to be 12 per cent the exempted schemes, according to market surveys, they usually earn a higher average return of up to 13.5–14.0 per cent. The funds under option (a) above are part of the public accounts since the moneys are kept in trust funds which are under the aegis of the government. These are usually deposited with the State Bank of India which in turn invests them according to the stipulated guidelines issued by CPFC from time to time.

The investment pattern of the scheme is stipulated by the Central Board of Trustees of the employees of the EPF. As of now, no investment is routed into private sector debt or equity investments in the capital market. The most recent pattern applicable from 1 April 1998 stipulated that 25 per cent of investment should be in central government securities, 15 per cent in central and state government guaranteed securities, 40 per cent in bond/securities of public financial institutions, public sector companies, and the Infrastructure Development Finance Company Ltd., and the balance 20 per cent in any of the earlier three categories as decided by the board of trustees.

To provide long term financial security to the families of industrial employees in the event of their premature death, the subscribers of EPF were compulsorily inclined in the Employees Family Pension Scheme (EFPS) which was initiated on 31 March 1971. This is done by diverting a portion of the employers' and employees' contribution of the EPF scheme. This family pension scheme has since been repealed after a new pension scheme known as Employees Pension Scheme (EPS), 1995 has come into force.

The Payment of Gratuity Act, 1972 is applicable to the employees of central and state governments, factories, mines, oil fields, plantations, ports, motor transport undertakings, companies, and shops and other establishments. The Act provides for a lump sum payment of gratuity made to workers at the rate of 15 days' wages for each completed year of service. The ceiling or the maximum amount of gratuity has been raised from Rs 50,000 to Rs 3.5 lakhs. In the case of seasonal establishments, gratuity is payable at the rate of seven days' wages for each season.

Employees Deposit Linked Insurance Scheme came into force with effect from 1 August 1976. All the employees who are members of the provident fund are also members of this scheme. The qualifying condition for this is a membership of the EPF having at least an average of Rs 500 in provident fund preceding death while in the service. On the death of a member, the person entitled to receive provident fund accumulation would be paid an additional amount equal to average balance in provident fund account of the deceased during the preceding 12 months. Maximum amount of benefit payable under this scheme, to which the employees do not have to make any contribution, is Rs 35,000.

Old age security provision underwent a significant change in 1995 when the EPS was introduced. The EPS is mandatory for all persons who become member of the provident fund from 16 November 1995. Provident fund subscribers, who were members of the family pension scheme, had the option to join this pension scheme. A minimum of 10 years of contributory service is required for entitlement to pension under the new scheme. According to latest rules, superannuation is payable on attaining the age of 60 years. Pension on a discounted rate is also payable on attaining the age of 50 years. When pensionable service is less than 10 years, the member has the option to remain covered for pension benefits till 60 years of age or claim refund of contribution, plus interest. The scheme provides for payment of monthly pension in the following contingencies: superannuation on attaining 60 years of age, retirement, death during service, permanent and total disablement, death after retirement, children's pension and orphan pension.

The EPS also allows withdrawal for house building, medical treatment, marriage, higher education, and disability and liberal survival benefits. Under the EPS, an employee is entitled to a minimum pension of Rs 1275 per month and a maximum of 50 per cent of the highest pay in the government (that is, Rs 30,000). All assets and liabilities of the erstwhile EPFS have been transferred to the new pension scheme. With the introduction of the EPS, employees' post-retirement income comprises a lump sum provident fund payment and a monthly pension. In other words, the benefits like the contributions have been bifurcated, the rationale of which is not entirely clear.

The new pension scheme is of DB type. The formula for calculation of monthly pension is as follows:

$$\text{Pension} = \frac{\text{Pensionable salary} \times (\text{pensionable years of service} + 2)}{70}$$

Thus, for a member with 33 years of service, the pension is 50 per cent of the pensionable salary, which is defined as the average of last 10 months' pay (plus DA). Under the scheme, neither the employer nor the employee is required to make any additional contribution from November 1995. The employers' share of the provident fund contribution representing 8.33 per cent of the wage is diverted to the pension scheme. The central government also contributes to the pension scheme at the rate of 1.16 per cent of the employees' wage. The balance 1.67 per cent share of the employer remains in the provident fund. The EPS 1995 is thus non-contributory as only employers contribute.

The 1995 pension scheme with DB appears to be a retrograde step in terms of financial viability of the scheme. It introduces a PAYG system that has been found in many countries to be a financial time bomb in the context of a population that is maturing.

1.3 Public Sector Undertakings

Employees in public sector undertakings (PSUs) are mostly governed by the EPF and Miscellaneous Provision Act 1952 which provides for the institution of a compulsory provident fund, family pension fund, and deposit-linked insurance fund for the benefit of employees in factories and establishments employing 20 or more persons. The provisions of this Act stipulate that a contribution of the monthly salary (basic wage + DA), together with a matching contribution by the employer shall be deposited in a public fund to be operated by the central government. The rates of contribution to the provident fund by both employers and employees are 10 per cent of the monthly salary. The accumulations in the provident fund earned, until recently, interest at 12 per cent per annum. That rate was reduced to 11 per cent in July 2000 and to 9.5 per cent from April 2001.

1.4 Pension Scheme in Banks and Insurance Companies

On the basis of a settlement signed by the Indian Banks Association and the All India Bank Workers Union, a pension scheme called BEPS as a second retirement benefit, in lieu of contributory provident fund, was introduced with effect from 1 November 1993. The scheme was compulsory for employees who joined the service of a bank on or after 1 November 1993 and optional for those who were already in the service of a bank. This pension scheme is on the pattern of the scheme applicable to central government employees. The scheme is financed from the entire portion of the employers' provident fund contribution, which is 10 per cent of basic salary (including DA). The main superannuation benefit (which is provided at the age of 60 years) after 33 years of service is a pension of 50 per cent of average of salary during the last 10 months of employment.

A similar scheme called IEPS was also introduced with effect from 1 November 1992 for employees in the insurance sector. The BEPS is administered by each bank under the aegis of a bipartite trust to manage the scheme, while the IEPS is administered by the Life Insurance Corporation (LIC) of India (Employees) Pension Fund Trust.

1.5 Role of Life Insurance Corporation

Under Section 30 of the Life Insurance Corporate Act, LIC is the sole provider of life insurance business in India. Hence, if any employer sets up privately administered superannuation fund as a supplement to the provident fund and employees pension scheme the firm can accumulate fund (in the form of an irrevocable trust fund) during the employment period of the employee concerned, but suitable annuities have to be purchased from LIC. Alternatively, the employer can have a superannuation scheme with LIC and pay suitable contributions for the employees in service. At present there are about 9 lakh members registered in the LIC pension scheme.

In the 1997 budget, the finance minister also allowed the Unit Trust of India to establish a pension scheme along the lines of that provided by the LIC. Therefore, an element of competition has now been introduced. The investment pattern that has to be followed by these funds, however, is identical to that enunciated earlier for the provident fund scheme.

1.6 Public Provident Fund

The Government of India established the Public Provident Fund (PPF) in 1968–9 to provide an instrument for long-term savings for those not covered by the formal pension system. Public provident fund has a medium-to- long-term maturity. However, loans can be taken after three years and withdrawals up to half the balance after seven years. The account can be closed after 15 years. Any member of the public can subscribe to the PPF with a minimum of Rs 100 in a year. Tax rebate of 20 per cent is provided on contributions up to Rs 60,000 per fiscal year. Deposits are mobilized through the banking and postal system network and depositors receive a passbook where transactions are recorded. The accumulated funds are held in the State Bank of

India and the Postal System and currently earn interest rate of 9 per cent per annum. The scheme has advantages for the informal sector in so far as the contributions are voluntary and payments can be made in cash, which avoids the burden of proving the source of income. Currently the coverage of the scheme is confined mainly to large cities and the number of accounts constitutes about only 1 per cent of the work force.

1.7 Social Assistance Programmes for the Elderly

Apart from the PPF, the main source of pensions for the informal sector is various social assistance programmes introduced at the central and state levels. Under the national old age pension scheme, central assistance at Rs 75 per month is provided to states for payment of old age pension to men and women who are of the age of 65 or more. In addition, all state governments and union territories have their own old age pension schemes under which pensions are paid at various rates. Also, several states such as Gujarat, Karnataka, Andhra Pradesh, Kerala, Maharashtra, and Tamil Nadu have pension schemes for agricultural workers. Because of the limited amount of resources available, these schemes benefit only a fraction of the elderly and only those who are destitutes. In addition, it is reported that in the regime of rationing necessitated by the gap between resource availability and needs, selection and grant of these pensions are not always transparent.

2. A Critique of the Indian Pension Systems

As in many other aspects of life, pension systems in India present a highly dualistic picture. A small privileged minority enjoys relatively generous pension provisions with a serious potential risk to the health of the fiscal system, while a predominant majority goes without any pension cover with serious risk to their financial wellbeing in old age.

2.1 Warning Signals in the Formal Sector

There are enough early warning signs to suggest that unless corrective actions are taken soon, the formal system of pension schemes will become a major burden on the fiscal system in the country within a decade, similar to what happened in Latin American and European countries in the 1980s. Three early warning signals are particularly noteworthy:

- First, life expectancy at retirement is increasing. Whereas a person retiring in 1970 was expected to live 14–15 years, a person retiring in 2001 can be expected to live 16–18 years and this trend is likely to continue. With increasing life expectancy, the number of persons receiving pensions will be increasing and, correspondingly, the amount of pension expenditures.

- Second, employment in government and the formal sector has been largely stagnant for some time, while the number of retirees is increasing and this will over time lead to a high dependency ratio (that is, the ratio of pensioners to workers). As noted here, in some cases the number of retirees may even exceed the number of workers.
- Third, and perhaps the most important recent event causing stress on the pension system is the implementation of the Fifth Pay Commission recommendations which led to a large increase in salaries (about 40 per cent on average) and which called for parity between those who retire in the future and those who retired earlier from similar positions. This retrospective adjustment to pensions (highly exceptional in worldwide practices) will enormously increase the pension burden on the government. Since the pension benefits are linked to the last drawn pay rather than average earnings over the working life, the sudden increase in pay will give a large increase to the future retirees. Moreover, to the extent the pay scales of employees in public sector enterprises and the private sector are sensitive to government pay scales, there is likely to be a significant increase in pension obligations of Employees' Provident Fund Organization (EPFO) without the financial backing provided by the accumulated contributions from the workers.

However, the issue of pension expenditures does not seem to be on the fiscal radar of the economic policy analysts in India. It is interesting that of hundreds of commentaries in the media on budget matters between mid-February to mid-March, 2000, hardly any mentioned the burgeoning burden of pensions in government finance. Even the *Economic Survey*, 1999–2000, a most comprehensive review of economic matters in the country, does not monitor pensions as a separate item in its review of public finance as it does for subsidies and interest payments.

In reality, rising pension expenditures are already contributing to busting the budget more than any other major item and over the next 10 years, they may become a major source of fiscal deficit as in many Latin American countries. This is likely to be the inevitable consequence of (a) the echo effect of rapid growth in government employment in the 'socialist' era of the 1960s and 1970s, (b) the increasing life expectancies of the retirees with improvement in medical facilities and living conditions, and (c) the current, largely unfunded, pension system for government employees in India. And once pensions are due, they are even more difficult to control than wages or interest payments or subsidies. One can try to downsize the government and reduce wage bill; one can reduce interest burden by faster repayment and/or reduction in interest rates; and with political will, even subsidies can be reduced. But pensioners cannot be retrenched and their benefits cannot be reduced except by unlawful withholding (which according to newspaper stories is unfortunately beginning to happen on a major scale in some parts of India). Prevention, rather than cure, is a better remedy for pension burden. That is why it is important to be aware of the time bomb that pension burden is for government finance in India and start initiating remedial measures.

Table 6.1 presents some key figures on revenue expenditures in the Union Budget. It is worth noting that:

- In 1999–2000, budget cost over-run on pensions were Rs 4173 crores, the single largest over-run item among the major budget categories and accounting for almost 30 per cent of the total over-run. They were nearly double the cost over-run in defence expenditures despite unanticipated defence expenditures due to Kargil!
- Between FY (fiscal year) 2000 and FY 2001, estimated pension expenditures will rise by a whopping 56 per cent as against the rise of 20 per cent in total revenue expenditures and 22 per cent in defence expenditures.
- In FY 2001, pension expenditures at Rs 15,843 crores will be more than those on all economic and social services combined (Rs 13,370 crores).

Yet pension expenditures shown in the budget are only the tip of the iceberg. For example, they do not include all the pension payments by the central governments, namely those in railways, posts and telecommunications, and to freedom fighters. Nor do they include the unfunded pension liabilities of public sector enterprises and unfunded liabilities of EPFO organization. And of course they do not include pension liabilities of state and local governments. Table 6.2 shows a more complete accounting of pension payments by the central

Table 6.1
Revenue Expenditures in Union Budgets of FY 2000 and FY 2001

(figures in Rs crore)

Revenue expenditure items	1999–2000 Budget estimates	1999–2000 Revised estimates	Difference between budget and revised estimates	2000–1 Budget estimates	Percentage in budget estimates between FY 2000 and FY 2001
Total revenue expenditures of which:	190331	204904	14573	228768	20.19
1. Interest payments	88000	91425	3425	101266	15.08
2. Defence revenue expenditures	33464	35873	2409	40661	21.51
3. Subsidies	23798	25692	1894	22800	–4.19
4. Pensions	10131	14304	4173	15843	56.38
5. Economic services	6176	6885	709	7183	16.13
6. Social services	5403	6900	1497	6187	14.51

Source: Budget documents for the year 2000–1.

government. It is noteworthy that:

- Total pension expenditures budgeted in FY 2001 are Rs 22786 crores, almost equal to the subsidies budgeted for the same year.
- The growth rate in budget provisions on pensions in FY 2001 is 57 per cent, nearly three times growth rate in total budget expenditures.
- Over the last 10 years, the growth rate in pension expenditures has been nearly 22 per cent per year, significantly higher than in GDP (about 16 per cent)
- In some areas, such as the army, pension expenditures have in FY 2001 become, for the first time, more than pay and allowances of current workers.

2.2 Pension Expenditures of States and Local Governments

Pension systems in states and local governments are basically similar to that at the centre. Thus even though state-wise figures could not be collected from the state budget documents, it is reasonable to assume

Table 6.2
Government Pension Expenditure

(figures in Rs crores)

Ministry/ Department	1990–1	1999–2000 Budget estimates	1999–2000 Revised estimates	Difference between budget and revised estimates	2000–1 Budget estimates	Annual percentage growth between 1990–1 to 2000–1
Defence, of which	1670.12	7344.9	11020	3675.1	11995	21.8
Army	–	6932.9	10333	3400.1	11037	–
(Pay and allowances)	–	(9200)	(9336)	136	(10317)	–
Navy	–	116	247	131	317	–
Airforce	–	296	440	144	641	–
Railways	902.1	3300	4094	794	5314	19.4
Civil	527.04	2800	3300	500	3865	22.0
Postal	150.27	514	730	216	850	18.9
Telecom	60.46	350	410	60	570	25.2
Freedom fighters	53.28	190	187	–3	192	13.7
Total (central govt.)	3363.27	14498.9	19741	5242.1	22786	21.09

Source: Budget documents for the year 2000–1 and Central Pension Accounting Office, Ministry of Finance and Ministry of Expenditure.

that the state budgets are facing problems very similar to those at the central level.

2.3 Pension Liabilities of PSUs

Many PSUs have unfunded pension liabilities which will impose a heavy burden for any restructuring that they may attempt. One useful indication of the magnitude of the problem is provided by an actuarial study done for Andhra Pradesh state-owned electricity companies.[1] The study estimated pension liabilities of present employees (about 60,000) at Rs 5000 crores. (This presumably leaves out the pension burden of current retirees.) If the pension burden estimated by this study can be applied to all PSUs (with a workforce of about 65 lakhs) the total pension liabilities of PSUs may be over Rs 4 lakh crores or over 20 per cent of GDP.

2.4 Wake-up call?

The budget figures on pension expenditures regarding a looming contingent liability represented by pensions should be taken as a wake-up call for the finance ministry. The total implicit pension debt of the public sector (that is, central, state, and local governments, PSUs, and unfunded liabilities of EPFO) may be over 50 per cent of GDP which is not unusual in the light of the experience of Latin American and Eastern European countries, some of which have implicit pension debt of more than 100 per cent of GDP. In India, this implicit debt would be more than the total domestic debt of the government (which is at present less than 50 per cent of GDP). And this implicit debt is as difficult to repudiate as the explicit public debt. When payments on the pension debt become due, they may exceed the current interest payments (as per cent of GDP) due at present. Fortunately, there is ample experience around the world on how to assess the burden and alleviate it. A serious study will have to involve international experts in this area and will cost time and money; but if it contributes to defusing the pension time bomb, it will yield a very high rate of return on the investment.

The seriousness of the financial risks facing the pension system in the formal sector can be elaborated further by looking at the situation in the railways and in EPFO.

[1]*The Business Standard*, 6 March 2000.

Indian Railways (IR) is one of the largest railway systems in the world under a single management which employed nearly 16 lakh workers in 1997–8. This large work force accounts for about 56 per cent of working expenses of the IR by way of salary, wages, allowances, and other benefits to the employees. In the railways, pensions are charged to the revenue of the year in which they are actually paid.

The issue of pension payment does not appear prominently in the railway budget but the facts presented in Table 6.3 show how rapidly it is growing and becoming a significant part of the current expenditure. Between 1990–1 and 2000–1, pension expenditures increased six-fold, nearly double the rate of increase of working expenses. As a result, the pension expenditures now form nearly 15 per cent of working expenses whereas they were about 8 per cent in 1990–1. The budget estimates of pension expenditure for 2000–1 are a whopping 61 per cent higher than budget estimates for 1999–2000.

Table 6.3
Growing Pension Payments as the Percentage of Expenditure

Year	Pension payments Rs cr.	Annual growth of pension payments (%)	Working expenses Rs cr.	Annual growth of working expense (%)	Pension payments as percentage of expenditure (%)
1990–1	892.40	12.7	11337.77	12.7	7.87
1991–2	1040.45	16.6	12572.78	10.9	8.28
1992–3	1251.43	20.3	14159.30	12.6	8.84
1993–4	1487.85	18.9	15261.17	7.8	9.75
1994–5	1686.00	13.3	16721.00	9.6	10.08
1995–6	2117.17	25.6	18678.77	11.7	11.33
1996–7	2508.92	18.5	21176.79	13.4	11.85
1997–8	3508.61	39.8	26109.80	23.3	13.44
1998–9	4144.03	18.1	28092.79	7.6	14.75
1999–2000(B.E.)	3300.00	–20.4	29040.00	3.4	11.36
1999–2000(R.E)	4094.00	–1.2	29884.00	2.9	13.70
2000–2001(B.E.)	5313.96	12.2	35552.00	19.0	15.00

Source: Explanatory Memorandum on the Railway Budget 2000–1, Appendix XIV Annual Report 1998–9, Statistical Summary—Indian Railways.

Looking ahead, it appears that the pension burden is likely to further increase rapidly for the next few years. Among the reasons for this increase, three deserve particular mention: rapid increase in labour force in the 1960s and 1970s, rapid increase in wages in recent years and increasing life expectancy of retirees. Table 6.4 presents the figures on growth of employment in the IR over the years 1950–1 and 1995–6. It is to be noted that the work force grew somewhat rapidly up to the year 1980–1 and has since stagnated at around 16 lakhs. This pattern of employment has several important implications for the pension burden. First the rapid growth in employment before 1980–1 will lead to an echo effect in terms of rapid growth in retirees as the workers complete their term of office. Already in 1995–6 the number of retirees was 10.4 lakhs, nearly 61 per cent of the workforce. With the echo effect of those employed around 1970–1 to come, the decade of 2000 may witness a rapid increase in the number of retirees. This, combined with the fact of increasing life expectancy of the retirees, makes it highly likely that by 2010, the number of pensioners will exceed the number of workers. This would mean that the dependency ratio which shows the number of retirees supported by one worker would reach an abnormal level of above 100 per cent of the railways. Moreover, in the wake of Fifth Pay Commission, wages of railway workers have increased significantly and as pensions are based not on lifetime wages but on last drawn pay, this will increase the pension burden significantly.

Table 6.4
Stagnant Number of Employees and Increasing Number of Pensioners

Year	Employees (lakhs)	Decade/annual growth of employees (%)	Pensioners (lakhs)	Annual growth of pensioners (%)	Pensioners as percentage of workforce (%)
1950–1	9.13	–	NA	–	–
1960–1	11.57	26.6	NA	–	–
1970–1	13.74	18.7	NA	–	–
1980–1	15.72	14.4	NA	–	–
1990–1	16.52	5.1	6.86	–	–
1991–2	16.54	0.1	7.26	5.8	44
1992–3	16.46	–0.5	8.19	12.8	50
1993–4	16.25	–1.3	8.63	5.4	53
1994–5	16.02	–1.4	9.00	4.3	56
1995–6	15.87	–0.9	10.40	8.2	61

Note: NA = not available.
Source: Central Pension Accounting Office—Ministry of Finance and Ministry of Expenditure, Year Book 1998–9, Indian Railways.

The current expenditure on wages and pensions may, in a few years time, consume the bulk of current receipts of IR and thus leave precious little for development expenditure. Already IR is facing a severe competition from other modes of transport. Without adequate resource for expenditure, modernization and development, it may well face on what the minister calls, a 'dangerous decline'.

EPFO is supposed to have annual actuarial review of its financial position. However, since the enactment of the Pension Act in 1995, the actuarial report of EPFO has not been made public. There are at least reasons to believe that the provision of the Pension Act of 1995 will impose financially unmanageable burden on EPFO.

- First, until recently, the contribution rate for beneficiaries under the Pension Act was 8.33 per cent of wages (plus 1.16 per cent as government contribution) and that is not sufficient to generate funds that can sustain 50 per cent replacement rate under normal conditions on rate of growth of wages and rate of return on pension funds. A 30 per cent replacement rate would be more plausible.
- Second, in the wake of acceptance of the Fifth Pay Commission recommendations, the wages of non-government workers are likely to increase in sympathy with those of government employees and since the present formula provides for replacement rate related to pay in the last 10 months, this would increase pension obligations of EPFO enormously.[2] An additional feature is retrospective adjustment to pensions to achieve parity between the old and new retirees from comparable positions.
- Third, and perhaps most important for EPFO, the switch to DB system is likely to increase the problem of compliance in paying contributions. The employees are now assured of a guaranteed pension according to a formula irrespective of whether or not EPFO succeeds in making the collections. The employees are no longer the pressure

[2]Some commentators are misled by the statement in the EPS scheme to the effect that 'the maximum pensionable salary shall be limited to five thousand rupees per month'. However, there is a qualifying clause with effect from 16.3.1996: 'Provided that at the option of the employer and employee, contribution paid on salary exceeding Rs 5000 per month from the date of commencement of this scheme or from the date salary exceeds Rs 5000, whichever is later, and 8.33 per cent share of the employees thereof is remitted into the pension fund, pensionable salary shall be based on such higher salary.

group, as they are under DB system, for making sure that their employers make the pension contributions. Under the circumstances, the EPFO will be saddled with pension liabilities not fully matched by their assets. It is important to emphasize that even though the new pension system replicates the practices prevailing in the government and many financial institutions, the task of collecting contributions from a large number of enterprises is fundamentally different in EPFO than it is in pension schemes managed by financial institutions such as banks and insurance companies.

There is clearly a need to make use of careful actuarial calculations on the financial burden assumed by EPFO under the 1995 pension scheme. However, back of the envelope calculations based on international experience suggest that the EPFO may have a shortfall of 30–50 per cent in meeting its pension obligations (assuming a cost of living adjustment to pensions) which will ultimately be a burden on the fiscal system in the country.

2.5 Lack of Provisioning for the Elderly in the Informal Sector

Traditionally the old age security in the informal sector was provided by the joint family system. However, there are now at least three important reasons why parents can no longer rely on children for old age security. First, with the progress in family planning the size of families is shrinking, particularly in urban areas. Second, quite often children's job opportunities take them away from their ancestral location and parents cannot always move with the children. Third, the value systems are changing with diminishing respect for the elderly and diminishing interest in learning from the experience of the elderly for social and economic activities of the young.

Family is of course one of the most enduring and powerful institutions developed in human society and every effort, in terms of public policy and value promotion, should be made to nurture family values which include support for the elderly. In fact, with increasing participation of women in the labour force, elderly parents can provide vital support for looking after the children in the same household. However, while working for strengthening of these family-based systems of old age security, one cannot ignore the reality that at present, in India, the condition of the elderly in the informal sector is worsening rapidly. Surveys done in urban as well as rural areas show the plight of the elderly, particularly the women. On present trends, a high percentage of the current 300 million workers in the informal sector in India are likely to sink into poverty and suffer from painful social exclusion when they reach old age. These new poor may not cause political instability but in terms of social justice and neglect of the Indian values of filial piety, this will constitute a veritable social time bomb for the country.

2.6 Missed Opportunity of Facilitating Labour Mobility

For increasing the productivity and competitiveness of the Indian economy it will be increasingly important to have labour mobility between the public and private sectors and within the private sector. There is very little doubt that the public sector in India has grown too large with the government involved in many activities where private sector can deliver the goods and services better and at lower cost. Over time, employment in the public sector may have to go down and labour reallocated from the public sector to the private sector. The current system of pension in the government with long defined benefit and long (20 year) vesting period, however, is a hindrance to labour mobility from the government sector. Even within the private sector, there is often an emphasis on buying loyalty of the staff through non-portable pension benefits. A plethora of pension systems with limited portability does not help mobility of labour. With increasing globalization of the Indian economy, exits from the declining industries and entry into the emerging industries would be necessary for employees at all ages and an absence of modern pension system with portable benefits would be a missed opportunity for facilitating such movements.

2.7 Missed Opportunity of Term Transformation of Savings

Pension funds are long term savings that are ideal for investment in long gestation investments in infrastructure including housing. However, under the present guidelines for investment of pension funds, most of these funds flow into government bonds of short and medium term maturity. Thus the infrastructure investment programmes are denied the opportunity of utilizing a potentially large pool of resources.

From the point of view of the government, the captive assets of pension funds are only short term attraction of doubtful long term value. By giving a guaranteed rate of return on pension funds, the government is assuming a contingent liability unconnected with market developments. Depending on movements in interest rates in the market, this could mean an unnecessary risk for the government finances. The annual flow of funds from the provident funds represent less than 10 per cent of capital receipts of the government and this should not, through the mechanism of guaranteed rate of return, become a constraint on pricing of government financial instruments. A more competitive system of investment of pension funds can earn better rate of return while reducing the rigidity in government borrowing programme.

India should learn from the experience of Euromerica and avoid introducing western style welfare oriented pension systems. The east Asian style of collective self-help oriented DC pension systems as in Singapore and Malaysia are more in line with the Indian practices and Indian realities. At India's stage of development, though, such systems cannot be introduced in a mandatory fashion in the near term. The key challenges therefore are two: (a) how to make the formal pension systems financially viable in India, and (b) how to introduce a voluntary pension system for the informal sector.

3. Comments on Some Recent Proposals on Pension System Reform in India

3.1 Strengths and Weaknesses of Dave Committee Report on Pensions

The first report of the expert committee for devising a pension system for India chaired by Surendra Dave, popularly known as the Dave Committee Report, is a good beginning, but only a beginning, for comprehensive examination of policy questions connected with old age security in India. In her tone-setting introduction to the report, Maneka Gandhi, the-then minister of state, Ministry of Social Justice and Empowerment, correctly points out,

> ... The steady elongation of life expectancy and declining birth rates are inexorably taking us towards an India where there will be such a large number of aged persons that a poverty alleviation programme, which aims to pay even a modest subsidy, would require a staggering expenditure much beyond the capacity of the government. Faced with such large numbers, it is apparent that the problem will have to be addressed through thrift and self-help, where people prepare for old age by savings accumulation through their decades in the labour force. The role that the Government can play in this enterprise is to create an institutional infrastructure to enable and encourage each citizen to undertake this task.

This statement emphasizing financial feasibility is particularly laudable coming from this ministry which under normal circumstances can be expected to be welfare oriented and lobbying for handouts underplaying the financial dimensions of such proposals. With such sound introduction, the Dave Committee goes on to make a number of useful observations and recommendations which include:

(1) Contribution rates to provident fund, pension, and other social security systems are already high and there is no need to step them up further.

(2) There should be tax disincentives for lump sum payments on provident funds and an annuity market with tax incentive should be developed.

(3) Each provident fund member should be allotted a unique identification/account number spanning across all provident funds—for comprehensive portability of account during job changes.

(4) The present contribution of 1.16 per cent by the Government of India to the EPS (which benefits only 10 per cent of the working force out of tax money paid by all citizens) should be channelled into National Citizen's Fund which will encourage, catalyse, and compliment all private sector efforts for the betterment of life of senior citizens in the country and be utilized for educating individuals about various security schemes, conducting research into areas concerning senior citizens and building infrastructure relevant to the social security industry.

(5) Customer service of the existing provident fund systems should be improved.

However, so far as the major recommendations of the report are concerned namely, (a) limiting early withdrawals, (b) deploying superior financial portfolio management and information systems so as to obtain higher rates of return, (c) expanding the coverage of existing provident fund systems so as to reach more workers, there is a need for more intensive deliberations than has been provided by the committee.

The Dave Committee undoubtedly worked in a difficult bureaucratic framework. While the project was initiated by the Ministry of Social Justice and Empowerment, its recommendations call for policy changes which are under the purview of the Ministry of Labour and the Ministry of Finance. The ownership by the relevant ministries of the policy proposals made by the committee was probably less than complete and the prospects of implementation of these reforms correspondingly less than rosy.

The bureaucratic context may also have played a role in the less than candid discussion by the Dave Committee of the problems faced by the current pensions and provident fund schemes as noted earlier. These financial risks facing EPFO as well as administrative problems of collecting the contributions and making timely payments argue for a consolidation of the present pension system under EPFO rather than expansion of its mandate. Yet the Dave Committee calls for increase in coverage under EPFO to include all establishments with the minimum number of employees reduced eventually to five.

The Dave Committee rightly highlights the importance of higher rates of return on provident and pension funds to improve the income of the retirees. It calls for increasing the share of equities in investment portfolio of these funds and recommends that

> fresh provident fund accretions, as well as earnings from investment of existing funds should be managed by professional, competing fund managers registered with the Securities and Exchange Board of India (SEBI).

The Committee compared the rate of return earned on provident funds in India with the higher figure for Chile, ignoring the point that in the Chilean situation in the past even the rates of return on government bonds were very high and more importantly, it overlooks the recent decline in the rate of return in Chilean funds. With regard to investment in equities, the issue of risks has to be taken more seriously than is done by the committee. As clearly shown by recent experience, the risks of equity investments for pensioners are considerable. Nor can we assume that the government authorities that may fail to make proper investments of pension funds would be able to provide effective supervision to private professional fund managers. The Indian experience with non-banking financial intermediaries does not justify the case that pension and provident funds should be entrusted to the professional managers irrespective of the wishes of account holders. An alternative line could be to recognize that the choice between bonds and equities is not a clear-cut technical issue. There is a choice between risks and returns involved. (It is not a case of win-win strategy in favour of equities as the committee seems to suggest.) An effort should be made to give the pension account holders some strategic choice about investment portfolio.

In fact, the committee seems to be torn between facing the Indian reality and falling for the fashionable Chilean model of private pension funds managers. On the one hand, it recognizes that 'In India, we have experienced a variety of scandals in the financial sector. This has led to legitimate concerns about liberalization of pension funds management'. Yet the committee goes on to recommend that to begin with six professional pension fund managers (PFMs) should be selected to manage the retirement funds. The choice of the six PFMs should be based on an auction, where interested fund managers would compete in bidding the lowest management fees (inclusive of all expenses). In what appears to be a blind copy of the Chilean model, the committee states (without giving any reason) that PFMs would need to be distinct entities exclusively doing pension asset management. Every five years, this bidding will take place afresh. The committee is concerned about the potential of fraud by PFMs: 'PFMs could indulge in a variety of malpractices, including violation of investment guidelines, front-running, use of trading mechanisms which are not in the best interests of individuals, market manipulation, etc'. Thus, the Indian Pensions Authority (IPA) is supposed to have enforcement machinery that imposes penalties upon errant economic agents, and evolve regulatory framework on an ongoing basis to avoid a recurrence of these lapses. If a fund has inadequate collateral, IPA would take over the assets of the fund, remove the PFM from the system, and assign the individuals to other PFMs. The PFMs would be required to supply a guarantee that they would not underperform the weighted average returns of all managers in that style by worse than 2 percentage points in a year. And to top it all, the government will purchase an insurance from insurance companies to compensate the pension account holders in cases where the final pension assets of a participant are smaller than the sum total of all contributions. Yet the whole elaborate system (with overtones of the Chilean system) is to basically transmit the instructions of individual participants. 'Individuals would be able to submit instructions with any "Point of Presence" (POP) which would transmit these to the depository, which would in turn implement them with the relevant PFMs. PFMs would only obtain a single instruction from the depository everyday which will drive the assets under their management.' Aware of the risks of fluctuations in individual stocks, the committee also recommends that 'for the first five years, all domestic equity investments should be implemented using index funds on the NSE-50 or the BSE-100 indices only. There should be no "active fund management" (where fund managers have discretionary control of which shares to buy)'. Under the circumstances, it is not clear what the role of the elaborately designed system of PFMs is. PFMs seem to be more of administrators for individual instructions rather than managers of funds. It is not clear if the committee envisages that the funds are transferred to PFMs or they remain with central depositories with PFMs directing the investments of funds. If it is the latter, why does the central depository not transmit the instructions of the individual participants directly to the brokers for allocation of the pension assets. With the development of IT, such functions can be and are routinely performed by brokerage houses in developed countries. No wonder, the board of trustees at EPFO is seeking 'clarification' of what the Dave Committee intended.

Leaving aside the specific proposals of the Dave Committee, the issue of appropriate investment of pension funds is an extremely important and urgent issue and deserves deep deliberations. Specifically, the problems of financial stress on the formal sector pensions are real and one should not throw out the baby (restructuring investment portfolio) along with the bath water (complex system of PFMs suggested by the Dave Committee). A prudent diversification of portfolio of provident funds can earn higher rates of return consistent with acceptable risks while contributing to accelerating economic growth in the country.

The committee also makes a strong case for limiting early withdrawals. Here again, there is some merit in limiting such withdrawals. But in order for this recommendation to be really persuasive, it is necessary to demonstrate that the effective rates of return earned on withdrawals which may finance the much needed expenditures for housing and other socially essential expenditures is less than that earned on provident funds. No such demonstration has been made by the committee.

At present the Public Provident Fund (PPF) is a key instrument for savings for old age security for the informal sector which accounts for 90 per cent of the working population in the country. The committee makes some useful recommendations such as renaming of the Fund, for increasing the tax-free annual contribution and, for allowing all commercial banks to serve as collection centres. But it does not recognize PPF's full potential for the informal sector and does not suggest any vigorous action to promote the Fund. Instead it calls for introducing a Public Pension Scheme with a percentage of contribution to PPF mandatorily earmarked for the new pension scheme. Given the problems of administration, such mandatory elements in PPF should be avoided, as should any move to defined benefit pension schemes for the informal sector as seems to be implied by the analogy with EPS.

In sum, the Dave Committee has made a great contribution by putting on the table a number of key issues in an important area. The opportunity should be taken to debate these issues nationally and form a national consensus.

4. Suggested Directions for Reform for India's Pension Systems

For designing an effective pension system in India, one may usefully begin with some reflections on the role of the state in economic and social development in India. In our opinion, India is at too early a stage of development to afford a welfare state. Continued clinging to that rhetoric will face serious implementation problems and enhance the tendency to empty rhetoric in economic policy-making. The 'minimalist state' approach, on the other hand, will condemn India to an unacceptably low rate of growth and is likely to be associated with increasing inequalities and social and political tensions. The 'developmental state' approach (illustrated, for example, by Japan, South Korea, Taiwan (China), Singapore, and mainland China) which seeks a partnership of the state with prices, markets, and the private sector in both economic and social spheres is more appropriate to India's circumstances. Adoption of such an approach will mean that pension system will be seen largely as a private rather than public good and it will be treated as a largely financial sector issue rather than a fiscal issue.

4.1 Rethinking the Concept of Retirement

The so-called demographic crisis may be more due to inertia in policy thinking than due to facts of demography. With improvement in health conditions, the work abilities and life expectancies of the elderly are improving. There is need for systematic study of how these factors are changing in India and what their prospects are over the next 50 years. To illustrate the importance of this point about the so-called demographic crisis, we assume that work abilities of a person aged 60 in 2001 will be similar to those of a person aged 65 in 2021 and of a person aged 70 in 2051. Thus the elderly will be defined as one aged 60 in 2001, 65 in 2021, and 70 in 2051 and in the same vein, an example of the elderly in India in different years is as follows:[3]

Proportion of 60+ in India in 2001: 7.1 per cent

Proportion of 70+ in India in 2051: 7.6 per cent

The cut-off point for definition of the elderly is the age when the life expectancy is about 15 years, the proportion of the elderly in India will change only marginally between 2001 and 2021, from 5.37 per cent for males and 5.48 per cent for females to 5.79 per cent for males and 6.23 per cent for females.[4]

Thus it seems that if the elderly are defined not in terms of chronological age but in terms of work ability, the rise in their proportion in the total population may not be as fast as often portrayed. The so-called crisis of aging may be, at least in India, more due to rigid policies on retirement than due to demographic factors per se.

4.2 Utilizing the Work Abilities of the Elderly

With increasing life expectancy and better health conditions, many retired people in India have substantial work abilities which can be of value in the market as well as in voluntary non-government organization (NGO) type activities. In many parts of India, elderly people are spontaneously developing mechanisms for keeping themselves busy while contributing to the society. There are cases where the elderly people are being brought in to improve supervision of municipal services. One hears of interesting experiments in combining old peoples' homes with orphanages and developing systems where the elderly informally 'adopt' orphans and the two play mutually supportive roles. The government or NGOs for the elderly should try to scale up these practices on a national level. Internet facility can also be increasingly used to match the supply of work capacities of the elderly at low cost and demand for their services. By utilizing these work abilities more effectively, the system can help to reduce the boredom of the retired and provide supplement to their financial security.

[3]Irudaya Rajan, S. 'Demography of Aging', paper presented at the Asian sub-regional seminar on Social Security for the Elderly, organized by Social Security.

[4]Irudaya Rajan, S., U.S. Mishra, and P. Sankar Sarma (1999), 'India's Elderly: Burden or Challenge?', New Delhi, Sage Publications.

As suggested by Maneka Gandhi in her foreword to the Dave Committee report, the Indian system should be basically one of self-help where people prepare for old age by savings accumulating through their years in the labour force. However, the government can and should play its role by helping the private sector and NGOs to create an institutional infrastructure and encourage each citizen to undertake this task. As a start, an effort should be made to set up an NGO, a Society for Elderly Persons in India, to provide a forum for discussion and action for promoting the collective self-help for the elderly.

4.3 A Reformed Public Provident Fund as the Main Pillar for Old Age Income Security in the Informal Sector

For reasons discussed earlier, for the vast majority of the people in India a mandatory pension system is not realistic. It may be most appropriate for Indian conditions to promote voluntary individual accounts for pensions. The PPF has many attractive features in the Indian context. It could be further improved through reducing options on early withdrawals and better investment of the funds.

In addition, it should be combined with a vigorous campaign along the lines of family planning campaigns highlighting the importance of savings for the old age particularly when the traditional support through children in the old age may no longer be available. The educational campaign should be combined with incentives in the form of tax benefits, allocation for housing and other scarce commodities and services and by allowing account holders to use part of their IRA balances as collateral for credits from the formal credit system. In addition the government could provide administrative support to the pension schemes in recognition of the positive externalities of pension funds. With regard to investment and management of pension funds too, schemes suitable to Indian conditions may need to be devised. The Chilean type of private single purpose pension funds may not be appropriate in view of the high costs of administering such funds and low confidence that such funds are likely to inspire in India today in view of the performance of private non-banking companies in India in recent years. For some time, the public trust in the safety of their long-term funds could best be assured by keeping them in government-owned institutions. However, with the advent of the internet, the intermediaries may be cut off in the management of such funds. The publicly held funds could be managed by the individual account holders and/or their advisers with limited power of attorney for management of funds only. To simplify the process, the investors may be given multiple choices for a limited number of times per year. But the basic point will be that the individuals will directly or indirectly manage their own individual accounts while the government provides safe custody for the funds. For those who do not want to participate in this respect, there will be a 'default clause', whereby investments will be managed by a board of trustees within some guidelines specified by the Parliament.

4.4 Portable Defined Contribution Pension System as the Main Pillar for the Formal Sector

Formal sector pension schemes (including those in the civil service) should gradually move toward portable DC schemes. It is high time to start thinking of various time paths for transition from the current unfunded or partially funded pension systems to funded systems. In view of the limited spread of the current pension system in India today, the transition may not be as costly as it was in Latin American or East European countries. But the greater the delay in starting the transition, the greater will be the costs in future. For railways and defence services where the pensions burden is high, the transition to funded schemes can be assisted by encashment of some of their land assets.

4.5 Improving the Rates of Return while Contributing to Accelerated Development

Improving the rates of return on pension and provident funds can go a long way toward improving the financial viability of the formal pension system in India.

Table 6.5 presents some basic data on rates of return on equities in India and the rates of return on fixed income securities computed by the authors. The rate of return on equities is equal to rate of appreciation of equity index plus rate of return through dividends. The rates of return on EPFO funds are assumed to represent returns on fixed income securities. These figures are derived from various issues of the Annual Report of Currency and Finance of the Reserve Bank of India and data from EPFO annual reports. To examine the relative returns and risks from investment in equities and in securities, simulations were made with regard to the pension funds situation of 10 hypothetical workers who begin their job during 1956 to 1966 and who retire after working for 30 years. It is assumed that wages increase at 4 per cent per year in real terms and the nominal wage increases are 4 percentage points above the increases in Consumer Price Index (CPI). It is assumed that 10 per cent of wages are put in pension fund every year. It is further assumed that the pension balance on retirement can be transformed into an annuity amounting to 10 per cent of the balance (which assumes life expectancy of 16 years on retirement and annual rate of return of 3 per cent in real terms). The annuity divided by the wage in the last year is the replacement rate (RR) (the retirement income as the percentage of last drawn wage) obtained by the pensioner.

Table 6.5
Replacement Rates on Retirement for 10 Hypothetical Workers
(rates in percentages)

Work-period	Average annual inflation (CPI)	Average annual rate of return of equities	Average annual rate of return on fixed securities	Replacement rates with investment in equities only	Replacement rates with investment in fixed securities only	Replacement rates with investment in equities for the first 20 years and in fixed securities for the last 10
1956–86	8.06	12.09	6.52	37	18	19
1957–87	8.14	12.05	6.79	38	19	21
1958–88	8.29	13.16	7.00	39	19	22
1959–89	8.25	14.25	7.28	52	20	23
1960–90	8.46	15.03	7.55	65	21	25
1961–91	8.73	16.42	7.83	84	20	26
1962–92	8.88	17.67	8.10	108	20	25
1963–93	8.98	17.39	8.38	91	21	27
1964–94	9.16	19.06	8.64	116	22	27
1965–95	9.07	18.27	8.90	80	22	36
1966–96	8.93	18.41	9.15	74	23	36

Source: Calculations are made by the authors on the basis of data obtained from the Reserve Bank of India bulletins and annual reports of EPO, various years.

Table 6.5 presents the replacement rates for 10 hypothetical workers who retired during the period 1986–96 with their contributions invested in equities or fixed income securities. It is striking that in all cases the RRs from investing in equities were double or more in comparison with cases of investing in securities. Thus at least in retrospect, the benefits of investing in equities for pensioners retiring during 1986–96 were very dramatic indeed.

The time profile of pension funds under two alternative approaches also indicates the differential risks faced by the pensioners. If a person started to work in 1964, his pension fund invested in equities, his replacement rate on retirement in 1994 would have been 116, but for the person who started working one year later and retired in 1995, the RR would have been only 80. It is however worth noting that even in the worst case, the pensioner's RR with investment in equities is significantly higher, more than double that of the person investing in fixed income securities. If, however, the pension funds move in a massive way to equities they may have a significant impact on returns on both equities and fixed income securities. In the absence of change in the supply of equities and securities, a demand switching may cause dramatic reversals of rates of returns on the two types, thus turning the past experience on its head. For a massive investor such as EPFO, the portfolio switch has to be considered in tandem with supply switches. If such a switch leads to augmenting the exuberance in the stock market and increase the costs of meeting financial needs of the government, it may not be a desirable step for the country at this time.

A more promising avenue in the near-term is to focus on an important potential new source of supply of long term debt instruments which can be achieved if the programme of securitization of housing and infrastructure loans is accelerated. These debt instruments can give more attractive rates of return (consider the double-digit rates of return in real terms guaranteed in many BOT (build, operate, transfer) contracts for infrastructure investments) than is given on government securities. With pension funds investments in these instruments, they can contribute to supplying long term savings to long term investments and thus contribute to development of the economy while reducing the risks of mismatch in the term structure of assets and liabilities in the financial sector.

There are thus many important challenges and opportunities for prudent diversification of pension and provident funds investment and there is a need for in-depth considerations of these various issues by an agency such as the Planning Commission, which can rise above ministerial rivalries and take a national viewpoint. For the next few years though, EPFO may adopt a simpler investment strategy than recommended by the Dave Committee. Such a strategy may include the following:

- Gradually increase the share of EPFO portfolio invested in BSE and/or NSE stock indices to, say, 30 per cent.
- Gradually increase the share of EPFO portfolio into securities backed by housing mortgages and other infrastructure loans to say another 30 per cent.
- Build up hardware and software for handling investments of individual retirement account holders according to their individual instructions.

4.6 Revising the Pension Act of 1995

As argued earlier in this paper, there is a worldwide trend in pension system to move from DB system to DC system. Thus it was a retrograde step when in 1995 the enterprise provident fund based on employer contribution was transformed into a DB pension system. It is highly likely that the EPFO will be unable to meet the provisions of the Pension Act without imposing unsustainable burden on the government. In order to make the enterprise pension system financially sound it may become necessary sooner or later to revert to DC system. In order to understand better the contingent liabilities created by the new Pension Act, the implications of the present system should be considered thoroughly with the help of a detailed actuarial model appropriate to the Indian conditions. The model once constructed can also be used to consider various options for gradual replacement of the new DB system by a DC system.

It is however important that we do not revert to the old system of lump sum payment on retirement. That system is somewhat anomalous with the rationale for government intervention for forced saving for old age. The main rationale for the mandatory pension system is that there is a risk of myopic behaviour on the part of workers and they may not voluntarily save enough for the old age with risk of possible demands on the state to prevent old age poverty. However, if the workers suffer from myopia during the working period, it is not reasonable to assume that they overcome that completely on the date of retirement. A lump sum runs the risk of myopia and insufficient provision in the old with growing risk of survival. It is important that an annuity market is created in India and the practice of lump sum payment on retirement is replaced in good part by annuities over life.

4.7 Changing the Age of Retirement

The age of retirement should ideally be decided in the light of (a) work ability of the elderly, and (b) the length of working life in relation to the period of survival after retirement. In view of improvement in health conditions and increasing life expectancy in India as well as delayed entry into service due to longer period of education and training, the age for retirement should be kept under review. A flexible policy on retirement age (and a graduated retirement policy) may be an important instrument for mitigating financial crisis in the pension system as well as for utilizing the work ability of the elderly. On the basis of evidence collected by the Fifth Pay Commission, it seems that for most of the government employees, there is no evidence of significant decline in work ability before age 62 and only marginal decline in ability by age 65. And this process of increasing work ability of 60 plus is likely to continue for some time. At the same time the age of entry into government service has been increasing. Thus both these trends would suggest that serious consideration should be given to raising the age of retirement. Increasing the age of retirement may also be a potent instrument for reducing the financial risk of the current pension system in the public sector and in EPFO. The Fifth Pay Commission estimate regarding the saving to the government as a result of increasing the age of retirement from 58 to 60 (Rs 3000 crores) is illustrative of the potential of such reforms.

It is sometimes argued that raising the retirement age is inappropriate because it will reduce the employment opportunities for the younger people. This argument was rightly rejected by the Fifth Pay Commission in so far as new employment was not an issue in view of the hiring freeze in the government sector and the small share of government employment in the total job picture of the country. There was also no visible increase in unemployment problem in the country in the wake of the government decision to increase retirement age from 58 to 60 in 1997.

Even if a decision is taken to increase the age of retirement to 65, it can only be implemented in stages. If the age of retirement is increased by one every two years, it will be 2010 before India will have retirement age of 65 which will be in line with the current practice in most OECD countries.

4.8 Revising Pension Benefit Formula

The pension benefit formula linking pension to the last drawn wages is unsustainable when wages are likely to increase fast. Instead an effort should be made to link pension to the average salary earned over the working period. In the Indian context the provident fund accumulated from the individual's contribution provides a ready reckoner of the wages earned during the lifetime of the worker. Pension could be made the annuitized value of the sum in the provident fund of the individual. The present practice of exempting from tax the lump sum receipts while taxing the annuities should also be reviewed. The cost of living adjustment to the pensions is inline with international practice but retrospective adjustment to pensions in line with current wage changes should be avoided.

4.9 Setting up a Social Security Commission for the Elderly

In sum, it seems that the present pension system in the formal sector in India constitutes a risk to fiscal sector stability as well as a hindrance to labour mobility essential for economic restructuring while the lack of an adequate pension system in the informal sector constitutes serious risk of dramatic increase in poverty for the elderly in India over the next decade or two. With proper reforms, this challenge can be converted into an opportunity that can defuse the financial time bomb of pension system, mobilize long term funds which can, by and large, meet the investment needs of infrastructure (as it seems to have done in Singapore), facilitate labour mobility and save the tens of millions of elderly from slipping into poverty over the medium and the long term.

The stake is high and there is a need for concerted and high level review of all the issues involved and designs a system appropriate for Indian circumstances. However, an expert design is not enough for such important social issues. There is need to built consensus in the government and the civil society behind the design, with experts willing to change the design as the interactions with the public suggest. After appropriate consensus and legislation, a statutory body may be created to implement the reforms. Throughout the process, ideas and financial assistance may be sought from the international development community but only if it is prepared to play a supportive role with the country firmly in the driver's seat.

7

Social Protection for the Informal Sector in India

Wouter van Ginneken

One of the key current global problems facing social security is the fact that more than half of the world's population (workers and their dependants) are excluded from any type of statutory social protection. They are covered neither by a contribution-based social insurance scheme nor by tax-financed social assistance. In sub-Saharan Africa and South Asia statutory social protection coverage is estimated at 5 to 10 per cent of the working population and decreasing. In India for example, in the mid-1990s not more than 10 per cent of workers were in the organized sector compared to more than 13 per cent in the mid-1980s. In Latin America coverage is roughly between 10 and 80 per cent, and mainly stagnant. Coverage is generally high in the 'cone' countries and low in central America. In South East and East Asia coverage can vary between 10 and 100 per cent, and is generally increasing. In most transition countries of Europe coverage varies between 50 and 80 per cent, while most developed countries have reached a coverage of practically 100 per cent.

The challenge for India, as for many other developing countries, is to design social protection schemes for the informal sector that are effective in protecting against poverty, and that at the same time promote productivity and employment. Since about 10 per cent of the

Indian working population and their dependants are covered by statutory social insurance, extension and reform of the statutory social insurance system could reach roughly another 5 per cent of the working population, that is, most regular and some casual wage workers in the informal sector. At the other end of the income scale are the 30 per cent of poor households who can be helped only by social assistance, together with other direct anti-poverty policies, such as food security measures and employment guarantee schemes. This leaves about 60 per cent of the working population—above the poverty line but not eligible or interested in statutory social insurance—who have some power to contribute to social insurance programmes that are tailored to their needs. So, the main challenge of a comprehensive social protection policy is to reach this majority of the working population.

The first section of this chapter defines the widening concept of social protection and attempts to identify the specific social protection needs of informal sector workers. The second section examines the reasons for low coverage under statutory social insurance schemes, and identifies some ways to extend their coverage. The third section highlights some of the emerging opportunities for so-called microinsurance schemes and attempts to draw some first lessons from these experiences. The fourth section identifies the various vulnerable groups that need social assistance and reviews some country experiences, while the fifth section proposes some experiments that would help to open up new ways of providing social protection to the informal sector.

1. Social Protection and Social Protection Needs

At the beginning of the 1990s Guhan (1994) argued that the 'contingency approach' of social security, traditionally used by the ILO and the developed countries, cannot be transferred to the developing countries, where poverty is caused by structural factors. Drèze and Sen (1991) as well as Burgess and Stern (1991) distinguish two aspects of social security, which they define as the use of social means to prevent deprivation (promote living standards) and vulnerability to deprivation (protect against falling living standards). In this article we shall focus on the protective aspect of social security, it being understood that social protection needs to be seen as an integrated part of a development policy that includes mainly promotional aspects.

For present puroposes we shall, therefore, use a wider definition of social protection (van Ginneken 1996 and 1998):

(a) the provision of benefits to households and individuals;
(b) through public or collective arrangements;
(c) to protect against low or declining living standards; and
(d) arising from a number of basic risks and needs.

The first element in this definition establishes that people derive individual rights from social protection. The second element defines the social element of social protection, that is, that it is provided through public or collective and often voluntary arrangements. The third element shows the distinction between protective and promotional social security policies. Finally, it makes the point that social protection is not only concerned with cash benefits and benefits in kind, but also with the cost of medical care and of some basic needs, such as education, housing, and nutrition.

Most formal sector workers have steady and high income patterns and are therefore in a position contribute regularly to social insurance. They generally have a long-term planning horizon, and given their regular earnings, they can provide for their retirement. This is not the case for most informal (sector) workers, who may not wish to save for retirement, since if they reach retirement at all, they will be supported by their children. Moreover, if they have the resources they may prefer to invest in their business, in land, or in their house. However, most informal (sector) workers 'are psychologically engrossed in their problems of immediate survival to such an extent that any concern or motivation to provide for a distant eventuality gets almost obliterated' (Singh 1994). Good health, the education of their children, and providing for death and disability are therefore much more immediate concerns for informal sector workers (van Ginneken 1999a).

Even poor households in India can spend between 5 and 10 per cent of their incomes on health care (Jain 1999). As a result of structural adjustment and privatization most governments are not able anymore to provide free access to basic social services. Health insurance is therefore the most pressing social protection need for most informal sector workers. Some of the reasons why informal sector workers would prefer social insurance schemes over individual spending and financing are the following (van Ginneken 1999b):

(a) by regular contributions, they can avoid indebtedness when they face large medical bills;

(b) as a group, they can negotiate on price and quality with private health providers; and

(c) within a group, they may be willing to spend on preventive and health promotion activities so as to keep down the cost of curative services.

2. Extending and Reforming Statutory Social Insurance

2.1 Obstacles to extension

In India the total contribution rate for statutory social insurance is now 28.5 per cent of the payroll. Formal sector wage workers share these contributions with their employers; however, self-employed workers are often not prepared to pay the full (workers' and employers') contribution by themselves.

Most social insurance schemes in developing countries have adopted a very cautious approach to the extension of coverage beyond the formal sector. Not only does this often result in the exclusion of the self-employed, family workers, domestic employees, and casual workers but it has also meant that restrictions have often been imposed on coverage for those who are in regular employment. The Employees Provident Fund (EPF) in India applies a combination of provisions to restrict membership. First, the employment must fall within the scope of one of 177 prescribed occupations, second, the establishment must have at least 20 workers, and third, until 1997, the establishment should have been operating for at least three years (infancy period).

In most developing countries the tendency has been for the restrictions based on legislation to be removed only slowly, because amendment of the legislation is a slow process which often has to be negotiated. Many schemes find it difficult to cope with the volume of administrative tasks associated with the operation of a social insurance scheme which requires the maintenance of accurate lifetime records for insured persons. These problems are intensified by the dependence of the administration on the cooperation of employers and insured persons in providing the necessary data accurately and regularly. So, there is a close connection between the extension of coverage and the administrative capacity of employers and the social security agencies.

Other factors affecting the extension process are a general lack of awareness among the excluded groups or perhaps even reluctance where the scheme is perceived either to be inefficient or not in their best interests. Some people (both employers and workers) feel overwhelmed by the bureaucratic obligations associated with registration under the formal social security scheme or may fear that entry into the 'public system' will have other unwelcome implications.

2.2 Extending the Personal Coverage of Statutory Social Insurance

In some developing countries the process of economic growth has resulted in the transfer of a large part of the labour force to the formal sector. In addition, in such countries the government had—and used—sufficient resources to subsidize the extension of the statutory insurance schemes. This has been the case in various countries from East and South East Asia. The most striking example is the Republic of South Korea, which achieved universal health insurance coverage in 1989 within about 12 years of the commencement of compulsory medical insurance in 1977 (Park 1992). This rapid extension was due to three factors: (i) the successful replication of five rural pilot projects that were set up at the end of the 1970s; (ii) a substantial (permanent) subsidy from the state; and (iii) a cost-containment strategy focused on moderation in medical salaries. Even though there are various inefficiencies in the Korean system, they have maintained full personal coverage in the aftermath of the East Asian crisis of 1997–8.

Approaches adopted by governments to integrate self-employed workers into the formal pension insurance programmes have met with very mixed success (Bailey and van Ginneken 2000). Some groups that are part of, or close to, the formal sector may be induced to join such schemes, but the self employed are usually not prepared to pay the 'double', that iss 'employers' plus workers' contribution. Some special schemes for these workers tend to have more success, particularly if the government is willing to subsidize. If individual self-employed workers are not willing to join, however, they have much greater opportunities for non-compliance than employees working in formal sector enterprises. In various developing countries governments have also attempted to create special schemes for casual and home workers outside the formal sector. These have had some success, in particular if such schemes were supported by earmarked taxes.

Another way to adapt pensions to the priorities and contributory capacities of different groups of workers would be to design benefit packages for the self-employed and the informal sector which would range from a basic core of social protection obligatory for all gainfully occupied persons to a more comprehensive provision which would be optional but subject to certain tests of membership. As noted in the first section, disability and survivors' benefits would be the first candidates for such a core package. Formal social insurance schemes would have a comparative advantage to deal with such benefits because insurance against these risks requires a large pool of contributors.

3. Promoting Microinsurance

Informal sector workers are increasingly setting up their own schemes in order to meet their priority social security needs. The mechanism used in these schemes is generally one of micro-insurance (Dror and Jacquier 1999), the concept of which conveys the following two main connotations: (i) the insurance is independently managed by groups and units at the local level; and (ii) the local unit is structured in such a way as to link up with multiple small area- and occupation-based units into larger structures needed for improved governance.

The analysis of such schemes (van Ginneken 1996) has shown that there are two fundamental requirements for the setting up of such self-financed social insurance schemes: (1) the existence of an association based on trust; and (2) an administration that is capable of collecting contributions and paying benefits.

There are various types of groups that organize informal sector workers. Some associations or organizations could be directly governed by the informal sector workers themselves (for example, producer and employer organizations, cooperatives and credit associations), or they could use some intermediate carriers such as trade unions, NGOs, and private insurance companies.

As noted in the first section, health insurance is the most urgent social protection priority for informal sector workers. The majority of the self-financed health insurance schemes provide primary health care services rather than coverage against hospital care costs. As shown in some of the recent literature (Bennett, Creese, and Monash 1998; ILO 2000) informal sector health insurance schemes can be classified into either high cost, low frequency events, or low cost, high frequency events and are designated as Type I and Type II schemes respectively in Table 7.1. Both types of schemes have different implications for variables, such as the frequency of service utilization and possibilities for cost control.

Table 7.1
Two Ends of The Health Risk-Sharing Spectrum

Type of scheme	Type I	Type II
Costs insured	Hospital care	Primary health care
Cost per intervention	High	Low
Frequency of utilization	Low	High
Ownership	Hospital	Community or association
Coverage	District	Community or association
Basis for premium setting	Actuarial study	Ability to pay

Source: Estimated by author.

Some of the self-financed health insurance schemes in India reflect the variety of circumstances and priorities. The SEWA health insurance scheme in India (Chatterjee and Vyas 1997) concentrates on hospital cost insurance and is part of a comprehensive social security scheme that also covers the contingencies of death, disablement, maternity as well as loss of working tools, house and property. The Action for Community Organisation, Rehabilitation and Development (ACCORD) scheme for tribals in Gudalur, Tamil Nadu is a hospital-based scheme, with its consequent problems of sustaining contributions (Eswara Prasad 1998).

In India there are various pension schemes that are fully financed by individual contributions. One example is the pension scheme by the Cooperative Development Foundation (CDF), an institute which aims at strengthening cooperatives and is mainly working with thrift and credit groups in Andhra Pradesh, as well as in Tamil Nadu, Karnataka, and Kerala. For social security a death relief fund has been constituted by CDF covering about 25,000 members. This scheme provides a form of life insurance, that is, a payment on the death of a member. The protection extends to the relief of all liability of surviving family members to repay any outstanding loans which the deceased member had taken from the thrift cooperatives. On reaching the age of 60 years or on withdrawing from the scheme, the deposit amount is returned with a 2 per cent bonus (Gupta 1994).

In India the benefits of social insurance have also been available to different categories of vulnerable groups under the various group insurance schemes subsidized with the Social Security Fund under the LIC. The most prominent example is the Rural Group Life Insurance Scheme introduced on 15 August 1995 in which insurance is available between ages 20 and 60 years for an assured amount of Rs 5000 (US$125), the premium being around Rs 60 per annum.

A preliminary assessment of these microinsurance schemes is that they have so far reached only a very small part of the poor and the informal sector workers. This is so because the schemes are not available in most areas, and when they are available, the poor and especially women have little or no knowledge about them. Most of these schemes are limited to small groups of workers, so that the administration costs are relatively high.

One important implementation and design issue is to define social insurance packages that are affordable and meet the priorities of workers. But there are a number of other issues that need to be analysed so as to establish conditions for replicating and extending such schemes. Some of these issues are:

- dependence on the input and charisma of one person or group of persons;
- dependence on money from outside for the scheme's long term financial viability;
- an evaluation of the implicit costs and the capacity of the scheme's administrators who are usually not remunerated;
- the possibility of pooling resources among different schemes; and
- the possible link-up with private insurance companies and/or social insurance agencies.

4. Cost-effective Social Assistance

A considerable number of developing countries have set up social assistance schemes that are aimed at people in need, who cannot be reached by employment or other social policies and who have not been able to protect themselves through social insurance. Such schemes are predominantly contingency-based as they limit means-tested support in cash or in kind to specific needy groups, such as widows, orphans, and old people without income and family support.

In mid-1995 the Government of India introduced the National Social Assistance Programme (NSAP) covering, amongst others, more than 10 million old-age pensioners. It consists of three cash benefits: a pension of Rs 75 per month for people older than 65 years, with low incomes and generally without relatives; a lump sum payment of Rs 5000 for families whose prime income earner dies before the age of 60 years; and a payment of Rs 300 per pregnancy up to the first two live births.

There are various difficulties associated with the administration of a social assistance scheme. These commence with the design of the system and the basis for distinguishing those persons among many who are poor and who should be potentially entitled to receive help and then determining to what extent account should be taken of support provided by (or expected from) other members of the household and family. A recent field study on the application of the Indian old-age social assistance scheme in Gujarat, Orissa, and Uttar Pradesh (Sankaran 1998) showed various cases of patronage, for example, at the selection stage, and of abuse, in particular in the case of cash payments. It also highlighted the various problems in determining a suitable means-test.

Thus in assessing the cost-effectiveness of social assistance schemes some of the questions that need to be addressed are:

- what are the responsibilities of the central and local government levels in the financing, administering, and fixing of the social assistance benefits;
- what should be the criterion for the means test (income, land, assets) and at what level should eligibility be determined (local government, local community);
- how to design corruption-free delivery mechanisms;
- the estimation of the implicit administrative costs incurred by the government; and
- to compare the cost-effectiveness of social assistance in relation to other social policy interventions, such as food for work, employment guarantee schemes, etc.

5. Proposals for Experimentation and Research

The widening of the social protection concept, as developed in the first section, implies the broadening of the social protection partnership. While for the formal sector it is logical to use the national tripartite formula of employers, workers, and governments, this partnership has to be broadened to make social protection work for informal sector workers. A larger role will have to be played by local governments, by associations that directly represent informal sector workers (such as cooperatives, mutual benefit societies, and communities) and by intermediary organizations that work on behalf of informal sector workers (such as workers' and employers' organizations as well as NGOs). In addition, there is room for greater participation of private insurance companies who, when correctly regulated and supervized, can provide a useful contribution in the form of efficient administration and management of social insurance schemes.

Little is known about the process of extension of social protection. It is therefore logical that for the near future activities in this area should be based on research and experimentation. At the end of this chapter, we propose four areas in which research and experimentation would be most useful.

The first priority would be to experiment with so-called area-based social insurance schemes which aim at full coverage within an area and which are mainly run by the (local) government in collaboration with a wide variety of possible social protection partnerships. In comparison with sector- or occupation-based schemes, area-based schemes have the advantage that administration costs are low and that local participation and control can be included in the design of the project. The core of such experiments should be on health insurance, but other elements of social protection could also be included. For India, two feasibility studies have already been carried out (van Ginneken 1997). The (sub) district would probably be the appropriate unit for the pilot project. If, say, two successful district-wide experiments were carried out and carefully documented, this could have an enormous impact on other districts in India. And, most importantly, coverage could be extended to other areas in relatively short periods, because district governments would be able to replicate the schemes under similar conditions.

A second proposal would be a detailed research on the implementation of the National Social Assistance Scheme. This research would find out what would be the best criterion for the means test. It would also investigate the various tasks that should be carried out at the central, state, and local levels. Issues, such as the mode of payment, a poverty assessment method for fixing budget ceilings at the district level, and the definition of mechanisms by which benefits can be adjusted for inflation. Finally, studies would examine the cost-effectiveness of social assistance, in comparison with other direct anti-poverty policies, such as food security measures and employment guarantee schemes.

A third proposal would be to experiment with local welfare funds for construction workers. In 1996 a central welfare fund was created for construction workers, financed by a tax on construction output. Construction workers constitute a sizeable proportion of the informal sector; they are vulnerable to occupational injury and have a high component of women in need of maternity assistance and crèche facilities. The aim of research and experimentation would be to see whether taxes are in fact collected, and to determine how the main social protection needs of these workers can be satisfied in a sustainable way.

A fourth proposal would be to study the monitored introduction of EPF and/or ESI benefits to small enterprises below the official limit of 10 employees. The aim of the study and the experiment would be to investigate the extent to which the EPF and/or ESI administration would be able to cope with such an extension, and what were the particular problems for employers and workers in these enterprises.

References

Bailey, C. and W. van Ginneken (2000) 'Coverage and its shortfalls' chapter 8, in C. Gillion, J. Turner, C. Bailey, and D. Latulippe (eds), *Social security pensions: Development and reform*, Geneva, ILO.

Bennett, S., A. Creese, and R. Monash (1998) *Health insurance schemes for people outside formal sector employment*, Geneva; WHO Division of Analysis, Research and Assessment, ARA Paper No. 16.

Burgess, R. and N. Stern (1991) 'Social security in developing countries: What, why, who and how?, in E. Ahmad, J. Drèze, J. Hills, and A.K. Sen (eds), *Social security in developing countries* Oxford, Clarendon Press.

Chatterjee, M. and J. Vyas (1997) *Organizing insurance for women workers: The SEWA experience*, Ahmedabad, SEWA.

Drèze, J. and A. Sen (1991) 'Public action for social security: Foundations and strategy', in E.J. Ahmad, J. Drèze, J. Hills, and A.K. Sen (eds), *Social security in developing countries*, Oxford, Clarendon Press.

Dror, D. and C. Jacquier (1999) 'Micro-insurance: Extending health insurance to the excluded', *International Social Security Review*, 52(1) pp. 71–97.

Eswara Prasad, K.V. (1998) 'Health insurance for tribals: ACCORD's experience in Gudalur, Tamil Nadu', in W. van Ginneken (ed.), *Social security for all Indians*, New Delhi, Oxford University Press.

van Ginneken, W. (ed.) (1999a) *Social security for the excluded majority. Case studies on developing countries,* Geneva, ILO.

——— (1999b) 'Social security for the informal sector: A new challenge for the developing countries', in *International Social Security Review,* Geneva, ISSA, 52 (1) pp. 49–69.

——— (ed.) (1998) *Social security for all Indians,* New Delhi, Oxford University Press.

——— (ed.) (1997) *Social security for the informal sector: Investigating the feasibility of pilot projects in Bénin, India, El Salvador and Tanzania,* Social Security Department Discussion Paper No. 5, Geneva, ILO.

——— (1996) *Social security for the informal sector: Issues, options and tasks ahead,* working paper for the Interdepartmental Project on the Urban Informal Sector, Geneva, ILO.

——— (1995) 'Employment promotion and the social safety net', in K. Griffin (ed.), *Poverty and the transition to a market economy in Mongolia,* New York, St. Martin's Press.

Guhan, S. (1994) 'Social security options for developing countries', *International Labour Review,* Geneva, ILO, 133(1), pp. 35–53.

Gupta, R.C. (1994) *NGO experiences in social security,* New Delhi, Friedrich Ebert Stiftung.

ILO (2000) *India—Social protection for the unorganized sector,* a report prepared for the UNDP under Technical Support Services-1, Geneva.

Jain, S. (1999) 'Basic social security in India', in W. van Ginneken (ed.), *Social security for the excluded majority. Case studies of developing countries,* Geneva, ILO.

Park, T.W. (1992) *'Cost-containment measures in the provision of hospital care under social security health care schemes',* report of the ISSA Regional Meeting for Asia and the Pacific on cost-containment measures applied under social security health care schemes, Social Security Documentation, Asian and Pacific Series, No. 15, Geneva, ISSA.

Sankaran, T.S. (1998) 'Social assistance: Evidence and policy issues', in W. van Ginneken (ed.), *Social security for all Indians,* New Delhi, Oxford University Press.

Singh, H. (1994) 'ISSA studies on extension of social security to unprotected groups in Asia and the Pacific', in T.S. Sankaran, R.K.A. Subrahmanya, and S.K. Wadhawan(eds.), *Social security in developing countries,* New Delhi, Har-Anand Publications.

8

Social Security in the Unorganized Sector in India

S. Mahendra Dev

1. Introduction

It is being increasingly recognized now that social security should be viewed as a rights-based concept and it is the duty of the government and civic society to provide social security for all the citizens, particularly the poor, of India. In other words, the conventional definition of social security which is more applicable to developed countries is being questioned. The recent literature on social security tried to widen the definition of social security in order to suit the requirements of developing countries.[1] At the same time it should not be so wide that there is a danger of putting all developmental activities under social security. It is useful to restrict the definition to public action (efforts of government and non-government) which leads to the promotion of capabilities and prevention of deprivation for the poor and vulnerable sections of society. Dreze and Sen (1989) distinguish between two different aspects of social security, viz., protection and promotion.

[1]Ahmed et al. (1991), Guhan (1994), Hirway (1995), Prabhu (1996), Sankaran (1996), Mahendra Dev et al. (2001).

The former is concerned with the task of preventing a decline in living standards as might occur, in say, an economic recession, or most drastically in a famine. The latter refers to the enhancement of general living standards and to the expansion of basic capabilities of the population and will primarily have to be seen as a long term challenge (Dreze and Sen, 1989, p. 16).

More than 90 per cent of Indian workers belong to the unorganized sector. The country has relied mostly on promotional measures (self-employment and wage employment programmes, etc.) for the unorganized sector. The neglect of conventional social security benefits for the poor workers is based on the assumption that in a country like India, the poor workers are so numerous and the problem of absolute poverty is so massive that comprehensive social security would be fiscally impossible. Given endemic unemployment and under-employment, a programme of unemployment benefits would attract a large fraction of the unorganized labour force and hence would be extremely costly. The focus and the bulk of spending in India, therefore, have been on 'promotional' forms of direct anti-poverty programmes as opposed to 'protective' interventions.

In recent years, the importance of protective type programmes (old age pensions, maternity leave, etc.) for the unorganized sector is being emphasized (Guhan 1994). It looks like most of the new employment in future may take place in the unorganized sectors characterized by poor conditions of work, low earnings, and lack of any social security. It would be an important concern of the public policy to see that a certain minimum measure of social security in the unorganized sector is ensured. Some of the targeted anti-poverty programmes have not been able to help the poor because of the problems of centralized approach and delivery systems. The protective type programmes such as old age pensions, widow pensions, survivor benefits, etc., provide a certain degree of financial support to poor or destitute persons facing specified adverse contingencies. Another potential advantage of protective schemes is simplicity and relatively low administrative costs if appropriately designed.

The most recent justification is the initiation of economic reforms in 1991. This led people to argue that there is a need for increase in social security programmes in order to face the negative consequences of reforms. It may be noted, however, that the problem of social insecurity had been severe even before the economic reforms were introduced. Many of the social security programmes are important whether we have economic reforms or not. It is true that reforms may create some new problems relating to social security and may necessitate some modifications in the existing programmes and introduction of new programmes.

The main objective of this chapter is to provide an overview of the various social security programmes for the unorganized sector. In an earlier study, social security had been divided into five components viz., food, employment, health, education, and women (Mahendra Dev et al. 2001). In this chapter the concentration is on preventive and protective schemes for the unorganized sector. More specifically, the following questions have been examined: what are the issues on social security for the unorganized sector? (second section); what are the social security programmes for the unorganized sector at the level of states and all India? (third section); what are the experiences at microlevel? (fourth section); what lessons can one learn from the Kerala and Tamil Nadu schemes and how to strengthen the programmes? (fifth section).

2. Some Issues under the Unorganized Sector

Who are the unorganized workers? The vast majority of the workforce including agricultural labour, construction labour, and labour in traditional leather tanning, handloom, fishing, forestry, salt making, household industry, etc., as also village artisans, coming under the generic categories of the unorganized sector are wholly out of any reckoning in the various statutory laws in the country. These workers are unprotected by legislation and most of them tend to be poor.

The questionnaire circulated by the National Commission on Rural Labour spells out the following as the generally recognized categories of unorganized rural labour:[2] (a) agricultural labour; (b) persons engaged in animal husbandry including sheep and goat rearing; (c) persons engaged in cottage and village industries including sericulture; (d) weavers and workers engaged in carpet manufacture; (e) rural artisans such as blacksmiths, carpenters, potters, and basket makers; (f) fishermen; (g) workers engaged in collection of raw hides and skin, tanning and leather work; (h) persons engaged in the production and collection of minor forest produce such as tendu leaves, gums, resins,

[2]This was quoted in Sankaran (1996).

essential oils, and sal seeds; (i) beedi workers; (j) workers engaged in brick making; (k) workers engaged in stone quarries, fire clay and lime; (l) building and construction workers; (m) contract and migrant labour; (n) workers engaged in the preparation of forest coops. marketing and felling of timber, preparation of charcoal, and loading and unloading of timber in forests; (o) workers engaged in khandasari units, saw mills, oil mills, etc; and (p) salt workers.

In addition, we have workers in the urban informal sector. Some of their problems are different from that of rural labour. Many components of the urban informal sector in the Indian context is, however, a phenomenon more of a rural than of an urban origin.

Table 8.1 gives data for the shares of unorganized workers by sectors in India. Around 90 per cent of the workers are in the unorganized sector. It is clear that in the aggregates as well as in virtually all sectors, the share of the informal sector has either remained the same or has in fact increased.

Table 8.1
Share of the Informal (Unorganized) Segment in the Workforce

(Percentage)

Sector	1972–3	1987–8	1993–4
Ag. and allied activities	99.3	99.3	99.4
Mining quarrying	21.8	54.7	59.0
Manufacturing incl. repair services	72.8	81.1	82.1
Electricity, gas, and water	Nil	Nil	Nil
Construction	73.0	90.0	89.9
Trade, hotel and restaurants	73.2	80.2	89.6
Transport, storage, and communication	36.5	62.8	71.1
Other services	61.1	58.0	66.1
Total	90.5	90.1	91.1

Source: Tendulkar and Sundaram (1995).

The data shows that in terms of additional generation of employment agriculture is still the dominant labour absorber if we ignore the drought year 1987–8 (Table 8.2). In future also, agriculture plays an important role in generating employment in India. Thus, in absolute number, the additions to the unorganized sector will be mostly in agriculture. It may, however, be noted that the elasticity of employment with respect to output would be lower for agriculture over time.

Table 8.2
Industrial Distribution of Additions to the Number of Workers
1972–3 to 1993–4

(Percentage)

Sector	1972–3 to 1977–8	1987–8 to 1983	1983 to 1987–8	1987–8 to 1993–4
Ag. and allied activities	49.85	51.09	16.17	62.74
Mining quarrying	0.40	2.06	2.06	0.70
Manufacturing incl. repair services	20.41	14.35	16.53	6.59
Electricity, gas, and water	1.03	0.30	0.30	1.05
Construction	0.24	5.85	25.50	0.71
Trade, hotel and restaurants	13.39	6.93	20.76	8.70
Transport, storage and communication	4.29	5.42	3.96	4.10
Other services	9.56	14.74	14.73	16.82
Total	100.00	100.00	100.00	100.00

Source: Visaria (1998): quoted in Anant and Sundaram (1998).

2.1 Some Issues under Employment

The workers in the organized sector who have regular employment and an assured source of income need only measures to protect their income when contingencies arise which tend to deprive them of the income or reduce it. In the case of the workers in the unorganized sector who have no regular jobs or assured income their primary need is employment security.

Casualization of Workers: The proportion of casual labourers for males and females in rural areas has increased from 22 to 36.2 per cent and 31.4 to 39.6 per cent respectively during 1972–3 to 1999–2000. The share of self-employed workers declined for both males and females.

The Problem of the Working Poor: In India, unemployment per se is not the main problem. Many people are working in the unorganized sector which is characterized by low earnings, poor working conditions, and lack of social security protection. Estimates given in Table 8.3 reveal that incidence of poverty is the highest for casual labour in rural as well as urban areas. In 1993–4, around 50 per cent of the casual workers were below the poverty line with 49.4 per cent in rural areas and 57 per cent in urban areas. The incidence of poverty declined for all the categories of workers over the last decade (Table 8.3). The rate of decline in poverty ratios, however, was the lowest for casual workers while it was highest for regular workers. From these results, it can be interpreted that casualization may be associated with immiserization in the sense of low incomes. Also the incidence of poverty for casual labourers and the self-employed was higher than that for the unemployed.

Table 8.3
Incidence of Poverty by Types of Workers and Unemployed
1983 to 1993–4

(per cent)

Worker types	Rural			Urban		
	1983	1987–8	1993–4	1983	1987–8	1993–4
Self-employed	38.5	32.4	28.3	44.3	41.2	34.0
Regular employed	32.7	26.5	17.5	26.9	24.5	18.3
Casual labourers	59.3	52.0	49.4	62.9	63.9	57.0
Total workers	44.8	38.4	35.2	40.8	38.4	32.0
Unemployed	33.0	38.5	21.1	40.1	36.0	27.1

Source: Estimated by the author based on NSS data.

2.2 Likely Scenario of Future Employment

The future employment scenario is likely to shift more towards the categories shown in Fig. 8.1

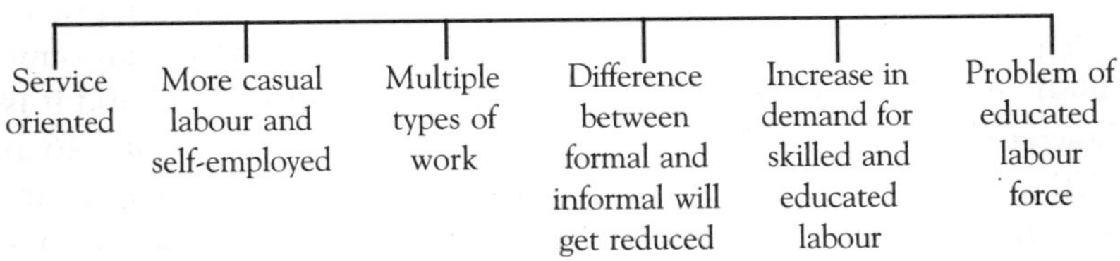

Fig. 8.1

The categories are elaborated here.

Service Oriented: The share of the tertiary sector (mostly services) in total employment seems to be larger than that of the industrial sector. This is in contrast to the experience of developed countries where the service sector followed after increase in the share of the industrial sector. The higher share of services in India could be due to people going to low productive jobs in the informal sector. In future also service sector employment will grow much faster than that of the industrial sector. The shift from agriculture and migrated workers will be absorbed more by the service sector than by the manufacturing sector.

More Casualization and Self-employment : With increase in labour market flexibility, casualization of labour will increase further in India. As noted earlier, casual workers report the highest incidence of poverty. Of course, it depends on the increase in their wages and how productively they are absorbed in the economy. Along with casualization, self-employment is also likely to increase, particularly among the young workers.

Multiple Types of Work, rather than one Job : The traditional type of sticking to one job for a month or year may change and move towards multiple types of work particularly in rural communities. People may work simultaneously in agriculture and non-farm activities. Similarly, they may work simultaneously as self-employed and casual workers. For example, poor communities work in diverse activities to cope up with risk of working in one activity.

Distinction between Formal and Informal Sector will get Reduced : Increase in labour flexibility after liberalization led to increase in sub-contracting by formal manufacturing sectors in developing countries. It also led to greater use of contract, temporary, and casual workers. Thus the differences between formal and informal sectors are getting reduced. A study on India provides estimates of production sub-contracting in Indian manufacturing industries as a source of flexibility (Ramaswamy 1999). An index of sub-contracting intensity is introduced and it is shown to have increased in aggregate manufacturing from about 9.46 in 1970 to 25.3 in 1993–4. It is shown that sub-contracting practices are concentrated in labour intensive industries producing consumer non-durables. The study found a non-linear relationship between factory size and sub-contracting intensity. Organizational diseconomies associated with large employment size seem to result in greater sub-contracting. The study also shows that the share of casual workers in large factory employment rose from 4.6 per cent in 1980–1 to more than 12 per cent in 1993–4.

Increase in Problems Relating to Educated Labour Force: With increase in education levels, the problems of the educated labour force will increase in India. The share of the educated among the unemployed population has been increasing. The educated may not get the traditional kind of regular jobs and they have to go in either for self-employment or casual work in rural as well as urban areas.

3. Social Security Programmes for the Unorganized Sector

Although the coverage is not high, several state governments have attempted to provide various protective social security measures for the unorganized poor and vulnerable sections of the society. Table 8.4 presents a list of various social security and welfare schemes at the state level.

Table 8.5 provides evidence on the coverage of schemes for selected states. In most of the states, old age pension schemes cover a large number of beneficiaries even in other schemes. Prasad's study (1995), however, indicates large interdistrict variations in the coverage of the social security schemes.

Initiatives in the Budget 1995–6: In the 1995–6 budget, the finance minister announced various schemes to help the unorganized and vulnerable sections.[3] These are: (1) National Bank for Agriculture and Rural Development (NABARD) will open an exclusive line of credit cooperatives and Regional Rural Banks for meeting the credit needs of scheduled tribes; (2) Loans to khadi and village industries through the banking sector; (3) NABARD will also extend refinancing to commercial banks for extending credit to cooperative handloom institutions; (4) Programmes mainly for rural areas: (a) one million houses to be built in 1995–6, (b) national social assistance scheme is announced. There are three components under this scheme, (i) minimum old age pension of Rs 75 per month to people above 65 years of age who are below the poverty line, (ii) lump sum survivor benefits to poor households on the death of primary bread earner or Rs 5000, (iii) pre-natal and post-natal maternity care to poor women, (c) Group Life Insurance Scheme.

Thus, for the first time an attempt has been made to introduce protective measures at the all India level.

[3]Details about the financing of these schemes will be discussed in the fourth section.

Table 8.4
State-Level Social Security and Welfare Schemes

1. *Old age pension*
   Andhra Pradesh (1960)
   Assam (1983)
   Bihar (1970)
   Gujarat (1978)
   Haryana
   Himachal Pradesh (1968)
   Jammu & Kashmir (1976)
   Karnataka (1965)
   Kerala (1960)
   Madhya Pradesh (1970)
   Maharashtra (1980)
   Orissa (1975)
   Punjab (1968)
   Rajasthan (1964)
   Tamil Nadu (1962)
   Uttar Pradesh (1957)
   West Bengal (1964)
2. *Pension for agricultural landless labourers*
   Andhra Pradesh (1984)
   Gujarat (1981)
   Kerala (1982)
   Tamil Nadu (1981)
3. *Destitute women*
   Tamil Nadu (1975, 1986)
4. *Maternity benefit*
   Gujarat (1975, 1986)
   Karnataka (1984)
   Kerala
5. *Physically disabled*
   Haryana
   Gujarat (1978)
   Kerala (1982)
   Tamil Nadu (1974)
   West Bengal
6. *Health and Medical under voluntary agencies*
   Maharashtra
   Tamil Nadu
   Voluntary health services (1963)
7. *Employment*
   Maharashtra (EGS)
8. *Relief for the educated unemployed*
   Gujarat (1979)
   Kerala (1982)
   Maharashtra (1979)
   Tamil Nadu (1980)
   West Bengal (1985)
9. *Self employment*
   Kerala (1982)
   Maharashtra (1980)
   Tamil Nadu (1985–6)
   Gujarat (1981)
10. *Group insurance schemes*
   Gujarat
   Kerala
   Maharashtra
   Orissa
   Tamil Nadu
   Bihar
   West Bengal
   Karnataka

Source: Statistical Abstracts and Economic Surveys at State Level, various issues.

3.1 Experiences of Kerala in Providing Social Security

Successive governments in Kerala have introduced a large number of social security and welfare schemes with the view to attaining the goal of reducing income insecurity among the weaker segments in society. It has the most wide-ranging set of schemes for the benefit of the unorganized

Table 8.5

Beneficiaries and Expenditure[a] for Various Social Security Schemes

Year/State and Scheme	Old age pension		Assistance to widows		Assistance to disabled		Pension to agricultural workers		Unemployment relief	
	Bene-ficiaries	Expen-diture	Bene-ficiaries	Expen-diture	Bene-ficiaries	Expen-diture	Bene-ficiaries	Expen-diture	Bene-ficiaries	Expen-diture
Gujarat										
1989–90	56,470	5.63	1813	20.96	865	6.35				
1990–1	58,622	9.05	2437	33.33	1445	1.09				
1991–2	63,658	9.04	2883	66.24	1088	1.31				
Kerala										
1988–90	57,321	13.47	1,20,244		66,764	69.84	30,06,347		2,15,456	23.54
1989–9	58,115	11.79	1,24,355		73,835	69.86	3,02,312		2,46,040	19.96
1990–1	27,795	12.77	1,33,401		77,372	87.52	3,23,781		2,64,314	19.35
Maharashtra[b]										
1989–90	3,21,576[c]	41.57	–						14,183	4.96
1990–1	3,40,557	41.46	–						12,206	5.29
1991–2	3,28,592	50.17	–						12,140	5.51
Orissa[d]										
1989–90	1,00,000	7.57	40,000	3.03	20,000	113				
1990–1	89,847	9.07	62,994	6.36	20,000	202				
1991–2	1,30,422	16.45	1,93,026	24.34	30,000	292	76,707	9.67		

Contd.

Year/State and Scheme	Old age pension		Assistance to widows		Assistance to disabled		Pension to agricultural workers		Unemployment relief	
	Beneficiaries	Expenditure	Beneficiaries	Expenditure	Beneficiaries	Expenditure	Beneficiaries	Expenditure	Beneficiaries	Expenditure
					Tamil Nadu					
1989–90	1,71,9722	103.1	1,28,820	90.9 (e)						
1990–1	2,13,213	122.3	1,60,997	105.3 (e)						
1991–2	2,32,821	133.7	1,91,140	205.9 (e)						

Notes: (a) Expenditures shown are in rupees in lakh; (b) Data not available for all the districts;(c) Data includes widows also as Maharashtra has no special schemes for this; (d) Scheme for agricultural labour introduced during 1991–2; (e) Includes pension to physically handicapped destitutes and destitute labour. 1 lakh = 100,000

Source: Prasad (1995).

sector (see Appendix Table 8.1). These schemes are implemented through institutional care measures and non-institutional measures. There are as many as 30 social security and welfare schemes in Kerala. The schemes are given in Table 8.6.

Table 8.6
Social Security and Welfare Programmes in Kerala

(a) *Schemes which are fully financed by the state*
Kerala agricultural workers pension scheme
Kerala destitute and widow pension scheme
Special pension scheme for the physically handicapped
Old age pension to craftsmen
Assistance to leprosy and cancer patients in indigent circumstances
Journalist welfare fund scheme
Cine Artists Welfare Fund Scheme
Financial assistance for men of arts and letters
Central–state scheme of financial assistance to artists in indigent circumstances
Financial assistance to widows for remarriage of daughters
Group personal accident scheme for school children
Unemployment assistance
Pension to sportsmen in indigent circumstances
(b) *Major schemes which are financed partly with state support*
Kerala cashew workers relief and welfare fund
Kerala handloom workers welfare fund
Kerala coir workers welfare fund
Kerala khadi workers welfare fund
Kerala construction workers welfare fund
Kerala advocate clerks welfare fund scheme
Kerala fishermen welfare fund scheme
(c) *Schemes which are financed outside the budget and operated by respective boards*
Kerala headloadworkers welfare fund
Kerala abkari workers welfare fund scheme
Kerala toddy workers welfare fund
Kerala motor workers welfare fund
Kerala artisan benefit fund scheme
Kerala state welfare fund board scheme
Kerala sports council sportsmen welfare and group insurance scheme
Kerala autorickshaw workers welfare fund
Kerala agricultural workers welfare fund
Kerala lottery agents welfare fund
Kerala document writers, scribes, and stampvendors welfare fund

Source: Rajan et al. (1999)

Fourteen out of 31 major schemes are entirely financed by the state government. The government spent about Rs 370 crores from the budget for social security and welfare programmes between 1986 and 1991 (Rajan et al. 1999). In 1992–3, the state had spent about Rs 80 crores which is 2.77 per cent of the revenue budget. The corresponding figure for all India was 1.02 per cent of the budget.

Social security programmes in Kerala are listed as:[4]

Protective: Primary health care through government health care centres (for all), public distribution system (for all except self-sufficient farmers producing foodgrains), supplementary nutrition schemes (for poor by self-selection), old age pension (for destitutes, widows, physically disabled, and informal sector workers), social insurance and other benefits through the institution of welfare funds (workers in the informal sector).

Promotional: Free school education up to 10 years (for all), distribution of house sites (for the landless), housing schemes (for the poor), income and employment oriented programmes (for the poor), special programmes for creation of entitlements and basic capabilities for depressed castes—that is, the scheduled castes and scheduled tribes (SC/ST)—in government jobs and higher educational institutions, affirmative action for intermediate castes (in government jobs and public higher educational institutions).

In this chapter, emphasis is laid on protective schemes. The most important schemes in terms of coverage are old age pensions for destitutes and rural labourers. The system of giving old age pension has come to occupy an important place in the social security provisioning in Kerala because its coverage, progressively being extended to most rural labourers, covered around 60 per cent of the old age poor in Kerala in 1991 under the two major pension programmes viz., destitutes and agricultural labourers (Table 8.7).

Another innovative programme in Kerala is the creation of welfare funds. In order to meet the demands of the informal sector workers, some kind of social insurance, and other non-wage benefits, a new institutional innovation was brought in the form of welfare funds. With the active support from trade unions, the government took the initiative to set up a fund through contributions from workers, employers, and the government (Kannan 1999).

[4]Kannan (1999).

Table 8.7
Beneficiaries and the Amount of Benefit Under Major Pension Schemes

Year	Old age destitutes			Physically handicapped, etc.			Agricultural workers			Fish workers		
	No.	Rs/ lakhs	Rs/ Capital/ Month	No.	Rs/ lakhs	Rs/ Capital/ Month	No.	Rs/ lakhs	Rs/ Capital/ Month	No.	Rs/ lakhs	Rs/ Capital/ Month
1990–1	181554	1277.00	58.61	76000	875.10	95.95	32378	2914.10	75.00	–	–	–
1991–2	182609	1401.32	63.95	84452	823.33	81.24	33523	1897.31	47.16	25757	–	–
1992–3	187310	1401.32	62.94	90306	895.23	82.61	34077	1451.46	35.49	25780	220.21	71.18
1993–4	187310	1630.00	72.52	90906	915.00	83.88	34565	2000.00	48.22	25780	220.21	71.18
1994–5	189263	1630.00	71.77	90906	915.00	83.88	34494	2000.00	48.32	27000	277.38	85.61
1995–6	132450	1727.33	108.68	91700	1085.05	98.60	31294	3457.28	92.06	30756	279.32	75.68
1996–7	142500	–	–	94800	–	–	31294	3457.28	92.06	26967	279.32	86.32

Source: Author's compilation.

3.2 Experience of Tamil Nadu

Tamil Nadu has been a pioneer in implementing protective social security. In this sub-section, we rely mainly on Guhan (1992 and 1993) which are probably the best studies in this field. The development strategies of the state reveal that there has been emphasis on welfare-oriented programmes.

The protective measures in the state can be divided into two categories viz., measures before and after the year 1989. The year 1989 is significant because the Dravida Munnetra Kazhagam (DMK) was re-elected in 1989 and the government introduced new measures and strengthened the old ones.

There were many social security schemes in the state even before 1989. Old age pension scheme was probably the first significant one to be introduced in the state in 1962. After that many pension schemes and welfare programmes were introduced. Some of them are: the Tamil Nadu old age scheme for destitute widows (1975), destitute physically handicapped pension scheme (1974), voluntary health services (1963), unemployment relief scheme (1980), self-employment promotion scheme (1983), supply of sewing machines to destitute widows (1974–5), marriage assistance to the daughters of poor widows (1982), marriage assistance to orphan girls (1986), incentive scheme for widow remarriage (1975–6), old age pension for destitute agricultural labourers (1981), group personal accident scheme for the workers in the match and fire works factories.

Guhan (1993) says that apart from the old age pension scheme of 1962 the other measures, mostly introduced since the mid-1970s, were limited in scale. Of course, these schemes indicate the commitment of the state government to extend protective social security benefits to the unorganized poor.

In 1989–90, the DMK government revamped and expanded its social security programmes. The main new initiatives of 1989 are: liberalized pensions, the liberalized accident relief scheme, the new survivor benefit scheme, the new maternity assistance scheme, and the new marriage grant scheme (Guhan 1993). As regards pensions, the reforms of 1989 increased the amount from Rs 35 per month to Rs 50 for all categories. There are five main types of pensions viz., Old Age pensions Normal (OAP Normal); Destitute Agricultural Labourers' Pension (DALP); Destitute Widows' Pension (DWP); Destitute

Deserted Wives' Pension; and Physically Handicapped Pension. In one year, there was around 27 per cent increase in the total pensions, the largest increase being in DDWP. The OAP (Normal) and DWP together constitute about 75 per cent of the total pensions. Guhan's estimate is that 0.732 million out of the total 4.4 million households (about 16 per cent) have been protected from contingencies which could have made them poorer.

3.3 Public Works Programmes

Given the magnitude of the problem of unemployment in the unorganized sector primarily in rural areas, the problem of unemployment cannot be tackled via the provision of unemployment compensation (Nayyar 1996). However, alternative means like labour intensive public works can play a helpful role in addressing the problem of employment security. They are easy to administer as they are based on self-targeting mechanism. There are many direct and indirect benefits due to public works programmes. An evaluation of Employment Guarantee Scheme (EGS) in Maharashtra shows that the programme has reduced unemployment in Maharashtra; has increased the incomes of many participating households; acts as an insurance mechanism; has impact on agricultural growth and agricultural wages; has made rural poor as a political force; and has considerable impact on women (Mahendra Dev 1996). These large scale employment programmes have also played an important role in prevention of famine in India. This experience illustrates the feasibility of certain kinds of social security arrangements, even in a poor country, when the government has adequate incentives to take action.

We feel that an unstated and probably equally important objective of EGS is to provide unemployment insurance. Hence even though the actual employment generated by EGS might be a small percentage of aggregate rural employment to the extent that it meets the seasonal slack, its welfare impact is much understated. As is well known, for a risk averse individual, the benefit of going from no employment to some employment in the slack season can be tremendous. One way to measure this is to quantify through an appropriately specified model, the utility of unemployment insurance.

Stabilization benefits: One of the most important aspect of EGS is its seasonally stabilizing effects on the incomes of the poor. If the programme's timing synchronizes with the agricultural slack season when the demand for labour is low, labourers are most likely to gain from the resulting income stabilization and consumption smoothing. Reducing fluctuations in income can be as important to the poor as raising average incomes. It can prevent acute distress and avoid the need for costly forms of adjustment, such as selling productive assets. In other words, even if the increase in employment and income is not very large compared with the aggregate needs, the existence of a form of income/ employment insurance can be quite significant. How valuable this insurance function of public works is will depend on other factors such as the ease with which employment is actually obtainable and the costs of alternative mechanisms, for example, credit.

4. Microlevel Arrangements of Social Security

The microlevel studies provide the arrangements of social security at the grassroot level. A study done at the Centre for Economic and Social Studies, Hyderabad (Galab 1999) provide the following arrangements in Ravirala village of Rangareddy district in Andhra Pradesh.

The study documents arrangements in terms of promotional as well as protective social security schemes for scheduled castes and toddy tappers. The coverage for public distribution system (PDS) is 98 per cent and 57 per cent for Development of Women and Children in Rural Areas (DWCRA). In the case of Training for Rural Youth for Self-employment (TRYSEM) and Jawahar Rojgar Yojana (JRY) the coverage is only 2 per cent. As regards protective schemes, the coverage of eligible members under pension schemes is better than that under other schemes (Table 8.8). The overall coverage is around 26 per cent. There seems to be an imbalance between the promotional and protective social security measures. Also, in many cases, the coverage of eligible households for the social security is inadequate in case of government implemented schemes. However, traditional institutions such as family is providing social security for the old aged in the study village. There are also indigenous community responses to provide social security among toddy tappers and fishermen communities. This is more in the nature of protective type security against sickness and loss of earning members of a family.

It is also worth noting the United Nations Development Programme (UNDP) initiatives for women. These are basically two

Table 8.8
Coverage Under Protective Social Security Measures Implemented by the State for Scheduled Caste and Toddy-tappers' Communities of Ravirala Village

Description of so. sec. measures	Caste affiliation of the households and their coverage								
	Scheduled castes (80)			Toddy-tappers (49)			SC+ Toddy-tappers (129)		
	Eligible	Benefited	Coverage %	Eligible	Benefited	Coverage %	Eligible	Benefited	Coverage %
Pension scheme	34	11	32.35	27	7	25.93	61	18	29.51
Maternity benefit scheme	8	1	12.50	2	1	50.00	10	2	20.00
Girl child protection scheme	5	0	0.00	1	0	0.00	6	0	0.00
All schemes	47	12	25.53	30	8	20.00	77	20	25.97

Note: Figures in parentheses indicate the total number of households.
Source: Galab (1999)

components viz., promoting institutions and initiating programmes of social security for each phase of life cycle of women; and interlinking with other agencies viz., banks, NGOs, and state institutions for accessing their programmes relating to social security. The details of these programmes are given in Table 8.9. Among other things, the organization at the village level has been promoted to address the social security problems of widows and destitutes and old age divorced and deserted women.

Galab's study also indicates that integration of traditional and modern institutions and their integration with the state has led to near universal coverage in social security with minimum transaction costs. This seems to have been reported by the members of self-help groups of UNDP.

5. Effectiveness of the Social Security Programmes

India has many promotional and protective social security programmes. But the main problem is inefficient utilization of funds under government programmes as well as by some of the NGOs. It is true that in a poor country like India, we need more social expenditure as compared to the relatively rich developing countries in Asia. More expenditure is particularly needed for poorer states where per capita expenditure priority sectors is very low.

Table 8.9
Institutions and Programme Initiatives and their Nature of Social Security for Women at their Different Phases of Life Cycle

Description of the stage of life cycle of women	Description of the institution promoted to tackle the social security problems	Description of the programme initiatives	Nature of social security (promotive/ protective/preventive)
Early childhood	Ammavadi	Early child care by providing education, recreational, and nutritional inputs	Promotional
Childhood	Girl child labour schools	Abolishing child labour, providing education bridge courses to put them into main educational stream, and providing recreational and nutritional inputs	Promotional
Adolescence	Balika sanghams	Education, skill formation inputs; roping them into economic activities, providing them with social awareness, sensitizing them on gender issues, making them self confident and preparing them to fight against social evils viz., child marriages.	Promotional + preventive
Womanhood			
a. Married women	Women SHGs	Social awareness, educational and skill formation inputs, undertaking economic activities, accessing health infrastructure, and social mobilization for collective social action for the delivery of public goods.	Promotional
b. Old women	Village organization	Social assistance	Protective
Disadvantaged women			
a. Widows and destitutes	Village organization	Jeevanjothi programme	Promotional
b. Divorced and desertion-prone	Village organization	Social mobilization against these processes	Preventive

Source: Galab (1999)

It may be noted, however, that importance should be given for effectiveness. In other words, we have to examine how efficiently funds are utilized and how much of it is reaching the poor.

Experience of Kerala

Economic, Institutional, and Political Factors

In terms of economic growth, Kerala can be considered a poor state; but her achievements in terms of basic needs and standard of living have been spectacular. For example, the infant mortality rate in Kerala was 13 per thousand whereas it was 110 in Orissa and 74 per thousand at the all India level in 1993. Direct public action on health and education are responsible for Kerala's success in levels of living. The differences in the success of health and education between Kerala and other states seem to lie more in the efficiency with which the facilities are effectively used rather than in the allocation of resources. Some people attribute Kerala's success partly to historical reasons. It may, however, be noted that the Malabar region was very much behind the Travancore and Cochin regions in social development when the state of Kerala was formed. But, the Malabar region caught up with the other regions in social development by the 1980s. The state action was responsible for these improvements. Apart from this, the role of public participation and local leadership is also important for Kerala's success (Ramachandran 1997).

Public action in health and education go far back into history, to the policies of the princely state of Travencore. After independence the successive governments have made notable efforts to extend health and education to everyone in the state. There is also historical evidence of the spread of health facilities to low caste backward communities in the then states of Travancore and Cochin. There is, however, some controversy on the levels of morbidity. In spite of good health record Kerala has the highest morbidity rate in India. One of the explanations for the high morbidity level in the state is the 'perception' factor. However, it is also noted that Kerala is a case of health transition from high mortality to high morbidity. In education, Kerala has achieved a unique position almost at par with developed nations.

The social movements such as caste-based reform movements (for example, the Izhava movement), missionary activities, and left movements have helped in raising human development and social security for the poor. The role of women is particularly important for higher levels of social development in the state. Similarly, historical factors have also played a significant role in spreading education and improving health facilities.

As regards protective schemes, because of the vigilance of various political parties and their unions and the checking measures at the village offices, one can assume that all those who receive pensions are more or less genuine (Kannan 1992). It shows that the protective social security schemes must have partly removed the contingent poverty of some sections of the population in the unorganized sector.

There are, however, some problems with the welfare funds of Kerala. It has been found that in some non-statutory welfare funds, workers have not been enthusiastic enough to enroll themselves because of what they consider to be insignificant benefits (Kannan 1999).

Experience of Tamil Nadu

The economic performance of the state has been lower but the quality of indicators are higher than those of all India. For example, total fertility rate in Tamil Nadu in 1986 was 2.7 whereas in all India it was 4.2. Tamil Nadu is, however, a pioneer in the implementation of the nutrition schemes and protective social security measures. There are two important state sponsored special nutrition programmes in Tamil Nadu, namely, Chief Minister's Nutrition Meal Programme (CMNMP) and Tamil Nadu Integration Nutrition Project (TNIP). The first programme which is considered to be the largest feeding programme in the world, is claimed to have raised the nutrition level of many school- going children. The TNIP showed that a limited package of health-linked nutrition interventions is operationally feasible in rural India in a cost-effective manner. Protective social security measures in Tamil Nadu have already been discussed. It is true that some shortcomings were found in one scheme in a district. But an overall evaluation of all the schemes in the state is yet to be done. Other states in India and also other developing countries can learn many lessons from the experiences of Kerala and Tamil Nadu on what can be done in the area of protective social security measures at reasonable cost to help the chronically poor who cannot afford loss of earnings as well as the drawbacks of such measures.

Apart from Kerala and Tamil Nadu, a few other states have also taken important initiatives in recent years. Employment guarantee scheme in Maharashtra, primary education in Himachal Pradesh and Madhya Pradesh, public distribution in Andhra Pradesh, and land reform in West Bengal are some examples. In contrast, in less developed states such as Bihar, Uttar Pradesh, and Rajasthan, there seems to be apathy towards the need to develop social security programmes.

The contrasting experiences of Kerala and Uttar Pradesh are shown in Dreze and Sen (1997). The reasons behind Kerala's success have already been mentioned. On the other hand, as Dreze and Gazdar (1997) say:

> ... in Uttar Pradesh, the high concentration of power and privileges deriving from the combined effects of inequalities based on class, caste, and gender has made for an environment that is extremely hostile to change and broad-based political participation (p. 106).

According to Dreze and Gazdar, there has been inertia in specific areas (land reforms, gender relations, basic education, local democracy) in Uttar Pradesh.

For making available the promotional and protective programmes effectively to the poor, decentralized access to information and social mobilization is important. These are elaborated here.

(a) *Decentralization*: There are many evaluations of the government programmes in India. The effectiveness of these programmes, however, is limited because of 'top down' approach, lack of people's participation, and poor delivery systems. However, there was one landmark achievement in the 1990s—the 73rd and the 74th Amendments to the Constitution. Nearly three decades later, since this idea was conceived, interest in decentralization revived at the political level and, for the first time, the Constitution provided a system of local government based on mandatory elections. Panchayats and nagarpalikas would be involved in all the social security programmes including identification of the poor for targeted programmes like new revamped PDS, self and wage employment programmes, health and education, and protective social security schemes. Reservations were made for women in panchayats for empowerment of women. But, as mentioned earlier, a large percentage of rural women are illiterate and the power may still be in the hands of the elite. It is true that mere involvement of panchayats may not provide social security to the poor. The accountability of panchayats should be improved. Several conflicts involving the transfer of financial resources and powers to local authorities remain to be resolved. Kerala and West Bengal decided to devolve 40 per cent of the plan funds to panchayats.

(b) *Access to Information*: One way of increasing the accountability of panchayats and other local bodies is to have right to information on the panchayat funds in all the promotional and protective schemes in villages. The people of Rajasthan have pioneered the recent struggle on the right to information. The initiative for this struggle came out of a process begun by the Mazdoor Kisan Shakti Sangathan, a people's organization working in central Rajasthan. The struggle which began to gain focus in 1994 through the organization of four public hearings in this region has now spread to other parts of Rajasthan with the involvement of a cross-section of citizens, organizations, and the media. The public hearings articulated the need for transparency and social audit of development expenditure. The demand for transparency in development expenditure of the state is a method by which the right may be realized.

(c) *Social Mobilization*: The main objective of social mobilization is to induce the poor to create participatory organizations based on direct and full participation of all members of different and varied socio-cultural backgrounds, irrespective of income, caste, gender, or other discriminating characteristics. The eradication of poverty or reducing it to manageable limits in India would require a major political approach and strategic thrust in which social mobilization of the poor to contribute to growth plays a critical role. Even for the success of government programmes the approach of social mobilization or empowerment of the people is important. The government should engage in strategic planning which includes creating an enabling framework, setting of objectives, committing resources, acting as catalyst—especially for capacity building—and engaging in a process of social mobilization which aims, inter alia, at putting the management of certain activities into the hands of people's organizations and the people themselves. NGOs and Community-Based Organizations (CBOs) play a vital role in strengthening the hands of the government. It may, however, be noted that there is also a need for accountability of NGOs and CBOs.

Apart from this, there are anti-poor biases built into a host of existing policies, regulations, and laws which cut across all sectors and vitiate any benefit that accrues to deprived communities.

5. Social Security for Old Age Population

As a further breakthrough in fertility and mortality is expected, the proportion of the elderly in India is likely to rise in the coming years. The number of the elderly in the population (age 60+) has increased from about 19.8 million in 1951 to 56.7 million in 1991 and their share in the total population has risen from 5.5 per cent to 6.8 per cent during the same period. According to the population projections prepared for the Ninth Plan, the number of those aged 60 and above will rise from 54.5 million in 1991 to 70.6 million in 2001 to 113 million in 2016. The share of the elderly in the total population is likely to increase to 8.9 per cent by 2016.[5]

Some characteristics of the old age population are given here (see Visaria 1998 for more details).

- The percentage of the old age population in rural areas (7.1 per cent) was higher than that for urban areas (5.7 per cent) in 1991.
- The proportion of elderly was almost the same for both males and females (6.7 per cent) in 1991 and is likely to increase faster for females in future.
- The proportion of illiteracy among the old age population is much higher than in the population aged 15 and over.
- The proportion of workers among the aged is higher than that in the total population. A majority of the workers among the elderly are self-employed (75 per cent for rural and 71 per cent for urban areas). Casual work is the second most important work for the aged.
- The special survey of NSS (National Sample Survey) for 1995–6 on aged show that about 30 to 31 per cent of the elderly males in rural and urban areas were fully dependent on others. The corresponding figures for females in rural and urban areas were 71 and 76 per cent.

The various small-sample surveys conducted in rural India reflects a greater degree of financial insecurity among the aged, and this insecurity is more pronounced in the case of females compared to males. Moreover, financial problems are more common among widows and among the elderly in nuclear families. The worries of the elderly

[5]According to some alternative projections, number of persons aged 60 and above will rise even more rapidly to 124 million forming 10.2 per cent of the total population by 2016. Visaria (1998) cautions about the data on the aged because of errors of age reporting which led to an overestimate of the number and proportion of the aged.

are on two fronts, one in relation to social strain and the other on economic independence. 'The worries on social relation aspect are much more complex compared to economic worries for those who live in nuclear families or are living alone' (James) 1994, p. 2336. The majority of the elderly also seem to be suffering from ill-health and poverty.

There is a need for a comprehensive policy for taking care of the problems of the elderly. Informal methods for obtaining income security, such as India's joint family system, are increasingly unable to cope with the enhanced life span and enhanced medical costs in old age. Hence there is an acute need for formal arrangements which can supplement informal systems. The programmes for old age can be in two forms: pension funds and health insurance.

Social Insurance for the Elderly: Social security for the elderly, or more appropriately, social insurance against poverty (income security) and ill health (health security) is a contractual arrangement that the elderly sign with the government, which in turn finances it by taxing the working young. The contract is 'paid for' by the elderly during their working lives, and they expect it to be honoured when they are old. This is why social insurance provision needs government intervention. A private provider cannot guarantee that the contract will be honoured since a private provider runs a risk of bankruptcy.

Pension Schemes: At present, less than 10 per cent of the workers between the ages of 20 and 59 (that is, workers in the organized sectors) are preparing for income security in old age using the existing formal systems. Almost all states and union territories have old age pension schemes. A few states such as Andhra Pradesh, Gujarat, Kerala, and Tamil Nadu also have special pension schemes for agricultural labour. Working of the pension schemes for the unorganized sector is, however, not satisfactory except in states like Kerala. The NSAP was launched by the central government in August 1995. Old age pensions to the poor of age 65 or above at Rs 75 per month is one of the components of NSAP. This is not enough to achieve income security for the elderly. There is a need for framing a comprehensive pension scheme covering the unorganized workers.

Health Insurance:[6] Any provision of health insurance to the elderly will necessarily involve the government because of market failure.

[6]For more details on health insurance for the elderly see Ranade (1998).

There is almost none or very little provision of health insurance to the elderly in India. Based on the surveys of the NSSO, National Council of Applied Economic Research (NCAER) and the National Family Health Survey it has been noted that the elderly population suffer from severe physical and mental conditions. Furthermore, increasing diagnostic and drug prices have also contributed to their vulnerability. There are three market products for health insurance that the elderly can access in the Indian market. They are: Mediclaim, Senior Citizens Unit Plan, and Bhavishya Arogya Yojana. The Mediclaim statistics show that the total number of people covered is a modest 1.3 million, of which the elderly probably constitute a small fraction. We can thus see that total coverage for health services for the elderly is miniscule, in that only a tiny fraction of the nation's 54 million elderly have assured medical services. Therefore, there is a need for designing a comprehensive health insurance scheme for the elderly with the support of the government.

6. Financing of Social Security

Many studies have shown that social sector expenditure declined considerably during the first few years of the reforms and this could affect human development indicators. The per capita expenditure in social services for all states together was lower in the post-reform period as compared to 1990–1. For poorer states the per capita expenditure in education and all social services declined considerably in the post-1991 period while rich states have not shown any decline in education expenditure. The expenditure patterns show that reforms would have affected the human development adversely particularly in the poorer states. It also suggests that there is a need for increase in the expenditure on the social sector in poorer states like Bihar, Madhya Pradesh, Orissa, Rajasthan, and Uttar Pradesh. If public policy concentrates on these states, India's human development would increase considerably.

Prabhu and Iyer (1999) make an attempt at examining the level and pattern of financing of social security in Indian states from a human development perspective. The basic postulate of their analysis is that financing of promotional, preventive, and protective social security by the government is necessitated on account of weak links between growth and human development. They classify social security expenditure into three categories (Table 8.10). The empirical analysis indicates that overall, the expenditures incurred by the centre and the states on social security are quite low in relation to the magnitude of deprivation in the country. The fiscal crunch for state governments began in the mid-1980s. The situation deteriorated in the 1990s with the initiation of economic reforms. The study observes a positive and fairly high correlation between ranking of states on the basis of tax to net state domestic product (NSDP) ratio and proportion of NSDP spent on social security. Thus, the question of social security provision is linked with fiscal reforms.

Table 8.10
Share of Government Expenditure on Social Security in Net State Domestic Product: Major States, 1991–5

State	Level 1 (Promotional)	Level II (Promotional)	Level III (Protective)	Total
Andhra Pradesh	1.56	0.58	0.19	2.33
Assam	3.38	0.30	0.20	3.88
Bihar	2.60	1.04	0.51	4.15
Gujarat	2.13	0.39	0.10	2.62
Haryana	1.29	0.17	0.63	2.09
Karnataka	1.95	0.43	0.44	2.83
Kerala	2.77	0.39	0.39	3.55
Madhya Pradesh	2.22	0.61	0.21	3.04
Maharashtra	0.95	0.33	0.15	1.44
Orissa	2.05	0.70	0.48	3.24
Punjab	0.98	0.09	0.26	1.33
Rajasthan	2.65	0.62	0.14	3.41
Tamil Nadu	2.64	0.42	0.38	3.45
Uttar Pradesh	2.16	0.65	0.23	3.04
West Bengal	1.45	0.41	0.21	3.07
Average	1.89	0.48	0.26	2.63
Centre	0.03	0.07	0.05	0.15

Note: Level I Expenditure on elementary education, rural and public health, family welfare, nutrition

Level II Expenditure on rural development and rural employment

Level III Expenditure on budget head social security and welfare

Source: Prabhu and Iyer (1999)

6.1 Source of Financing Social Security and the Available Options

It may be noted that public action for social security does not mean that it is the responsibility of the state only. Local communities and NGOs also have an important role to play in providing social security for the poor.

The state, however, will continue to have a major role in providing social security for the poor. There are various options available for mobilizing resources for financing social security. The Human Development Report (1990) provides the following options for financing human development: (a) Taxes: raising of extra resources by reducing tax avoidance and tax evasion; (b) Discriminating user fees: improvement in social services so that the better-off pay for services, poorer sections pay nothing more than nominal fees—particularly for primary education and primary health care; (c) Voluntary organizations contributions; (d) Reallocating budgetary resources within sectors: shifting expenditure from low priority to high priority uses, say, from curative to preventive health or from tertiary to primary education; and (e) Reordering budgetary priorities across sectors: shifting expenditure from military to social sectors.

A mix of the options including shifting defence expenditure can be used for financing social sectors in India. For example, Guhan (1993) advocates a case for mobilizing additional resources in the form of direct taxes for social assistance in India. According to his calculations, a moderate surcharge on the incomes of the top 12 per cent of households (about 20 million households) can be expected to yield about Rs 1400 crore per annum which would meet the likely cost of the package.

According to one estimate, if the government imposes 2 per cent tax on the gross assets of the top 500 companies, the corporation tax collection will rise by Rs 1130 crore. If such a tax on the entire corporate tax is imposed, the revenue will be higher. Such a tax revenue can be used for different purposes including expenditures on social sectors.

Also note that the bulk of the expenditure on education and health is incurred by the states. For example, in 1994, states accounted for around 90 per cent of the total expenditure on medical and public health. Therefore, the role of the states is more important than that of the centre in building capabilities.

Lastly, options like the SEWA insurance schemes (Table 8.11) and other innovative programmes which can increase financial viability of the programmes on social security have to be explored.

Table 8.11
Particulars of the Integrated Insurance Scheme of SEWA Bank and SEWA

Type of work	Risk coverage (Rs)	Annual premium (Rs)	Insurer
Sickness (health insurance)	1000	30.00	SEWA
Accidental death of a member (women) (including partial disablement)	10000	3.50	United India Insurance Company
Accidental death of a member's husband (widowhood) (including permanent disablement)	10000		United India Insurance Company
Loss during riots/flood/fire/ theft, etc.	2000	8.00	United India Insurance Company
–loss of work equipment	(Maximum)		
–loss to the hut/house	3000 (Maximum)		
Natural death (accidental death)	3000 25000 (double)	15.00	Life Insurance Corporation
Maternity	300	–	SEWA

Source: Chatterjee and Vyas (1998).

Lessons From East and South East Asian Crisis: The recent East and South-East Asian crisis provides some lessons for India. First, developing countries have to be cautious on capital account convertibility. Second, there should be checks and balances on private sector activities with liberalization of economy. Third, and most important lesson, is that there should be enough safety nets for the poor including workers and the unemployed in a liberalized economy.

The dramatic reversal from economic growth to contraction has had such a major impact on employment in the South East Asian economies that much after the onset of the crisis, unemployment is still increasing (Table 8.12). 'As a result, the social crisis is defined by the loss of employment, which includes increases in total unemployment, retrenchment, underemployment in the informal sector, and reversals in occupational trends, wage cuts and increasing poverty' (ILO 1999). 'In the absence of social protection in the region, economic and social hardships arising from the crisis have been borne directly by workers and their families themselves' (ILO 1999).

Thus, one of the lessons from the South East Asian crisis is that countries should have social protection measures to protect the poor from unemployment and decline in incomes.

Table 8.12
The East Asian Crisis: Changes in Unemployment Rates and Levels 1996–8

	Unemployment Rates (%)			New Unemployed (millions)	
	1996	1998	Most recent estimates	1998	Most recent estimates
China	3.0	5.0 to 6.0		3.5	
Hongkong	2.8	4.8		0.1	
Indonesia	4.1	9.0 to 12.0	15 to 20	4.8 to 7.6	12 to 15
Republic of Korea	2.6	7.6		1.2	
Malaysia	2.5	6.7		0.4	
Philippines	7.4	13.1		1.7	
Thailand	1.1	4.4	8	1.7	2.8
Total				13.4 to 16.2	20.6 to 24.7

Source: ILO estimates based on national sources.

7. Concluding Observations

The main objective of the present chapter is to provide an overview of the various social security programmes for the unorganized sector. It is being increasingly recognized now that social security should be viewed as a rights-based concept and it is the duty of the government and the civil society to provide social security for all the citizens of India, particularly the poor. In other words, the conventional definition of social security which is more applicable to developed countries is being questioned. The recent literature tried to widen the definition of social security in order to suit the requirements of the developing countries.

It is known that around 90 per cent of the workers in India are in the unorganized sector and they do not have proper social security programmes. The future employment is likely to be created mostly in the unorganized sector. Our review of protective social security programmes show that many state governments have introduced some programmes. The impact of these programmes on the poor and vulnerable sections seems to be substantial. However, their effectiveness in other states is not as significant as that for Kerala. Political, economic, and institutional factors helped for the successful implementation of the social security schemes in Kerala. In other states, particularly in the northern states, political support for social security programmes has been missing.

It may be noted that economic growth and human development should go together in order to create opportunities for the unorganized sector workers. Economic growth is not correlated with some of the human development indicators. For example, the infant mortality in Uttar Pradesh was five times higher than that of Kerala with both having the similar levels of poverty in the 1980s. Kerala has higher human development but the economy (both agriculture and industry) has been stagnant and unemployment rates are high. Punjab and Haryana have very high per capita incomes but gender inequalities are much higher than in the southern states. The association between poverty and child mortality is also weak. The basic point is that there is no 'problem region' in India. Each state has its own problems. In general, the northern (except Punjab and Haryana where, however, gender bias is evident) and eastern states such as Bihar and Orissa show lower social development as compared to southern states.

As regards finances for social security programmes, there is a need for more funding particularly in poorer states. It is possible at least in the medium run to allocate more funds if measures are taken to improve both economic growth and human development. As mentioned earlier, public action does not mean that we should depend on only government programmes. The microlevel arrangements presented in the chapter have shown that community programmes (traditional as well as modern) are also important in providing social security for the unorganized sector.

The economic reforms introduced in the country in 1991 would lead to greater economic opportunities for the population. However, in the context of marketization, there is a substantial section of society which does not have the resource power to enter into market operations. The government and those who are already in the market have responsibility for providing social security for the large sections of unorganized workers and other vulnerable groups who are out of the market. One important lesson India can learn from the recent East and

South East Asian crisis is that there should be enough safety nets for the poor including workers and the unemployed in a liberalized economy.

References

Ahmad, Ehtisham, Jean Dreze, John Hills, and A. Sen (1991) *Social Security in Developing Countries,* Oxford, Clarendon Press.

Anant, T.C.A. and K. Sundaram (1998) 'Wage Policy in India: A Review', *Indian Journal of Labour Economics.*

Chatterjee, Mirai and J. Vyas (1998) 'Organizing Insurance for Women Workers: The SEWA Experience', Ahmedabad, SEWA (mimeo).

Dreze, Jean and A. Sen (1989) *Hunger and Public Action,* Oxford, Clarendon Press.

Dreze, Jean and Harris Gazdar (1997) 'Uttar Pradesh: The Burden of Inertia', in J. Dreze and A. Sen (eds), *Indian Development: Selected Regional Perspectives,* Oxford University Press, New Delhi.

Galab, S. (1999) 'Some Micro-Level Arrangements of Social Security in Andhra Pradesh', *Indian Journal of Labour Economics,* July–October, 1999.

Guhan, S. (1994) 'Social Security Options for Developing Countries', *International Labour Review,* 133 (1).

——— (1993) Social Security for the Poor in the Unorganized Sector: A Feasible Blueprint for India in K.S. Parikh and R. Sudarshan (eds), 1993, op.cit.

——— (1992), 'Social Security Initiatives in Tamil Nadu 1989', in S. Subramanian (ed.), *Themes in Development Economics, Essays in Honour of Malcolm Adiseshaiah,* Oxford University Press, New Delhi.

Hirway, Indira (1995) 'Social Security for the Indian Poor in the Context of Structural Adjustment', in G.K. Chaddha and A.N. Sharma (eds) 1997, *Growth, Employment and Poverty,* Vikas.

James, K.S.(1994), 'Indian Elders: Asset or Liability?' Economic and Political Weekly, 29(36).

Kannan K.P. (1999), `State-assisted Social Security for poverty alleviation and human development: Kerala's record and its lessons', paper presented at the seminar on *Social Security in India,* organized by the Institute for Human Development, New Delhi, 15–17 April 1999.

——— (1992), *Labour Institutions and the Development Process in Kerala,* Trivandrum: Centre for Development Studies.

Mahendra Dev, S. (1996) 'Experience of India's (Maharashtra) Employment Guarantee Scheme: Lessons in Development Policy', *Development Policy Review,* 14 (3).

Mahendra Dev, S., P. Antony, V. Gayatri, and R. P. Mamgain (eds) (2001) *Social and Economic Security in India,* Institute for Human Development, New Delhi.

Nayyar, Rohini (1996) 'Unemployment Compensation and Employment Services in India', *Indian Journal of Labour Economics,* 39 (2).

Prabhu, Seetha (1996) 'Promotional and Protective Social Security During Economic

Reform', Working Paper 96/8, Department of Economics, University of Bombay, March 1996.

Prabhu, K.S. and Sandhya V. Iyer (1999) 'Financing Social Security in India: A Human Development Perspective', *Indian Journal of Labour Economics*, July–October 1999.

Eswara, Prasad, K.V. (1995) 'Social Security for Destitute Widows for Tamil Nadu', *Economic and Political Weekly*, 30 (15).

Rajan, I., U. S. Mishra, and P. S. Sarma (1999) 'India's Elderly: Burden or Challenge?', Sage Publications, New Delhi.

Ramachandran, V.K. (1997) 'On Kerala's Development Achievements', in J. Dreze and A. Sen (eds), 1997, *Indian Development: Selected Regional Perspectives*, New Delhi, Oxford University Press.

Ramaswamy, K.V. (1999) 'The Search for Flexibility in Indian Manufacturing: New Evidence of Indian Outsourcing Activities, *Economic and Political Weekly*, 34(6), pp. 363–8.

Ranade, A. (1998) 'Health Insurance for the Elderly', Mumbai: IGIDR, (mimeo).

Sankaran, T.S. (1996) 'Social Security in India in the Unorganized Sector', Discussion Paper, project of UNDP on *'Studies on Human Development'*, Centre for Development Studies, Thiruvananthapuram.

Tendulkar, S. D. and K. Sundaram (1995) 'Macroeconomic Policies and Poverty in India: 1966-67 to 1993–4', paper prepared for ILO, New Delhi.

UNDP (1990) *Human Development Report*.

Visaria, P. (1998) 'Demographics of Aging India', Institute of Economic Growth, New Delhi, (mimeo).

Appendix Table A8.1

Social Security and Pension Schemes in Kerala

Name of the scheme	Qualifying/Eligibility conditions	Year of starting assistance 1992–3	Rate of assistance	Amount spent (Rs in lakhs)	No. of persons received
Kerala destitute pension scheme	Above 65 years age for widowed destitute, no age limit, monthly income not to exceed Rs 100	1960	Rs 65 pm is also being paid to those widows who have one or more minor children	1401.32	187310
Special pension scheme for the physically handicapped, disabled and mentally retarded persons	Disabled persons who have minimum 40% disability, medical certificate necessary; beneficiaries' monthly income Rs 75 or family income not to exceed Rs 5000 per annum	1982	Rs 85 pm	895.23	90306
Pension to sportsmen	Income should not exceed Rs 300 pm, minimum age 45 years.	1978	Below 60 years Rs 100 pm, between 60 and 70 years Rs 150 pm, above 70 years Rs 200 pm	157	
Agricultural Workers' pension scheme	Eligible age is above 60, annual family income should not exceed Rs 15000	1980	Rs 70 pm	1451.46	340776
Kerala cashew workers relief and welfare scheme	Cashew workers above the age of 60 years	1989	Rs 100 pm for workers and Rs 200 pm for workers under the category of staff	41.02	103000

Cont.

App. Table A8.1 Cont.

Name of the scheme	Qualifying/Eligibility conditions	Year of starting assistance 1992–3	Rate of assistance	Amount spent (Rs in lakhs)	No. of persons received
Kerala khadi workers welfare scheme	Khadi workers having 10 years of services and of 60 years of age	1990	Rs 60 pm	0.09	11286
Kerala handloom workers welfare scheme	Handloom workers above the age of 60	1989	Rs 75 pm	10.84	24514
Kerala coir workers welfare scheme	Coir workers above the age of 60	1989	Rs 75 pm	37.50	383394
Kerala construction workers welfare scheme	Construction workers having one year service and attained 60 years of age	1991	Rs 75 pm	0.53	210000
Abkari workers welfare scheme	Abkari workers having 5 years of service and 60 years of age	1990	The minimum pension is fixed at Rs 200 and maximum pension Rs 300 depending on the length of service	NA	12845
Kerala head load workers welfare scheme	Minimum 3 years of service	1983	Accident benefit at Rs 10,000, fund to be used for pension bonus, death insurance scheme, super-annuation assistance, etc.	0.90	16
Financial assistance to widows for the marriage of their daughters	Yearly income of the family should not exceed Rs 3000	1978	Rs 1250	110.00	11000

Cont.

App. Table A8.1 Cont.

Name of the scheme	Qualifying/Eligibility conditions	Year of starting assistance 1992–3	Rate of assistance	Amount spent (Rs in lakhs)	No. of persons received
Tree climber's Welfare Scheme	Financial assistance is given to workers in the event of total accidents and permanent total disability following the accident	1980	Rs 10000	12.50	128
Unemployment assistance	Financial assistance is given to those who wait for employment in the live register of employment exchange for more than 3 years	1981	Rs 60 pm	16119.63	253798
Welfare fund for journalists	Financial assistance is given to the working journalists, their dependents in distress. The annual income should not exceed Rs 3600	1975	Varies from Rs 100 to Rs 300 pm	7.24	192
Welfare fund for cine artists	Financial assistance is given to cine artists in distress. The annual family income should not exceed Rs 3600	1975	Rs 300 pm	5.14	145
Students accident insurance scheme	All students	1989	Rs 10,000 in the case of total accidents which cause total disability in, the case	NA	58000

Cont.

App. Table A8.1 Cont.

Name of the scheme	Qualifying/Eligibility conditions	Year of starting assistance 1992–3	Rate of assistance	Amount spent (Rs in lakhs)	No. of persons received
			of minor injuries assistance is subjected to a maximum of Rs 500 in a year		
Kerala toddy workers' welfare fund		1970	PF contribution at 16% of total wages, gratuity at 50% of the monthly average of wages and other facilities		46000
Kerala advocate clerk welfare scheme	NA	1985	After 5 years of contribution Rs 1650 is given, after completing 30 years Rs 10000	2500	
Pension to sportsmen	The income should not exceed Rs 300 pm, minimum age 45 years	1978	Below 60 years Rs 100 pm, between 60 to 70 years Rs 150 pm, above 70 years Rs 200 pm	NA	157
Kerala artisans and skilled workers welfare scheme	Artisans and skilled workers above 68 years	1991	Death benefit of Rs 10000, Rs 500 as medical and disability assistance at Rs 100 per month; scholarship for children; maternity benefit at Rs 500 for two live births for women members, retirement benefit, etc.	NA	278595

Cont.

App. Table A8.1 Cont.

Name of the scheme	Qualifying/Eligibility conditions	Year of starting assistance 1992–3	Rate of assistance	Amount spent (Rs in lakhs)	No. of persons received
Kerala motor workers welfare fund		1986	Retirement benefit PF etc. A member will get about Rs 12000 for 5 years of contribution and Rs 60,000 if continues as member for 15 years		29332
Kerala freedom fighters pension scheme		1971	Rs 500 pm	660.50	12000
Financial assistance to leprosy and cancer patients	Leprosy and cancer patients are covered; certificates from hospitals are to be produced; income of the patients not to exceed Rs 50 pm	1976	Rs 100 pm	31.75	5300
Kerala fishermen's welfare scheme	Bonafide fishermen who have completed 60 years of age	1987	NA	220.21	25780
Kerala labour welfare fund scheme		1989	NA	NA	405706
Self-employment scheme	Unemployed persons	1980	Rs 600 pm	15.92	2653

Note: NA—Not available.
Source: Rajan et al. (1999).

9

Employment Generation Policy and Social Safety Nets in India

Alakh N. Sharma

1. Employment and Labour Policies in Retrospect

1.1 Strategy for Employment Generation During Planning Period

Employment expansion—at a pace adequate to absorb the unemployed and those entering the labour force and also for ensuring that this is brought about at rising levels of productivity and incomes—has been an important concern of development policy in India. The overall approach adopted in the early years of planning emphasized utilization of labour for development rather than tackling the problem of unemployment as such. Unemployment was not perceived as a major problem warranting independent treatment either in plan modelling or in plan programmes (Papola 1992, p. 300). The first Five Year Plan followed a strategy based on a long term perspective with a focus on acceleration in the growth rate of the economy. The plan showed some concern about the problem of underemployment and made some proposals for employment generation in agriculture and allied occupations, irrigation, and villages and small industries and services in the urban context (Planning Commission, 1953) The second Five Year Plan (1956–61) recognized the poor performance on the employment front, reflected in an increase in the backlog of unemployment and underemployment (Planning Commission 1956, p. 27). The plan accorded a relatively higher priority to the capital goods sector along with the objective of increasing the role of cottage and small industries for augmenting the supply of consumer goods. However, the thinking on employment continued to be dominated by factors such as the critical role of investment, labour productivity, importance of the use of machinery, and new techniques for higher productivity. The plan's thinking on the sectoral pattern of employment became crystallized around the position that a shift of workforce from agriculture towards mining and modern small and large industries and transport, construction and communication is inherent in the very process of development. The Third Plan (1961–6) hardly showed any change in the basic strategy towards employment generation. The plan emphasized the area approach in order to respond to the needs of the specific occupational and skill groups (Planning Commission 1962, p. 160).

The backlog of unemployment at the start of the Second Plan and the net addition to labour force during the period 1956–61 were estimated at 50 lakhs and 80 lakhs respectively, which could be taken care of over a period of 10 years with the envisaged growth rate of GDP at 5 per cent per annum. Employment creation was thus treated as a corrolary of the development process in the early plans.

During the 1960s and the 1970s the Indian economy experienced an average growth rate of around 3.5 per cent per annum. Employment growth was around 2 per cent per annum during the period 1961–83, as against the rate of growth of labour force at 2.5 per cent during the 1960s and 1970s leading to a rise in the backlog of unemployment from 50 lakhs in 1956 to 1 crore 10 lakhs in 1977–8. The shift in the structure of employment during this period was also very small compared to changes in the structure of output. The share of agriculture and allied sectors in GDP declined from 54 per cent in 1960–1 to about 39 per cent in 1983–4, while the share of agriculture in employment declined from 73 per cent in 1961 to only 69 per cent in 1983 implying thereby a relative deterioration in average productivity and income levels in agriculture. Estimates of poverty based on levels of consumption expenditure derived from large scale sample surveys initiated in the early 1970s also showed that about 54 per cent of the rural population was below the poverty line defined in terms of the average total consumption expenditure of the households for meeting the per capita norm of 2400 calories in rural areas and 2100 calories in urban areas. These trends in the incidence of unemployment and levels of poverty raised doubts about the efficacy of growth in tackling these problems. Although the Fourth Plan (1969–74) stressed greater investment in industry and infrastructure by the public sector in the wake of prolonged recession, some target group oriented programmes along with some ad hoc self and wage employment programmes were initiated, which provided only some relief. By the mid-1970s employment was regarded as the most important challenge to be met in the Fifth Plan (1974–9) and a solution was sought primarily in changing the pattern of growth. A view that growth alone could not take care of these problems soon emerged leading to the introduction of a number of special employment programmes in the late 1970s.

Acceleration of growth rate while attempting to deal with the problem of unemployment and poverty through special employment programmes thus became a central element of the strategy of the Sixth and Seventh Five Year Plans. Accordingly, many special programmes for poorer groups including women, tribals, unorganized urban poor, etc. were launched (Planning Commission 1980). Groups of people such as bonded labour, child labour, the educated unemployed, also attracted specific attention. While the economy experienced a relatively high growth of about 5.5 per cent per annum during these plans (Sixth and Seventh) employment growth was estimated to be only 1.8 per cent during 1978–88 and unemployment to have risen to about 1.5 crores by that year and further to 1.7 crores by the end of 1991–2 (Planning Commission 1992). And this was so in spite of the implementation of special employment programmes having been implemented on a large scale during the 1980s. Thus, arguments that neither a higher growth rate nor special employment progammes per se could provide an effective solution to the problem of unemployment began to be advanced in the early 1990s and the need for an employment oriented growth strategy was emphasized. The Eighth Plan sought to adopt a strategy which combined a high level of growth with an emphasis on employment generation which would ensure faster growth of employment intensive sectors, sub-sectors, and activities. The launching of the Plan coincided with the initiation of economic reforms in India.

The strategies of the Eighth Plan included (i) a faster and geographically widespread growth of agriculture; (ii) development of infrastructure and marketing arrangements for agro-based and allied activities; (iii) an expanded programme of development and utilization of wastelands; (iv) development of an appropriate support and policy framework for the growth of non-agricultural activities in rural areas; and (v) laying greater stress on meeting the needs of the small and decentralized manufacturing sector as a major source of industrial growth. The Plan also provided for revamping of training systems to introduce greater flexibility and responsiveness to labour market trends and larger involvement of users of the system's output, and provision of opportunities for upgradation of skills of the employed workers as also for the development of entrepreneurship for the actual and potential self-employed. The Ninth Plan (1997–2002) recognized the importance of productive work and the primary objective of the Plan was to generate greater productive employment in the growth process itself by concentrating on sectors, sub-sectors, and technologies which are more labour intensive in regions characterised by higher rates of unemployment and under-employment. It also laid stress on the quality of employment, regional dimensions of employment, tackling the problem of educated unemployment and the need for increasing agricultural productivity for ensuring the productive absorption of the labour force. The Plan also focused on special employment programmes, particularly those relating to wage employment.

The Tenth Five Year Plan (2002–7) is being launched, when there is deceleration in the growth rate of employment generation (from over 2 per cent during 1983–94 to about 1 per cent during 1994–2000) and second generation of economic reforms including labour market reforms is being sought to be introduced. The Approach Paper to the Plan targets a growth rate of 8 per cent in GDP and envisages to provide gainful high quality employment to the addition to the labour force over the Tenth Plan period. According to the Approach Paper,

> the growth strategy of the Tenth Plan must ensure rapid growth of those sectors which are most likely to create high quality employment opportunities and deal with the policy constraints which discourage growth of employment. Particular attention would be paid to the policy environment influencing a wide range of economic activities which have a large employment potential (Planning Commission 2001a, p. 5).

The approach paper as a whole lays considerable emphasis on qualitative aspect of employment. In order to enable the poor to access the opportunities and to ensure consistency between the requirements and the availability of skills, emphasis will need to be placed on skill development. It also pleads for the continuing need to supplement the impact of growth with special programmes aimed at special target groups which may not benefit sufficiently from the normal growth process.

1.2 Ingredients of Labour Policy

The essential ingredient of social policy concerning labour and employment, particularly during the first three decades of planning, has been to treat labour not as a mere resource for development, but as a partner in and beneficiary of social and economic development. This philosophy of labour has its roots in the national movement. In fact many of the legislative provisions for protecting labour were enacted before independence which were further strengthened later. Accordingly, comprehensive legislations relating to conditions of work in various sectors, which already existed earlier, were strengthened; provisions of social security were made comprehensive and expanded to include various kinds of risks. Further, detailed laws governing industrial relations and industrial disputes were enacted, and a mechanism for fixing and implementing minimum wages was developed. The basic philosophy behind all these measures was to ensure that labour is not exploited by being employed in sub-human conditions; or subjected to unfair practices in respect of payment of wages, dismissals and retrenchments. While payment of wages is reasonable and fair; minimum security is provided against risks (such as injuries and accidents at work), sickness, maternity, and old age. Industrial relations have provided a measure of job security by specifying procedures for settlement of industrial disputes and also stipulating restrictions on employers in laying off and retrenching workers. The basic idea behind all these comprehensive and well meaning protective measures adopted for labour was that some section of the workforce was the relatively weaker partner vis-à-vis capital in the production process and that in a poor country like India it was desirable to safeguard them not only on considerations of social justice, but also for promoting an appropriate industrial and productive climate.

The legislative measures taken in India have often been described as excessive and have been held responsible for slowing down the growth of employment by discouraging investment and growth. It has also been argued by many that, as such, protection is provided to only a small section of the workforce (nearly 8 per cent in India), the generation of employment will take place mostly in the unprotected unorganized sector with deplorable conditions of work and as a result the proportion of protected workers would decline. In the process, the very objective of providing social protection to a majority of workers gets defeated.

In the earlier years of planning when the expectations of economic growth were higher and unemployment was not thought to be a serious problem, the issues did not draw much attention. However, with the significant slowing down of employment growth in the organized sector during the 1980s and also the not so encouraging trends in the 1990s the debate has intensified in recent years, more so after the introduction of economic reforms in the early 1990s. It has been argued that overprotection to a small section of workers is not only inimical to growth of employment, but also goes against social justice as the number of workers with deplorable conditions of work is increasing. Of late, restrictive provision in this regard have come under attack, as they are supposed to negate an 'exit policy' considered necessary for industrial restructuring and attracting foreign investment.

2. Trend and Pattern of Employment and Unemployment in Recent Years

2.1 Trend in Employment Growth

Employment in India has grown at an average annual rate of around 2 per cent over the past five decades or so (Table 9.1). The growth rate has varied in different sub-periods—it grew at less than 1 per cent during the 1950s, but over 2 per cent during the 1960s. The 1970s saw an employment growth of slightly lower than 2 per cent per annum, which decelerated to about 1.8 per cent during the 1980s. During the early 1990s it further decelerated but rose a little to over 2 per cent after 1992. But the later half of the 1990s has shown considerable decline in the employment growth to about 1 per cent.

The growth of employment needs to be seen in relation to the demand for and supply of labour. The demand for labour is basically determined by the rate and pattern of growth, particularly the former. The economy registered an annual average growth rate of around 3.5 per cent in GDP from 1950s to 1970s and over 5.5 per cent during the 1980s. The growth rate decelerated to below 4 per cent in early 1990s, but again accelerated over 6 per cent during 1992–7 and 1997–2000. The growth rates, of course, fluctuated over different sub-periods, as can be seen from the estimates of GDP growth in different five year plans and during the intervening annual plan periods (Table 9.1).

Table 9.1
Growth Rate of GDP and Employment

Plans	Annual Average Growth Rates	
	GDP	Employment
1951–6(First Five Year Plan)	3.6	0.39
1956–61 (Second Five Year Plan)	4.2	0.85
1961–6 (Third Five Year Plan)	2.8	2.03
1967–9 (Annual Plans)	3.9	2.21
1969–74 (Fourth Five Year Plan)	3.3	1.99
1974–9 (Fifth Five Year Plan)	4.8	1.84
1980–5 (Sixth Five Year Plan)	5.7	1.73
1985–90 (Seventh Five Year Plan)	5.8	1.89
1990–2 (Annual Plans)	3.4	1.50
1992–7 (Eighth Five Year Plan)	6.5	2.44
1997–2000 (Three years of Ninth Five Year Plan)	6.1	0.98 *

Note: *Pertain to the year from 1993–4 to 1999–2000.
Source: Planning Commission, Government of India, Five Year Plan Documents.

One of the reasons for the slow growth of employment during the 1950s, apart from the slower rate of GDP growth, was that large investments were made in infrastructure industries which had a low potential for direct employment generation and relatively long gestation periods. As a result employment during this period grew slower even in relation to the low GDP. As a result of the secondary effects of heavy investments made earlier, the growth of employment was faster even with low GDP in the 1960s. Although the growth in GDP picked up since the mid-1970s and accelerated during the 1980s, the growth in employment did not pick up correspondingly. This was largely because a significant component of the GDP growth came from productivity growth. Further, the industries which grew faster were not employment intensive. The recent decline in the growth of employment is being attributed to the increasing capital-intensity of the economy as well as the much slower growth of the labour force than had been expected.

The results of the 50th round of the NSSO have shown a sharp decline in the growth rate of employment (UPSS) from 2.04 per cent per year in the period 1983 to 1993–4 to only 0.98 per cent in the period 1993–4 to 1999–2000, which has raised considerable concern.[1] Although this deceleration in employment is associated with an equally sharp decline in the rate of growth of the labour force from 2.29 per cent in the period 1987–8 to 1993–4 to only 1.03 per cent in the period 1993–4 to 1999–2000, there is no doubt that the employment growth has been inadequate—the growth rate of employment is less than the growth rate of the labour force indicating an increase in the unemployment rate. When seen in terms of sectoral distribution, it is observed that the deceleration in the employment growth during 1994–2000 is basically due to the stagnancy of agricultural employment as compared to the period 1983 to 1994 when agricultural employment grew by about 1.5 per cent per annum. As a result, the proportion of workers employed in agriculture, which declined from 68.5 per cent in 1983 to 64.8 per cent in 1993–4, declined more sharply to 59.8 per cent in 1999–2000. Another sector which has stagnated is the services. In fact, these two sectors—

[1]The NSSO comprehensive surveys provide estimates of employment and unemployment on the basis of three criteria—the Usual Status (US), the Current Weekly Status (CWS), and the Current Daily Status (CDS). Under the US criterion, estimates are available on the basis of the Usual Principal Status (UPS) and also by taking into account the subsidiary gainful status of persons categorized as not working in principal status (UPSS). In the CWS, a person is considered employed if he/she was engaged for at least one hour on any one day of the preceding one week in any gainful activity. While estimates of employment and unemployment based on UPS, UPSS, and CWS criteria are in terms of person, those based on CDS basis are in person days. While UPS estimates of employment could be considered as representing the magnitude of stable employment since they represent the number of persons who are employed for relatively larger part of the year, those on the basis of UPSS and CWS take note of those with intermittent employment also. Estimates based on CDS criterion are the most inclusive inasmuch as they provide an idea of the person days of employment of those with stable employment as well as those with intermittent work.

agriculture and services which comprise large share of employment—have almost zero employment elasticity during 1994–2000 as against 0.50 during 1983–94 (Table 9.2). Employment in sectors like trade, construction, financial services and transport, storage and communication has grown faster than the average and the share of these sectors in total employment, therefore, has increased. The share of manufacturing to total employment has also increased but only marginally (Table 9.2).

Table 9.2
Employment Growth and Elasticities in Different Sectors
1983–2000 (UPSS)

	Annual growth rate (%)		Employment elasticities	
	1983–94	1994–2000	1983–94	1994–2000
Agriculture	1.51	–0.34	0.50	0.00
Mining+quarrying	4.16	–2.85	0.69	0.00
Manufacturing	2.14	2.05	0.33	0.26
Elect., gas and water supply	4.50	–0.88	0.52	0.00
Construction	5.32	7.09	1.00	1.00
Trade	3.57	5.04	0.63	0.55
Transport, storage, etc.	3.24	6.04	0.49	0.69
Financial services	7.18	6.20	0.92	0.73
Community, social and personal services	2.90	0.55	0.50	0.07
All sectors	2.04	0.98	0.41	0.15

Source: Planning Commission 2001b.

In a developing country like India the availability of employment does not capture the whole scenario and hence the quality of employment should be taken into account. This is evident from the fact that overall rate of unemployment in the country as per UPSS criterion was as low as 2.23 per cent in 1999–2000 and even on CDS criterion it goes up only to 7.3 per cent, whereas the percentage of people below poverty line is as high as 26.1. Obviously the problem is that of the 'working poor' as the productivity of employment is very low. The low productivity of employment is basically because of low educational and skill levels of the workers. About 44 per cent of all workers in 1999–2000 were illiterate and another 22.7 per cent had schooling only up to the primary level. Further, only 10.1 per cent of the male workers and 6.3 per cent of the female workers passed specific workable skills in rural areas in 1999–2000. Although the percentages were higher in urban areas, still they were very low—only 19.6 per cent for male workers and 11.2 per cent for female workers. The level of vocational skills in the labour force in India compares very poorly not only with the developed countries, but also with several developing countries. Only 5 per cent of the labour force in the age group 20–4 years has vocational skills.

Another important aspect related to the quality of employment is the status of employment. As high as 53 per cent of the total workforce in all sectors was engaged in self-employment in 1999–2000—the proportion was 56 per cent in rural areas and 42 per cent in urban areas (Table 9.3). Self-employed is a heterogeneous category consisting of big cultivators, high income earning professionals (such as doctors and lawyers), as well as a large majority of poor people like marginal farmers, hawkers and artisans. The share of self-employment has declined from 58.9 per cent in 1977–8 to 52.9 per cent in 1999–2000—the decline has been largely in rural areas. The share of regular salaried employment, which is the best form of employment, has fluctuated around 14 per cent for the economy as a whole—as expected it is much higher in urban areas at around 40 per cent and lower in rural areas at around 7 per cent. However, there is a sharp increase in the share of casual employment overtime—it increased from 27.2 per cent in 1977–8 to 33.2 per cent in 1999–2000 (Table 9.3). The increase is sharper in rural areas where it increased from 29.7 per cent in 1977–8 to 37.3 per cent in 1999–2000, reflecting the displacement of marginal cultivators and their conversion into agricultural labourers. Although the rise in the proportion of casual employment usually reflects the deterioration in the quality of employment, it is worth mentioning that increase in the casualization in the 1990s has been associated with the a rise in the growth of real wages (Table 9.4). Male as well as female wages registered considerable rise during 1994–2000 as compared to 1988–94.

An important aspect of the employment situation in India is the distinction between the organized and the unorganized sector. The size of the organized sector, characterized by higher earnings and job security, is small—it was only about 7 per cent of the total employment in 1999–2000. Over two-thirds of total organized sector employment is in the public sector. Over the years the organized sector employment has grown more slowly than the total employment,

Table 9.3
Distribution of Workers (Usual Status) by Category of Employment

(per cent)

Year	Category of employment		
	Self-employment	Regular salaried	Casual
Rural Areas			
1977–8	62.6	7.7	29.7
1983	61.0	7.5	31.5
1987–8	59.4	7.7	32.9
1993–4	58.0	6.4	35.6
1999–2000	56.0	6.7	37.3
Urban Areas			
1977–8	42.4	41.8	15.8
1983	41.8	40.0	18.2
1987–8	42.8	40.3	16.9
1993–4	42.3	39.4	18.3
1999–2000	42.1	40.1	17.8
Total			
1977–8	59.9	13.9	27.2
1983	57.4	13.9	28.7
1987–8	56.0	14.4	29.6
1993–4	54.8	13.2	32.0
1999-2000	52.9	13.9	33.2

Source: NSSO Surveys on Employment and Unemployment.

Table 9.4
Growth of Average Daily Wage Earnings in Rural India
(1993–4 prices)

	Rural males		Rural females	
	1987–8 to 1993–4	1993–4 to 1999–2000	1987–8 to 1993–4	1993–4 to 1999–2000
Public works	1.55	3.83	1.90	5.04
Casual labour in agriculture	1.36	2.80	2.34	2.94
Casual labour in non-agriculture	1.33	3.70	1.32	5.07
Casual labour in all activities	0.77	3.59	1.95	3.19

Source: NSSO Surveys on Employment and Unemployment for 1987–8, 1993–4 and 1999–2000.

reflecting the faster growth of employment in the unorganized sector. Organized sector employment grew at an average of 1.20 per cent per annum during 1983–94 but the growth rate was as low as 0.53 per cent between 1994 and 1999. This deceleration was entirely due to the slowing down in employment in the public sector from a growth rate of 1.52 per cent per year between 1983 and 1994 to a negative growth of –0.03 per cent per year during 1994–9. On the contrary, the organized private sector grew at the rate of 1.87 per cent per annum between 1994 and 1999 as against the growth rate of only 0.45 per cent between 1983 and 1994. As can be seen from Table 9.5 though the overall proportion of organized sector employment has come down only marginally between 1993–4 and 1999–2000, the proportion has considerably decreased in construction, transport, storage and communication, and financial services. Manufacturing, construction, trade, and transport are such sectors where there is a large concentration of unorganized workers.

Table 9.5
Organized Sector Jobs in Employment by Industry

Industry	Employment 10 lakhs				Share of organized sector (per cent)	
	1993–4		1999–2000			
	Total@	Organized sector*	Total@	Organized sector*	1993–4	1999–2000
Agriculture	242.46	1.48	237.56	1.39	0.61	0.58
Mining and quarrying	2.70	1.09	2.27	1.01	40.37	44.49
Manufacturing	42.50	6.40	48.01	6.75	15.05	14.06
Electricity	1.35	0.97	1.28	1.00	71.85	78.13
Construction	11.68	1.23	17.62	1.18	10.53	6.70
Wholesale and retail trade	27.78	0.45	37.32	0.49	1.62	1.31
Transport, storage and communication	10.33	3.11	14.69	3.15	30.11	21.44
Financial services	3.52	1.53	5.05	1.65	43.46	32.67
Community, social and personal services	32.13	10.93	33.20	11.49	34.02	34.61
All sectors	374.45	27.18	397.00	28.11	7.26	7.08

Notes: *As on 31.3.1993 and 31.3.1999; @As on 1.1.1994 and 1.1.2000.
Source: DGE&T for employment in organized sector; 55th Round Survey of NSSO for total employment.

Thus the trend and available evidence suggest that the bulk of the growth in employment in future will come from the unorganized sector only. How to ensure that this sector can provide a sufficient supply of high quality job opportunities is a major challenge, which should be addressed seriously by the employment planners.

2.2 Trends in Unemployment

In India the open unemployment rate is low (mainly because of high participation rate of the poor). The unemployment rate is as low as 2.23 per cent in 1999–2000 as per UPSS criterion (which refers to percentage of individuals in the labour force classified as unemployed) but it rises to 7.32 per cent based on the CDS criterion (which refers to the percentage of unemployment in terms of person days) (Table 9.6). The recent years have shown a rise in the unemployment rate. The UPSS measure shows a modest increase in the rate of unemployment in the 1990s from 1.9 per cent in 1993–4 to 2.23 per cent in 1999–2000, but the CDS measure shows a sharper increase

Table 9.6
Unemployment Rates: Alternative Measures

(per cent of labour force)

	Usual principal status (UPS)	Usual principal and subsidiary status (UPSS)	Current weekly status (CWS)	Current daily status (CDS)
Rural				
1977–8	3.26	1.54	3.74	7.70
1983	1.91	1.13	3.88	7.94
1987–8	3.07	1.98	4.19	5.25
1993–4	1.80	1.20	3.00	5.63
1999–2000	1.96	1.43	3.91	7.21
Urban				
1977–8	8.77	7.01	7.86	10.34
1983	6.04	5.02	6.81	9.52
1987–8	6.56	5.32	7.12	9.36
1993–4	5.21	4.52	5.83	7.43
1999–2000	5.23	4.63	5.89	7.65
All India				
1977–8	4.23	2.47	4.48	8.18
1983	2.77	1.90	4.51	8.28
1987–8	3.77	2.62	4.80	6.09
1993–4	2.56	1.90	3.63	6.03
1999–2000	2.81	2.23	4.41	7.32

from 6.03 per cent to 7.32 per cent. It is important to note that all the four measures show an increase in unemployment rate reversing the decline witnessed in the precious period. Female unemployment rates are significantly higher than male unemployment rates though the difference has narrowed down over time and was almost completely eliminated in rural areas in 1995–2000 (Table 9.7). Female unemployment in urban areas was 9.8 per cent compared with 7.2 per cent for male unemployment. As a matter of fact, as the number of women, particularly in urban areas, entering into the labour market is likely to increase in future, the employment strategy has to take effective steps to generate employment suitable to women workers.

Table 9.7
Unemployment* among Males and Females

(per cent of labour force)

Survey period	Rural areas			Urban areas		
	Male	Female	Persons	Male	Female	Persons
1977–8	7.1	9.2	7.7	9.4	14.5	10.3
1983	7.5	9.0	7.9	9.2	11.0	9.5
1987–8	4.6	6.7	5.3	8.8	12.0	9.4
1993–4	5.6	5.6	5.6	6.7	10.5	7.4
1999–2000	7.2	7.3	7.2	7.2	9.8	7.7

Note: *Unemployment rate on current daily status basis.
Source: NSSO Surveys on Employment and Unemployment.

The unemployment rates are significantly higher in the younger age groups, in the crucial age group of 15–29 years, the unemployment rate (CDS) was as high as 12.1 per cent in 1999–2000 (11 per cent for rural and 15.5 per cent for urban) as against 7.2 for the population as a whole. Another important aspect of the unemployment situation is the very high rate of unemployment among the educated compared to those with lower levels of education. The unemployment rate (UPSS) for the illiterates is as low as 0.2 per cent rising to 1.2 for literates up to primary school and 3.3 per cent for middle school. For the category of educated (secondary and above) the rate was 7.1 per cent, which is more than 3 times the unemployment rate on the UPSS basis for the population as a whole (Table 9.8). This difference clearly indicates the large mismatch between expectations and available employment opportunities for the more educated and highlights the need for employment strategies to focus on employment quality. This mismatch is more evident in the case of the unemployment of educated youth. The unemployment rate for educated (secondary and above) persons in the age group of 15–29 in 1993–4 was as high as 18.5 per cent—the rate was much higher at 27.3 per cent for having technical education. It is important to note that the incidence of unemployment among educated youth, both for general and technical education declined sharply between 1993–4 and 1999–2000, although the rates are still very high. However, most of the employed educated youth are joining the labour markets as either self employed or casual workers, which shows that the informal sector is increasingly absorbing more and more educated workers because of limited opportunities in the organized sector.

Table 9.8
Unemployment* by Level of Education

(per cent of labour force)

Education level	Unemployment rate 1987–8	1993–4	1999–2000
Not literate	1.1	0.2	0.2
Literate upto primary	1.9	0.9	1.2
Middle	5.3	3.4	3.3
Secondary	8.7	6.2	5.5
Higher Secondary	–	8.7	7.8
Secondary + Higher Secondary	–	7.1	–
Graduate and above	9.9	9.3	8.8
Educated (secondary and above)	9.0	7.7	7.1
All	2.7	1.9	2.2

Note: * Unemployment rates on usual principal and subsidiary status basis.
Source: NSSO Surveys, 43rd Round (1987–8), 50th Round (1993–4), and 55th Round (1999–2000).

3. Manufacturing Sector Employment, Industrial Restructuring, and Labour Adjustment

A major concern, that has been often expressed, is the continued declining rate of growth of employment in the manufacturing sector. Manufacturing employment, constituting about 10 per cent of the total employment, which grew at an annual average rate of 5.83 per cent during 1973–8, could experience a growth rate of only 2.92 and

2.62 per cent during 1978–83 and 1983–8, respectively. The growth rate further declined to 1.70 per cent during 1988–94—the period which witnessed a recovery in many sectors. During 1994–2000 the growth in manufacturing employment was recovered only marginally—2.05 per cent. It needs to be noted that this decline has not taken place because of deceleration in the rate of growth of this sector (even during 1988–94, the growth rate was 5.10 per cent), but due to falling elasticity of employment which declined from 1.14 during 1973–8, to 0.53 during 1978–83, and further to 0.42 and 0.33 during 1983–8 and 1988–94 respectively. The elasticity further declined to 0.26 per cent during 1994–2000.

The declining trend in the organized manufacturing sector employment has been a matter of considerable debate in recent years. It has been attributed by many scholars to the rigidities in the labour market leading to high labour adjustment cost (Lucas 1988; Fallon and Lucas 1991; Ahluwalia 1992). These rigidities have been mainly of two types: job security provisions; and lack of any relation between productivity and wages. It has been argued that the legal provisions of job security and institutional factors such as the trade unions make it difficult to adjust the workforce of enterprises necessitated by the requirements of technological change and efficiency. It is also contended that the inflexibility caused by legal provisions and unions has discouraged enterprises, at least in the organized sector of the Indian industry, from expanding employment as they fear that it will not be possible for them to reduce it subsequently if warranted by compulsions of competitive efficiency. According to Fallon and Lucas (1991), employment in the organized manufacturing would have been 17.5 per cent higher in the absence of job security regulations.

The considerable increase in real wages has also been held responsible for the sharp fall in the registered manufacturing sector. According to Fallon and Lucas (1991), the faster growth of industrial wages relative to consumer prices for industrial workers, abetted by union militancy and job security provisions, resulted in a significant long term reduction of employment during 1959–60 to 1998–2002. According to Ahluwalia (1992), a 34 per cent increase in the real wages of manufacturing sector workers between 1980–1 and 1985–6, significantly contributed to a decline in employment during that period.

Papola (1994), taking into account pros and cons of the

employment generation vis-à-vis rigidities in the Indian labour market, has examined the issue in detail. Citing recent trends at disaggregated levels and findings of some studies, he has concluded that the real wage increase during the 1980s does not seem to be important in promoting employers to opt for capital intensive technologies which led to stagnation in employment in the Indian manufacturing industries. According to him, the real wage increase did not necessarily lead to higher unit labour cost that should have discouraged employers from expanding employment and resorting to labour intensive techniques as high increases in real wages were generally closely associated with high increase in labour productivity across industry groups. Overall the correlation coefficient between annual increases in wages and productivity during 1970–1 to 1987–8 for all industries works out as high as 0.91; in most industries it was higher than 0.70, significant at 1 per cent level (Papola 1994). Further, Nagraj (1993) doubts even the extent of the real wage increase in the manufacturing sector. His estimate for the period 1979–80 to 1988–9, shows that about one half of the observed increase in earnings per worker during this period, at 3.2 per cent per annum, was accounted for by an increase in the number of man days per worker, and earnings per man day, in fact, increased only by 1.6 per cent per annum. According to the data from Occupational Wage Surveys, the wage rate per worker per day showed a still lower increase in real terms (Nagraj 1993).

As such, wage increase does not seem to be a very important factor in reducing the employment in the organized manufacturing sector. This is also corroborated by the fact that by and large organizations and industry have not made wage increase their main targets of reform in the labour market. In fact minimum wages have always been set lower than the prevailing market wages in industry and as such their rationality has also not been questioned. Most of the industries' organizations as well as several scholars have found that the job security regulations which were strengthened during the 1980s by changes in law restricted the flexibility in the labour market. Changes made in the Industrial Disputes Act 1976 made it necessary for enterprises employing 300 or more workers to seek government permission to effect lay-offs, retrenchments and closures, and later in 1982 these provisions were made applicable to establishments employing 100 or more workers. It has been argued that because of these rigid provisions the employers were highly reluctant to increase the number of employees, because if required by consideration of efficiency and competition, they were to reduce their workforce they would not able to do so due to the delays involved and refusal of permission by the government. As such, the industries either opted for more capital intensive technologies or contracted out an increasingly large volume of work to smaller enterprises where the provision of government permission did not apply.

Although, the stringent job security regulation may be one reason for the slower growth of employment, this may not be the sole or even major factor in restricting growth in employment in the organized manufacturing sector. As noted by Papola (1994), the decline in employment in this sector during the 1980s was largely accounted for by a large reduction in employment in only two major industry groups—cotton textiles and food products, which account for one-third of the total employment in the organized sector. These two industries experienced a decline of more than 3.5 per cent per annum during the 1980s, which was mainly due to the closure of a large number of mills due to sickness caused by several reasons and rationalization of many of them to overcome obsolescence. Most other industry groups including those with high wage levels and capital intensity, experienced growth in employment. It should be noted also that the decline in employment in the organized manufacturing sector is not accompanied by a faster rate of growth in the unorganized manufacturing sector. In fact, both organized and unorganized manufacturing sectors have shown a continuous decline in the growth rate of employment since early 1970s. Thus slow growth of employment in the aggregate cannot be attributed mainly to protective labour legislation and unionism.

An important reason for the decline in the growth of employment seems to be structural and technological characteristics of the industrial growth induced primarily by demand and efficiency considerations. That is why manufacturing growth during the 1980s has been contributed mainly by capital-intensive sectors like chemicals, fertilizers, petroleum products, and electrical machinery or by industries such as food products which, though labour intensive, have experienced rapid rate of technological change. As a matter of fact, during the 1980s the economy as a whole including agriculture, became less and less employment-intensive as reflected in the declining employment elasticities in all the major sectors.

It will be interesting to see the pattern of employment growth in organized manufacturing in recent years and compare this with the earlier years. The analysis of organized manufacturing from 1973 to 1997 reveals a revival in the organized manufacturing employment (Goldar 2002). The growth rate of total manufacturing employment as a whole during the period 1990 to 1997—the period of economic reforms—was about 3 per cent per annum compared to only about 1.6 per cent during 1973 to 1989 (Table 9.9). This has been accompanied by very high growth in capital intensity and labour productivity. However, the rise in real emoluments (which includes wages and other benefits) have been rather low. Apparently this has been achieved by buoyant demand conditions as reflected by about 9.35 per cent growth in gross value added in the manufacturing sector as a whole. However, because of increasing capital intensity, employment elasticity declined from 0.45 during 1973–89 to 0.16 during 1989–97. It is worth noting that this kind of growth has been achieved even with existing job regulations.

Table 9.9
Growth Rate of Value Added, Employment Elasticity, and Real Wages in Organized Manufacturing, 1973–7

	1973 to 1989	1990 to 1997
Gross value added	6.18	9.35
Employment	1.60	3.09
Real wages per worker	3.15	1.16

Source: Goldar (2002).

The evidences at microlevel also point towards the increasing labour market flexibility in the wake of economic reforms in India. A comprehensive survey of about 1300 firms scattered over 10 states and nine important manufacturing industry groups, shows that between 1991 and 1998, employment increased at the rate 2.84 per cent per annum (Deshpande et al. 2001). Non-manual employment increased at 5 per cent per annum whereas manual employment increased at 2.29 per cent. This increase in total employment was brought about by increasing the share of non-permanent employees and increase in manual employment by increasing the share of women workers. Smaller firms grew faster than bigger firms. Firms, which increased sales, increased manual employment as did those which employed contract workers. Employees who increased fixed capital per worker reduced manual employment. Employers increased employment but only of one or other category of non-regular flexible workers.

It was found that as a whole over the seven years of liberalization (between 1991 and 1998) dualism in the labour market increased. The share of permanent manual workers declined from close to 68 per cent in 1991 to 64 per cent in 1998. Not only did the share of non-permanent workers increase but the share of the casual among non-permanent workers increased even faster. It is the big firms that resorted to the greater use of non-permanent workers. Holding all other factors constant, firms that employed 50–99 workers as also those that employed 500 or more workers, increased the share of non-permanent workers significantly between 1991 and 1998. Also, firms employing 500 workers or more increased the share of temporary workers. Casual employment did not show an association with size of employment. Women workers were mostly employed in large firms. Firms that employed 1000 workers or more accounted for more than 75 per cent of all women workers. Firms that employ a higher share of non-permanent workers also employ a higher share of women. Firms that employ 50–99 workers and those that employ 500 and over also report an increase in the share of female workers.

The study found that in the sample firms basic wages are determined largely by minimum wage level and to a very small extent by collective bargaining in the larger firms. Payment of separate DA was reported by only 12 per cent of the firms whereas consolidated wage was reported by 75 per cent. Collective bargaining was associated with separate DA, other allowances, and higher rates of bonus. The study showed that both unionized and non-unionized firms increased the capital intensity of the firm. Hence, unions could not be blamed for forcing employers to adopt capital intensive technology. Union absence appears to be slightly more conducive to the growth of employment than union pressure. Holding other factors constant, firms with unions paid the unskilled and skilled workers about 17 per cent more than those without unions. The greater the share of women in employment, the lower was the wage paid both to the unskilled and skilled male worker but the higher the share of contract, the higher the wage paid to the skilled worker. Generally unions raised the wages of the unskilled more than those of the skilled thereby reducing wage differentials based on skill. Taking all the evidence of what unions do and their limited presence in manufacturing it seems unlikely that their impact would be intolerably strong (Deshpande et al. 2001).

Some other studies done at the microlevel also point out that flexibility in the labour market has increased after the introduction of economic reforms in India.[2] In spite of the existence of labour laws, firms have been able to retrench a large number of permanent workers. As a whole, union power has declined and employers' militancy has increased. The closure of a large number of units has also led to unemployment of a large number of workers.

From the discussions so far, one should not hasten to conclude that there is no rigidity in the Indian labour market. Irrespective of its impact on employment, a degree of protection to labour may lead to inflexibility in labour adjustment required for restructuring of enterprises in the interest of competitive efficiency. In the wake of liberalization, this problem has been brought into centre stage and there has been frequent demand by the industry and foreign investors to have some kind of 'exit' policy—the right of hiring and firing.

In this respect the provisions of the Industrial Disputes Act which lays down conditions and procedures for retrenchment of workers have been widely criticized. It is contended that the provisions are so restrictive that reduction in workforce or closures is extremely difficult even if the employer is agreeable to pay the compensation as required under the law. This is because under the law prior permission of the government is required to retrench workers or effect closures in the case of enterprises employing more than 100 workers and such permissions are generally not granted by the government (mostly state governments)

Although, in spite of these obstacles, many enterprises were able to adjust their workforce by rationalization and technological changes, the process has not always been fair. Several routes have been found out—illegal closures by not paying electricity bills, etc.. All these have only added to the problem of labour—they are neither paid their wages nor their due compensation. This has also resulted in significant industrial

[2]See Sharma and Sasikumar (1996) who studied 233 firms located in Ghaziabad district and 16 fertilizer factories in different parts of the country. Also see Sharma (1997) for a review of the implication of economic reforms on labour and poverty at microlevel.

sickness as well as prevalence of redundancies leading to their uncompetitiveness. Although unions have generally resisted any legislative or executive move to make closure and retrenchment easier, in recent years unions at enterprise level have generally been found to be accepting the inevitability of adjustments in workforce in the face of globalization and industrial restructuring.

4. Economic Reforms and Safety net Measures

4.1 Labour Redundancies and National Renewal Fund

When the economic reforms in India were introduced in 1991, it was feared that a large number of workers would become redundant in the wake of economic restructuring. There is no firm estimate about the extent of redundancy in India in the wake of restructuring, but available evidences point towards significant numbers. According to one estimate, the potential labour redundancy would be around 4.4 million in the organized sector as a whole (which account for 16.5 per cent of total employment in the sector) (ILO–SATT 1996). The bulk of the potentially redundant labour is in the service sector. Indeed, public services, which account for more than two-thirds of all potentially redundant labour, appear to be the most important reservoir of surplus labour. Further, much of this surplus exists at the level of state and local governments. Recognizing the problem of redundancy and the need for rehabilitation, the Government of India, immediately after initiating the reforms in 1991, declared its intention to protect the interests of labour, enhance their welfare, and equip them to deal with the inevitable technological change.

The government set up a mechanism in the form of an organization called the Board of Industrial and Financial Reconstruction (BIFR) to examine and decide whether the sick private and public sector enterprises could be revived with restructuring or would have to be closed down. Several public sector units have been privatized through a policy of disinvestment. In the case of public sector enterprises, the pronounced policy of the government is to effect closures or retrenchments only as a last resort, after all avenues of reviving the unit and maintaining employment were exhausted. And where these measures were inevitable, a National Renewal Fund (NRF) was constituted in 1992–3 to enable enterprises to pay reasonable separation benefits, and assist the workers rendered redundant by their retraining and redeployment. The NRF had three parts: (a) an employment generation fund (EGF) to provide resources for approved employment schemes, to regenerate employment opportunities for employees affected by industrial restructuring in the unorganized sector; (b) the NRF to deal with the immediate requirements of labour in sick units arising from revival or closure of such units; and (c) an insurance fund for employees (IFE) to deal with the future changes in employment structure in the context of changes in technology and modernization.

The NRF was designed to provide assistance specifically for (i) retraining, redeployment and counselling and placement of workers rendered surplus; (ii) payment of compensation to such workers; (iii) payment of interest subsidies to enable financial institutions to provide soft loans for meeting the funding requirements of labour arising out of restructuring of weak units; and (iv) approved programmes for employment generation.

Till 2000–1, on account of Rs 30.60 billion was spent under NRF. (It has been abolished vide Government of India notification No. 7(4)2000, July 12, 2000). While the main objective of NRF was to help in retraining, counselling, and redeployment of affected workers, and also employment generation, both in the organized and the unorganized sectors of the economy, a major part (92.8 per cent) of the NRF expenditure was utilized for compensation payment under VRS.

Thus only 7.2 per cent of the NRF (Rs 2839.62) has gone for non-VRS activities like survey of workers, counselling, retraining, and redeployment during the period 1992–3 to 2000–1. The expenditure on employees assistance centres was a minuscule 0.32 per cent of NRF expenditure and 11.31 per cent of non-VRS expenditure. Also, the non-VRS allocation in NRF declined over the years—up to June 2001, 114,094 workers were surveyed of which 73194 were counselled, 55374 retrained and only 19043 redeployed. Thus about 40 per cent of VRS availees were retrained and merely 13.7 per cent could be redeployed under NRF (Mamgain, Parashar, and Datta 2001).

Displacement of a large number of the workforce through the mechanism of VRS without equipping them with adequate skill and training to reenter the job market, has resulted in a huge loss of productive manpower. Though, no major study has been undertaken to follow up the post-VRS vocation of the labour, a few studies have pointed out that a majority of these redundant workers have joined the unorganized sector as 'new poor' (Roy Choudhary 1996; Datta 2001). Roy Choudhary finds that 25 per cent of the displaced workers who are working as casual labourers, are not employed even for a full week, Displaced workers also face income loss—the average income of those re-employed dropped by about 44 per cent (Noronha 1999). Datta (2001) finds that though more than half the VRS availees could have found employment within a period of six months, most of them took self-employment in agriculture in their native village. This is a social waste of human potential and raises question about the 'training' objective of the NRF.

Thus the overall performance of retraining for redeployment under NRF has been extremely poor. This is a matter of concern because it shows that retraining is not perceived as a skills improvement strategy for redeployment. Counselling may also act as an important factor in popularizing retraining, though in some cases it has been restricted only to giving advice regarding optimum utilization of VRS funds received. An important factor responsible for the limited interest in training can be the time that elapsed between displacement and availability of counselling. Counselling should, therefore, begin early—ideally, right from the time when those potentially affected by retrenchment have been identified.

All this makes it extremely desirable to strengthen the retaining activities. At the outset, the focus of retraining should not be 'just some other skills for employment but enhancing core skills and intellectual skills of the workers which make them more flexible and adaptable and useful to the changing pattern of production'. As more and more industrial firms undertake restructuring and start operating in leading-edge technologies, the requirement of enhancing the core skills and higher order cognitive skills would become more important. This is a requirement not only for retraining but, even more importantly, for the initial training system. Sustainability of employment will depend on this focus (Chandra 1999).

Second, retraining of better educated high level workers should also be taken up. Even though many in these categories have not been displaced from central public sector undertakings in the first wave of restructuring, they may also be affected in future and would require retraining interventions for redeployment. Entrepreneurship development, training and preparing workers for careers in consultancy may be particularly important for this category.

Third, only fully equipped and recognized training institutions with relevant background and experience should be selected . While some effort has been made in this direction, there are instances of inappropriate institutions being entrusted with the responsibility of retraining.

Last, retraining should also focus on developing proper work culture and attitudinal development. Many private sector employers are not keen to hire workers displaced from organizations whose work culture they distrust. They also believe that these workers may not have the right attitude to be productive and efficient in their environment.

Apart from retraining in skills relating to potential jobs or self-employment opportunities, it is important to impart job search training to the displaced workers. There are examples that such training has yielded good results and reduced the duration of unemployment. The job search training would also help to enlarge the worker's vision about the potential jobs that he or she can choose from. It would also help in locating relevant information on jobs, preparing suitable bio-data, writing meaningful job applications and developing the techniques of facing interviews.

The scheme for retraining has been initiated but only on a very modest scale. A much better scheme for retraining and redeployment needs to be expeditiously operationalized with the active involvement and participation of industry so as to ensure that the relevant type of training is imparted and re-employment is ensured.

It has been rightly suggested that costs involved in labour adjustment including retraining of redundant workers should also be borne by the industry through an Industrial Renewal Fund, which may be financed by levying a cess on industry or better still by contribution from industrial units. While there is a continuing need for training and retraining within industries, a retraining and redeployment mechanism should also form part of industry and the government could act as a facilitator. This is because (i) the retraining programmes organized by the government have built-in rigidities and do not respond quickly to the market signals; and (ii) industry as a group has a better knowledge of the emerging skill needs and also the sources of demand for them and as such it can act promptly both in respect of retraining and redeployment.

4.2 Major Anti overty and Employment Programmes

A number of poverty alleviation and employment programmes have been operational in India, particularly since the beginning of the 1980s. After economic reforms some new programmes have also been introduced and restructuring of the old programmes has also been done. These programmes were perceived to be important safety measures in the wake of economic reforms. Some basic features of each of these major programmes and an overview of their performance are attempted here, as a backdrop to an assessment of their adequacy in the present day context.

(i) Self-employment Programmes

(a) *Integrated Rural Development Programme (IRDP)*

The programme was formally started in 1980–1 in all blocks of the country though it was initiated in 1978–9 in a limited form. From April 1999, it has been restructured and merged with SGSY. It provides support to the rural households below the poverty line, with a package of assistance consisting of a subsidy and a bank loan to enable them to acquire productive assets like livestock, manufacturing, and processing equipment and business space. It also stipulates a minimum coverage of disadvantaged groups and women. In order to provide training support for self-employment under the programme and to provide special focus on women and children, two sub-programmes allied to IRDP, namely, TRYSEM and DWCRA were also put in operation.

Since the initiation of the programme till March 1999, a total sum of Rs 33953 crores has been spent including subsidy by union and state governments under IRDP. Around 54 million households have been provided assistance so far. The average level of investment per beneficiary household was about Rs 3000 during 1980–5, about Rs 9000 during 1992–5 and about Rs 20,787 during 2000–1 which was about 40 per cent in the form of government subsidy. The average investment per family in real terms did not increase much particularly after the reforms. Similarly, under the TRYSEM, 45.56 lakh youths had been trained from 1980–1 to 1998–9 and 2.73 lakh groups were formed with 41.45 lakh members under the DWACRA during 1982–3 to 1998–9.

The programme, as envisaged in its design, has succeeded to some extent in reaching the poor and amongst them the more disdvantaged groups like the SC and ST. According to the concurrent evaluation of the programme, about 88 per cent of the assisted families belonged to the destitute and very poor groups as per official records of their pre-assistance income, but the percentage of assisted families in these two groups was about 47 according to the assessment at the time of the evaluation (Government of India 1990). The results of the concurrent evaluation of IRDP by the programme evaluation organization of the Planning Commission revealed that 14.8 per cent of the beneficiaries could cross the revised poverty line of Rs 11000 (at 1991–2 prices) (Planning Commission 2001c). The concurrent evaluation also shows that a poor individual beneficiary under IRDP without any skill or experience could not improve his income, and those who did succeed, possessed better skill. The rate of success is higher where individual beneficiaries have formed a group. It is easier to organize a better training for such a group. The experience of DWACRA in Andhra Pradesh has been widely thought to be a successful one. IRDP has been more successful in those regions where both infrastructure and markets were well developed. The evaluation shows that indebtedness has increased among the IRDP beneficiaries which raises doubts about the viability of the projects in generating adequate employment and income.

The programme also suffered from certain serious limitations as an effective instrument to raise the income levels of assisted households substantially and permanently to lift them above the poverty line. First, though the programme is termed as integrated it is, in fact, not at all integrated with other development programmes of the area and thus tend to ignore input and market linkages and infrastructure requirements of assisted activities. Second, in relation to the requirements of meeting a quantitative target in terms of the number of families covered, the identification of activities and projects often tends to be arbitrary, and viability and sustainability aspects are often neglected. Third, the provision of outright cash subsidy often leads to misappropriation of benefits due to lack of a stake and interest from the beneficiaries. The recovery performance under the programme was relatively poor—41 per cent as on March 1986. Fourth, there was an implicit assumption that the prospective beneficiaries possessed information and skills to be able to choose viable options, had access to raw materials, and were aware of markets. These are the disabilities from which the poor suffer which the IRDP did not take into account, particularly those relating to the community decision-making. Fifth, there are bureaucratic red-tapism and delays at several levels of implementation of the programme. Last, there was no follow-up either by bankers or government agencies.

(b) *Swarna Jayanti Gram Swarozgar Yojana*

With the addition of several programmes, viz., TRYSEM, DWACRA, Supply of Improved Toolkits to Rural Artisan (SITRA) and Ganga Kalyan Yojana (GKY) in IRDP over the years, there has been a complete lack of sectoral integration in their implementation as each one started operating as an individual programme and focused entirely on achieving its own goals. With a view to ensuring sectoral integration and making poverty alleviation programmes more meaningful, these are merged into a single programme—the SGSY, with effect from 1 April 1999.

The SGSY aims at establishing a large number of micro enterprises in the rural areas with an emphasis on the 'cluster' approach. In each block four to five key activities are to be identified based on their resource endowments, occupational skills, and the availability of markets. The results of evaluation of the scheme are yet to be known. However, since SGSY is still a credit-cum-subsidy programme, it is feared that the scheme may face similar difficulties as in the case of IRDP unless the old loopholes and shortcomings are removed effectively.

The credit disbursed during the year 2000–1 was Rs 1445.30 crore against the target of 3205 crore, thus showing an achievement of 45 per cent of the target. The average per beneficiary family investment was Rs 20787. A total of 4.93 lakh Self Help Groups (SHGs) were formed under SGSY since its launching in 2000–1 and only 27,205 SHGs were able to take on economic activities.

The overall progress of the programme during its years of operation has been rather slow. In spite of a shift in the emphasis from individual oriented to group oriented, the former continued to be a dominating feature of the programme. The level of utilization of funds, credit disbursement, per family investment and credit subsidy ratio were low (Planning Commission 2001c)

(ii) Wage Employment Programmes

Short term wage employment on public works has been an old and conventional device used by the government to provide relief to the poor households from the hardships caused by drought, flood, and other natural calamities. The first major programme called 'Food For Work' was initiated in India during the 1970s. Subsequently, National Rural Employment Programmes (NREP) and Rural Landless Employment Guarantee Programme (RLEGP) were started with the objectives of providing gainful employment to the unemployed and underemployed and building community assets and rural infrastructure.

(a) *Jawahar Rozgar Yojana, and Employment Assurance Scheme*
The experience of implementation of NREP and RLEGP showed that the large investments made in generating employment did not yield commensurate returns in terms of creation of durable and useful assets. Even on the employment generation front, the administrative procedures were not cost-effective and thus a sizeable part of the funds got utilized in overheads. With a view to remove some of these shortcomings a new programme, Jawahar Rozgar Yojana (JRY), was launched on 1 April 1989 by merging NREP and RLEGP. Some basic changes in the modus operandi of the implementation were also introduced. The basic objectives of the programme, remained the same. However, the creation of additional employment opportunities for the unemployed and underemployed was emphasized as a primary objective, and the creation of sustained employment by strengthening rural economic infrastructure and assets in favour of the rural poor and improvements in the quality of life in rural areas as a secondary objective. A major change introduced in JRY in 1993–4 in comparison with the earlier programmes, was that funds based on pre-determined criteria would be provided to every village panchayat for utilization towards employment generation in various works within the village to be decided by the village panchayat itself based on the overall guidelines provided by the central and state governments. Since the inception of JRY, 737.65 crore man days of employment have been generated up to March 1999. The total expenditure during the same period was about Rs 302 billion.

The Employment Assurance Scheme (EAS) was launched on 2 October 1993 in 1778 identified backward blocks situated in the drought prone areas, desert areas, tribal areas, and hill areas. Since April 1997 the scheme has been extended to all the rural blocks of the country. The scheme provides for assured employment of up to 100 days during the lean agricultural season to those seeking work, and the work would be of an unskilled manual type. The secondary objective is the creation of economic infrastructure and community assets for sustained employment and development. Persons above 18 years and below 60 years of age who need and seek employment under the EAS are required to register themselves in the village panchayats where they are residing. They have to be provided work within the area of the block where they are residing, if employment is not available within that panchayat area itself. The wages paid to the workers under the EAS are the minimum agricultural wages for unskilled labourers fixed by the state government concerned.

EAS has been restructured in 1999–2000. It is now an allocation-based scheme under which the funds are shared by the centre and state in the ratio of 75.25. The allocation of funds to the state is made on the basis of incidence of poverty and district-wise allocation within a state on the basis of the index of backwardness.

According to a concurrent evaluation by the Ministry of Rural Development during 1993–4, about 11 days of employment per person were generated by JRY during the reference period of 30 days preceding the date of survey. In some comparitively poor states such as Madhya Pradesh and Orissa JRY workers got work for less than 10 days per month. As the average employment per participant is about 11 days in a month, at wage rates of Rs 33.36 per day, it would mean a supplementary monthly income of Rs 369 to the household—earning about 40 per cent of the poverty line threshold. Thus JRY seems to have contributed substantially to the family income of the poor. The concurrent evaluation also shows that the selection of beneficiaries was largely as per the criteria— 82 per cent of the JRY workers were poor. However, there are large variations across the states. The percentage of non-poor beneficiaries was quite high in Punjab (56 per cent), Andhra Pradesh (51.7 per cent), Bihar (22 per cent), Karnataka (34 per cent), Kerala (32 per cent), and Uttar Pradesh (30.2 per cent). Among the major weaknesses of the programme as pointed out by the concurrent evaluation of the Ministry of Rural Development (1993–4) are the delay in the completion of work owing to lack of funds (47 per cent of work), non-adherence to the guidelines for providing 30 per cent employment to women (women's share in employment generated was only 16.6 per cent), type of asset to be created—40 per cent for watershed development and 20 per cent for minor irrigation, link roads, building for schools, etc..

The conflict between employment generation and asset creation objectives, common to all wage employment programmes, has assumed greater significance in the case of JRY, particularly in view of its large outlays. It is, therefore, argued that while the provision of additional gainful employment to the rural poor is the primary objective of the programme and which is being met to a significant extent, it is desirable to ensure that such large outlays help simultaneously create useful community and productive assets for sustaining development and employment generation in rural areas.

With an objective to develop village infrastructure, JRY has been strengthened and restructured as Jawahar Gram Samridhi Yojana (JGSY) with effect from 1 April 1999. The primary objective of JGSY is the creation of village infrastructure including durable assets at the village level and assets to enable the rural poor to increase the opportunities of sustainable employment. Another objective is to generate supplementary employment for the unemployed rural poor. Though there is no sectoral earmarking of resources under JGSY, 22.5 per cent of allocation must be spent on schemes for SC/ST families living below the poverty line and 3 per cent for the creation of barrier-free infrastructure for the disabled. Nearly 30 per cent of employment opportunities are to be reserved for women. Under the programme, each village panchayat has to prepare an annual plan, which shall be approved by the Gram Sabha. Priority will be given to the completion of incomplete works. The village panchayats are empowered to execute work schemes up to Rs 50,000 without seeking any technical approval. Since 1999 till October 2001, 62.27 crore man days of employment have been generated under JGSY and total expenditure incurred is Rs 49.52 billion.

As regards EAS, its success in providing employment has been rather limited. According to the Comptroller and Auditor General's Third Report of 1995, the EAS provided 18 days and 16 days of employment during 1994–5 and 1995–6, respectively. The evaluation of EAS by PEO of the Planning Commission during 1995–7 shows that the scheme provided about 30 days of employment and benefited about one-fourth of the job seekers under it. Non-poor households were also found to have been the beneficiaries of EAS (Planning Commission 2001c). The scheme also suffered from several limitations, for example, extremely low levels of fund utilization, poor coverage, bogus reporting, and providing employment without assets entailing the risk of again falling below poverty line. It has been suggested by many that in order to improve efficacy of the programme and ensure that the poor and unemployed get up to 100 days of employment in lean agricultural season, the programme should be restricted to backward areas characterized by poor agriculture, chronic poverty, and hunger.

(iii) Urban Employment and Anti-poverty Programmes

Special programmes for employment generation and poverty alleviation in India have concentrated mostly in rural areas as the problem of poverty exists mainly in these areas. Over the years, it has been realized that poverty in urban areas is as persistent as in rural areas. The unemployment rates as revealed by NSSO surveys have always been higher in urban areas than in rural areas. Studies also show that urban poverty is relatively high among the self-employed households which account for about two-fifths of urban population. It was, therefore, decided to initiate some anti-poverty and employment generation programmes in urban areas as well. The first initiative in this direction was taken in 1986 with the introduction of the Self Employment Programme for Urban Poor (SETUP). It provided assistance to the urban households living below the poverty line for starting self-employment ventures on the basis of a bank loan up to Rs 5000 of which 25 per cent was to be a government subsidy. During the four years, 1986–90, as many as 9 lakh persons were assisted under the programme, with a total capital subsidy of Rs 1.2 billion from the government and Rs 3.7 billion of bank loans. The programme was scaled down as the banks, through which it was implemented, showed scant interest in it.

(a) *Nehru Rozgar Yojana*

A major initiative in promoting urban employment was taken in 1989 with the introduction of the Nehru Rozgar Yojana (NRY). It aims at providing employment to the urban unemployed and underemployed poor, through wage work and self-employment ventures as well as upgradation of housing for the poor. The earlier scheme (SETUP) was merged into NRY, with effect from 1992–3. The NRY consists of the following three schemes:

(i) Scheme of Urban Micro Enterprise (SUME): Under this scheme, the unemployed and underemployed persons belonging to poor families are encouraged to set up small enterprises in service, petty business, and manufacturing. The assistance is given on a bank loan-cum-subsidy basis. The scheme is applicable in all urban settlements.

(ii) Scheme of Urban Wage Employment (SUWE): Under this scheme, wage employment is sought to be provided to the unemployed and underemployed persons from poor families in public works in urban settlements with less than 1 lakh population. The works to be undertaken are to be decided by urban local bodies and could be in the nature of construction of public utilities. The total expenditure for this programme in 1999–2000 was Rs 177.81 crore.

(iii) Scheme of Employment through Housing and Shelter Upgradation (SHASHU): This scheme aims at improving the shelters of the urban poor through repair, construction, and additions to their existing housing units. The assistance consists of government subsidy of 25 per cent of the cost subject to a ceiling of Rs 1000 and loan from the Housing and Urban Development Corporation (HUDCO), at a concessional rate of interest and with a repayment period of 10 years. The scheme is applicable to urban settlements with a population of 1 lakh to 20 lakhs.

It may be noted that even if the envisaged targets were fulfilled and the programmes effectively implemented, the coverage of the programme would still be too meagre in relation to the magnitude of the problem in urban areas. The total wage-employment generation in terms of man days under NRY accounted for about 2 per cent only of the estimated 1492 million man days of unemployment in urban areas in 1990. It may, however, be noted that all urban unemployment cannot be sought to be tackled through wage employment in public works. A large part of the urban unemployed are educated and openly unemployed looking for regular full-time work. The need and scope for wage employment programmes like the rural JRY are limited in urban areas, but self-employment offers a substantial scope in urban settlements, particularly in the informal sector. The SUME scheme under NRY seems to be a very limited attempt in this regard in relation to the magnitude of unemployment.

(b) *Swarna Jayanti Shahri Rozgar Yojana*

Swarna Jayanti Shahri Rozgar Yojana (SJSRY) was launched in April 1999 subsumming the earlier urban poverty alleviation programmes, viz., NRY, UBSP and the Prime Minister's Integrated Urban Poverty Eradication Programme (PMIUPEP). The objective of the scheme is to provide gainful employment to the urban unemployed or underemployed poor by encouraging them to set up self-employment ventures or provision of wage employment. There are two schemes under SJSRY—the Urban Self-Employment Programme (USEP) and the Urban Wage Employment Programme (UWEP).

USEP has three distinct components: (i) assistance to individual urban poor for setting up of gainful self-employment ventures; (ii) assistance to group of urban poor women for self-employment—the scheme is called Development of Women and Children in the Urban Areas (DWCUA); and (iii) training of beneficiaries, and other persons associated with the urban employment programme for upgradation and acquisition of vocational and entrepreneurial skills.

(c) *Prime Minister's Rozgar Yojana*

Prime Minister's Rozgar Yojana (PMRY) was launched in urban areas during 1993–4, and the most important national level scheme for promotion of self-employment launched earlier, that is, Self Employment for the Educated Unemployed Youth (SEEUY), has been subsumed in it since then. PMRY has been extended to rural areas from 1994–5. The objective of the scheme is to provide self-employment opportunities in industry, business, and services to up to one million in the group of 18 to 35 years, who have passed or failed in matriculation examination or qualified from ITI or who have undergone a government sponsored technical course for a minimum duration of six months, and have a family income not exceeding Rs 24,000 per annum from all sources. The entrepreneur is required to contribute 5 per cent of the project cost as margin money and the balance of 95 per cent would be sanctioned as composite loan by banks without any collateral guarantee. The central government would provide subsidy at the rate of 15 per cent of the project cost subject to a ceiling of Rs 7500 per individual. During the first year of its implementation (1993–4), 32,000 cases were sanctioned against a target of 40,000. The target for 1994–5 was 2.20 lakh against which about 1.77 lakh cases were sanctioned. For the year 1997–8, the target was 2.20 lakh and 2.61 lakh cases were sanctioned and 1.57 lakh case were disbursed. The target for 1998–9 was 2.20 lakh beneficiaries.

An evaluation of PMRY (IAMR 2000) revealed that it generates employment for about 2.4 persons per unit. Though many more youth are seeking assistance under PMRY, almost half of the total applications are rejected by the taskforce committees of the district industries centres, mainly due to inadequate technical skills. Also, there is a lack of public campaigns focusing on various aspects of PMRY like eligibility, funds availability, skill requirement and market. An important aspect of PMRY is that three-fourths of the beneficiaries invested from their own resources in addition to the amount provided by bank loans and subsidy.

(iv) Adequacy of Existing Programmes in the Context of Economic Reforms

It was generally recognized by the government, international financial institutions, and independent scholars that the structural adjustment programme introduced in 1991 may have an adverse effect on the poverty and employment situation, particularly during the initial years when stabilization measures were to be strictly followed. That adjustment involves a social cost, the burden of which may particularly fall on the poor, was recognized, and the need for evolving an appropriate safety net to minimize hardship to the poor was emphasized in various official policy documents and statements.

The existence of large scale employment and anti-poverty programmes was generally regarded as a point of advantage in dealing with the possible adverse effects of stabilization and structural adjustment on the poor. The World Bank's Country Economic Memorandum of 1992, for example, observed that India is better equipped than many other developing countries to ensure that the adjustment process is carried out without serious adverse effects on the poor, as it has well equipped poverty alleviation programmes and a variety of other special programmes. Therefore, the approach to the provision of a safety net has been primarily in terms of expanding these programmes with some modifications to improve their effectiveness.

The approach of the government to provide a safety net to the poor against the possible adverse effects of the structural adjustment programme has generally been that of treating it as an integral part of the overall poverty alleviation strategy. Poverty, in any case, is a widespread phenomenon, and the objective of minimizing the hardships of the poor during the period of structural adjustment would best be met by ensuring that the overall strategy and programmes for poverty alleviation are suitably revamped and expanded. Given the vast magnitude of poverty, unemployment and underemployment, it would not be feasible to try to remove them on the basis of direct government expenditure. Such expenditure should be enhanced to the extent that resources permit and the coverage of existing programmes should be substantially expanded. But the extent to which poverty could generally be alleviated and adverse effects of structural adjustment on the poor could be mitigated would primarily depend on the pace at which the generation of productive employment opportunities is accelerated. And that, in turn, would depend on how quickly the economy can attain a high and sustainable growth rate. Fortunately, India has been able to quickly absorb the shock of adjustment and the growth rate of the economy has been over 6 per cent during the last few years. Although poverty levels have not risen in India during reforms, it continues to be high and hence there is need for the continuation of direct measures for poverty alleviation and employment generation.

However, all efforts are needed to streamline and strengthen the delivery mechanism of these anti-poverty and employment programmes so as to increase their better targeting and effectiveness. Often want of better coordination among different programmes has been listed as an important reason behind the poor performance of these programmes. The government's recent efforts in merging the several programmes into one may be able to remove this lacuna to some extent.

Another important reason behind the less than satisfactory performance of these anti-poverty and special employment programmes has been the lack of people's participation. It has often been said that the approach seems to be more technocratic and top-down in implementing these programmes with poor delivery systems (for more on this, see Mahendra Dev 1996). However, an important landmark in the 1990s has been the 73rd and 74th Amendments to the Constitution bringing about significant decentralization by providing for a system of local government based on mandatory elections. This provides an opportunity to strengthen the panchayats to effectively implement the various anti-poverty employment schemes. The panchayats must serve as the principal agencies of programme implementation. The experiences of implementing such schemes in West Bengal and Karnataka have shown that there is enormous potential in this regard. Gaiha's study (1996) with regard to the performance of two major anti-poverty interventions—JRY and IRDP, shows that while development is associated with a better performance of anti-poverty interventions, decentralization displays a consistently stronger association. This is an important finding as some recent studies have drawn pointed attention to the potential for different forms of community initiative in the area of poverty alleviation. However, success achieved through decentralization will depend to a large extent on whether acute inequalities in endowments have been eliminated. In such a setting, the panchayats would be free from the domination of rich and powerful landlords and would be more responsive to the needs of the rural poor (Gaiha 1996).

Apart from decentralization, the organization of the poor and the prospective beneficiaries needs to be encouraged. It has been found that people's organizations can play an important role in ensuring the effective implementation of these programmes. The essential point is that whatever the form of the organizations that emerges, the poor must become aware of their collective strength and organize themselves accordingly. The NGOs and community-based organizations can also play an important role in creating an environment for social mobilization and for promoting poverty alleviation programmes.

5. Conclusions and Policy Implications

The discussions in this chapter show that the strategy adopted for tackling the issues of poverty and unemployment is a two-track one in which the benefits of normal growth process are supplemented by social safety nets. This seems inescapable at least as long as the present high levels of poverty persist. As Bhagwati (1988) points out, 'the optimal strategy for poverty alleviation is bound to be a mixed strategy involving some consideration of the direct and indirect approaches'. It is important to recognize that while some elements of a direct approach are unavoidable as long as significant poverty persists, it is perhaps best to view this as a necessary safety net while relying on broader-based growth processes to provide sustained growth to income levels for the bulk of the population. A question that is sometimes raised in this context relates to the relative efficacy of the two tracks in this strategy. Special employment programmes like JRY claim investible resources, which could otherwise have contributed to the growth process. A study on costs and benefits of the rural works programme in India has indicated that the benefits accruing from such employment programmes contribute directly to the growth process, thereby reducing the force of the 'growth foregone' argument.

Notwithstanding the desirability of such schemes, it may be useful to concentrate allocation of resources on areas with higher levels of poverty, unemployment, and underemployment rather than spreading these resources thinly over the entire country. Although there is bound to be resistance over this step, ways should be found to overcome it. The importance of these programmes also lies in their capacity for holding the wage rate and for creating some infrastructure in the rural areas, which are added to the already existing stock of infrastructure every year. In wage employment programmes, the emphasis has been more on employment creation than on the building of infrastructure of a durable or productive type. Although in recent years there has been some changes in the approach to the infrastructure building, emphasis on creation of durable infrastructure is still rather weak. The creation of infrastructure like minor irrigation, watershed development, and roads will enhance agricultural productivity and will thereby increase employment in agriculture on a more sustainable basis. In the face of persistence of high levels of poverty along with increasing casualization of the labour market, this kind of safety net mechanism seems to be desirable, but its linkage with the growth process is also essential.

As the process of reforms in the economy gets intensified—and the indications are that it would be—the issue of labour market reforms would be an important agenda. As we have discussed earlier, the employers need some kind of flexibility in adjusting the workforce in the face of global competition. It will be a real test of the Indian system to combine efficiency with safeguarding the genuine interest of labour. In a poor country like India adequate separation benefits to workers should be assured. The vulnerable group of workers may be paid relatively better compared to others. Utmost care and balance is needed while undertaking labour market reforms so that labour is not put to great disadvantage. While laws relating to job security should be relaxed there is a need to make minimum wage provisions even more comprehensive. Minimum wages in India are extremely low and very often they are lower than poverty-line wages. There have been suggestions for evolving some kind of national minimum wage in the country, but because of opposition from several quarters it has not taken off. There are some valid arguments in favour of formulating a national minimum wage and it should not be rejected outright on the plea that it would increase the rigidities in the labour market.

The changes in the labour market show that measures to tackle unemployment problem need to concentrate on creation of regular employment opportunities through diversification of the economy. The importance of such a strategy also emerges from the long term changes that have come about in the structure of chronic open unemployment in favour of the educated. Further, as the 'educated component' of female unemployment has exceeded that of male unemployment in urban areas, and unemployment rates for urban females, educated or otherwise, have not come down since 1983, strategies should include women's accessibility to education and skills which are relevant and responsive to the needs of the economy. Gender differentials in skill and expertise levels and gender biases operating in the labour market have to be removed to enhance levels of utilization of the female labour force. It is also revealed by employment structure that while there is a declining trend in the level of rural unemployment, the structure and characteristics of the unemployment among males as well as females in rural areas are fast becoming like those of urban areas. The rural non-farm sector can also be made buoyant by creation of sustainable and productive employment opportunities through the diversification of the economy and development of a variety of relevant skills and expertise among rural workers to enable them to gain access to the emerging employment situation.

From the Eighth Plan there has been greater emphasis on skill development and vocationalization of education, but so far not much has happened. While private training institutions (that is, computer centres, manager training institutes, etc.) have expanded at a phenomenal rate, they have been mostly of inferior quality. Appropriate skill development and training institutions which can cater to the emerging needs of the labour market are extremely lacking and unfortunately the efforts by the government have been only disappointing in this regard.

Agriculture will continue to play a dominant role in the creation of employment. As the average income of a worker in the agriculture sector is extremely low, the emphasis should be on creating the productive employment and not treating it as a residual sector for the surplus labour. Development of agriculture in backward regions has very high potentiality of creating employment and reducing poverty. In agriculture, the potential for indirect employment in the form of agro industries like food processing seems to be higher than direct employment. Allied activities like dairy development has also a high potential for employment.

According to some estimates, there are about 30 to 40 per cent post-harvest losses in many agricultural commodities particularly fruits and vegetables. Agro processing in general and food processing in particular is going to be an important sector for value addition and has a large potential for employment opportunities. These opportunities exist in oilseeds, cotton, marine products, poultry, cashew, vegetables, fruits, mushroom, and floriculture, apart from the traditional plantation industries of tea and coffee. All these have a large export potential as well as expanding domestic market, which can create significant employment. But a concerted policy and action plan is needed to develop them by adequate investment, suitable technological upgradation, and proper marketing.

Although employment in the manufacturing sector has shown deceleration in growth, it seems that there has been some recovery very recently. Textile products, chemicals, leather products, transport equipment, etc. have shown relatively good performance on the employment front and efforts should be taken to consolidate this trend.

Above all, it is the informal sector—either in rural or urban areas but mostly in the latter—where most of the employment is going to be created. It will be in manufacturing as well as services, but the trend shows that services have much more potential of employment than manufacturing. This sector has so far been completely neglected by planners and that is why it is characterized by low productivity. The sector has both self-employed and wages workers, but most of them work under deplorable working conditions with low earnings. A well planned support system should be provided for the growth of this sector in the form of marketing, credit, training, upgradation of technology, etc.. For enhancing the capabilities of vulnerable workers in the informal sector a proper blend of education and training is extremely desirable. The workers in this sector, who are extremely vulnerable and practically devoid of any safety net mechanism, accept the statutory minimum wages which are generally below poverty-line wages. Even these wages are mostly not implemented. How to develop a proper safety net mechanism for the workers in this sector along with increasing its productivity is a challenge which must be met if an effective dent on poverty has to be made.

REFERENCES

Ahluwalia, Isher J. (1992) *Productivity and Growth in Indian Manufacturing,* New Delhi, Oxford University Press,

Bhagwati, Jagdish (1988) 'Poverty and Public Policy', *World Development,* 16(5).

Chandra, Ashoka (1999) 'The Role of Training in Productivity: the Objectives of NRF', in M.L. Nandrajog (ed.), *National Renewal Fund—A Look Ahead,* New Delhi, International Labour Organisation.

Datta, R.C. (2001) 'Economic Reforms, Redundancy and National Renewal Fund: Human Face or Human Mask', *The Indian Journal of Labour Economics,* 44(4).

Deshpande, L.K., Alakh N. Sharma, A.K. Karan, and S. Sarkar (2001) *Economic Reforms and Labour Market Flexibility,* Institute for Human Development, New Delhi (mimeo).

Dreze, J., and A. Sen (1997), *Indian Development: Selected Regional Perspectives,* New Delhi, Oxford University Press.

Fallon, P. and R. Lucas (1991) 'The Impact of Changes in Job Security Regulations in India and Zimbawe', *World Bank Economic Review,* 5(3).

Gaiha, R. (1996) 'Do Rural Public Works Influence Agricultural Wages? The Case of the Employment Guarantee Scheme in India', *Oxford Development Studies,* 25(3).

Goldar, Bishwanath (2002) *Trade Liberalisation and Employment: The Case of India,* Working Paper, forthcoming, Geneva, ILO.

Government of India (1990) *Concurrent Evaluation of Integrated Rural Development Programme: The Main Findings,* Department of Rural Development, New Delhi.

IAMR (2000) *Evaluation of Prime Minister's Rozgar Yojana,* Institute of Applied Manpower Research, New Delhi.

ILO-SAAT (1996) *India: Economic Reforms and Labour Policies,* New Delhi.

Kannan, K.P. (1992), *Labour Institutions and the Development Process in Kerala,* Centre for Development Studies, Trivandrum.

Lucas, R.E.B. (1988) 'India's Industrial Policy', in R.E.B. Lucas and G.F. Papanek (eds), *The Indian Economy: Recent Developments and Future Prospects,* New Delhi, Oxford University Press.

Mahendra Dev, S. (1996) *Poverty and Human Development in India: Regional Dimensions and Policy Issues,* Working Paper, Institute for Human Development, New Delhi.

Mamgain, R.P., Vandana Parashar, and Indira Datta (2001) 'Rehabilitation of Redundant Workers: The NRF Experience', *The Indian Journal of Labour Economics,* 44(4).

Nagraj, R. (1993) 'Employment and Wages in Manufacturing Industries in India: Trends, Hypothesis and Evidence', Indira Gandhi Institute of Development Research, *Discussion Paper No.* 98, December.

Noronha, Ernesto (1999) 'Duration of Unemployment and Re-employment', *Management and Labour Studies,* 24(2 and 3), April.

Papola T.S. (1994) 'Structural Adjustment: Labour Market Flexibility and Employment', *The Indian Journal of Labour Economics,* 37(1), New Delhi.

——— (1992) 'The Question of Unemployment', in Bimal Jalan (ed.), *The Indian Economy*, New Delhi, Viking.

Planning Commission (2001a) *Approach Paper to the Tenth Five Year Plan*, New Delhi.

——— (2001b) *Report of Task Force on Employment Opportunities*, New Delhi.

——— (2001c) *Report of the Working Group on Rural Poverty Alleviation Programme*, New Delhi.

——— (1999) *Ninth Five Year Plan, Vol. 1*, New Delhi

——— (1992) *Eighth Five Year Plan, 1997–2002*, New Delhi.

——— (1980) *Joint Evaluation of Employment Guarantee Scheme of Maharashtra*, Programme Evaluation Organization and Directorate of Economics and Statistics, Government of Maharashtra, New Delhi.

——— (1962) *Third Five Year Plan*, New Delhi.

——— (1956) *Second Five Year Plan*, New Delhi.

——— (1953) *First Five Year Plan*, New Delhi.

Ramaswamy, K.V. (1999) 'The search for Flexibility in Indian Manufacturing: New Evidence on Indian Outsourcing Activities', *Economic and Political Weekly*, 34(6), pp. 363–8, February 6–12.

Roy Chowdhary, S. (1996) 'Industrial Restructuring, Unions and the State; Flexible Mill Workers in Ahmedabad', *Economic and Political Weekly*, 31(8).

Sharma, Alakh N. (1997) *Economic Reforms and Labour: Evidences from Micro Level*, Institute of Economic Growth, New Delhi (mimeo).

Sharma, Alakh N. and S.K. Sasikumar (1996) *Structural Adjustment Programme and Labour*, V.V. Giri National Labour Institute, NOIDA (*mimeo*).

UNDP (1990), *Human Development Report (1990)*, Oxford University Press, New York.

